19 W'hale by

MONASTERY AND SOCIETY
IN THE LATE MIDDLE AGES

Selected account rolls from
Selby Abbey, Yorkshire, 1398–1537

Selby Abbey from the north-east (Photograph by Dianne Tillotson)

MONASTERY AND SOCIETY IN THE LATE MIDDLE AGES

Selected account rolls from
Selby Abbey, Yorkshire, 1398–1537

Edited and translated by
John H. Tillotson

THE BOYDELL PRESS

© John H. Tillotson 1988

First published 1988 by The Boydell Press
an imprint of Boydell & Brewer Ltd
PO Box 9, Woodbridge, Suffolk IP12 3DF
and of Boydell & Brewer Inc.
Wolfeboro, New Hampshire 03894-2069, USA

ISBN 0 85115 489 1

British Library Cataloguing in Publication Data

Monastery and society in the late Middle Ages:
  selected account rolls from Selby Abbey,
  Yorkshire, 1398–1537.
  1. Selby Abbey (North Yorkshire) –
  Accounting – History – Sources
  I. Tillotson, John H.
  271'.009428'45   BX2596.S4/
  ISBN 0-85115-489-1

Library of Congress Cataloging-in-Publication Data

Monastery and society in the late Middle Ages.
  Bibliography: p.
  Includes index.
  1. Selby Abbey (Selby, North Yorkshire) –
History – Sources.   2. Selby (North Yorkshire) –
Church history – Sources.   I. Tillotson, John H.
BX2596.S46M66 1988   271'.1'042845   87-21861
ISBN 0-85115-489-1

∞ Printed on long life paper
made to the full American Standard

Printed in Great Britain by
St Edmundsbury Press, Bury St Edmunds, Suffolk

CONTENTS

ACKNOWLEDGEMENTS

My work on the Selby Abbey account rolls commenced more than a decade ago and the debts of gratitude incurred during that time are too numerous to acknowledge in full, not least to the many undergraduate students who have utilized successive versions of this book in their courses. The primary task of transcription and translation of the documents was made possible by two periods of study leave from the Australian National University in 1973 and 1979, which provided the opportunity for extended research in English archives and libraries together with the freedom for uninterrupted writing. I am grateful to the following institutions and their staffs for assistance in these years: The East Riding of Yorkshire County Record Office, Beverley; The Department of Palaeography and Diplomatic, University of Durham; The Brynmor Jones Library, University of Hull; The Lincolnshire Archives Committee, Lincoln; The Public Record Office, London; The Department of Manuscripts, British Library, London; The Westminster Diocesan Archives, London; The Department of Local History and Archives, City Libraries, Sheffield; The York Minster Library; and the Borthwick Institute of Historical Research, York.

Many individuals have, of course, also contributed generously to the writing of this book, none more so than Miss E. Poyser, the archivist at Archbishop's House in London, and Mr N. Higson, archivist at Hull University, who have been unfailingly helpful over many years. Their hospitality has made work on the archives under their care a pleasure. Mr G. S. Haslop of Hemingbrough and Professor R. B. Dobson at the University of York have made available to me their knowledge of Selby Abbey and its records, and I am grateful both for this valuable help and for their encouragement of my own project. My friend Dr Jack Ravensdale provided in his beautiful house at Landbeach the perfect environment for the work of translating medieval documents, and I benefited greatly from discussions with him about particular points of difficulty. Among my colleagues at the Australian National University, Mr Leslie Downer and Professor John Molony have been repeatedly consulted and always ready to provide expert advice. Whilst my friend Mrs Barbara Ross has helped at various points with her experience of editing monastic account rolls.

The thirteen accounts translated in this volume form part of two larger collections: the Londesborough manuscripts deposited on loan in The

Brynmor Jones Library, University of Hull; and the Selby Abbey manuscripts at The Westminster Diocesan Archives, London. I wish to express my gratitude to the owners of these documents, Lord Londesborough and the Cardinal Archbishop of Westminster, for making them freely available to researchers and for granting ready permission to publish them.

The task of preparing this book for publication has been a lengthy one involving many hands and much advice. I am grateful to successive Deans of the Faculty of Arts for their patience and generous provision of funds for word-processing; to the readers appointed by the Faculty Publications Committee for helpful comments on the original draft; and to the word-processors who have worked on the manuscript, most particularly Mrs B. Hutchinson, Mrs J. Knobel, and Miss D. Mathews. My wife Dianne shared with me the task of compiling the indexes, provided the photographs that adorn the text, and generally provided the stimulus and support without which the work would never have been brought to completion. Finally, I have to thank the members of the Faculty Publications Committee for their sympathetic consideration and support of the project over an unduly prolonged period, and the Australian National University for making publication ultimately possible with a generous subsidy.

The help and advice acknowledged above has undoubtedly made this a better book than it would otherwise have been. For the errors and inadequacies that remain in translations, commentary, or elsewhere, I alone am responsible.

John H. Tillotson
Canberra 1984

MAPS AND ILLUSTRATIONS

ABBREVIATIONS

CCR   *Calendar of the Close Rolls preserved in the Public Record Office*
CFR   *Calendar of the Fine Rolls preserved in the Public Record Office*
CPL   *Calendar of Entries in the Papal Registers relating to Great Britain and Ireland: Papal Letters*
CPR   *Calendar of the Patent Rolls preserved in the Public Record Office*
HUL   Hull University Library
OED   *Oxford English Dictionary*
PRO   Public Record Office, London
RP   *Rotuli Parliamentorum; ut et Petitiones, et Placita in Parliamento*
VCH   *The Victoria History of the Counties of England*
WDA   Westminster Diocesan Archives
YAJ   *Yorkshire Archaeological Journal*
YAS   Yorkshire Archaeological Society

INTRODUCTION

INTRODUCTION

I

'The reule of seint Maure or of seint Beneit,
By cause that it was old and somdel streit
This ilke Monk leet olde thynges pace,
And heeld after the newe world the space.'[1]

Geoffrey Chaucer's monk, with his cheerful disinclination to follow rules
that were too strict for the more relaxed ways of the modern world,
provided the impulse from which this collection of Selby Abbey account
rolls has grown, as he has provided the starting-point for many discussions
of late medieval monasticism. Because the characterization is so vivid, some
have believed him copied from a real personality and there have been
plausible attempts to identify the model from which he was drawn.[2] For
others he is typical of the monks of his time, whether or not he existed in
life as well as literature, representing institutions that had replaced the
rigour, zeal, and piety of former times with the comfortable existence of
celibate gentlemen's clubs. In any assessment the quiet satire of the portrait
raises intriguing questions about the quality and purpose of the religious
life in the late fourteenth and early fifteenth centuries. Was learning really
despised, hunting a popular monastic recreation, gourmandizing common?
Had the world too much invaded the cloister; and if monasteries were no
longer either spiritual or intellectual powerhouses, where then was their
function in late medieval society to be found?

Before approaching these questions it is important to consider the ideals
of the Christian life which the monks of Selby Abbey could be seen as
committed to uphold. Theirs was a Benedictine monastery, a community
vowed to the lifelong service of God according to the precepts set out in
the Rule of St Benedict, composed in sixth century Italy and kept fresh in
the minds of its followers by daily readings from its provisions in Chapter.
The moderation and humanity of St Benedict's Rule have been frequently
and no doubt rightly remarked, quoting his own introductory words:

---

[1] F. N. Robinson (ed.), *The Works of Geoffrey Chaucer*, Oxford, 2nd edn, 1957, pp. 18–19.
[2] See D. Knowles, *The Religious Orders in England*, II, Cambridge, 1955, Appendix I,
pp. 365–366, and A. R. Myers (ed.), *English Historical Documents*, IV, 1327–1485, London,
1969, p. 785.

'Therefore must we establish a school of the Lord's service: in founding which we hope to ordain nothing that is harsh or burdensome.'[3] Yet this may be seen as relative to the more extreme asceticism of early forms of monasticism. As Professor Brooke has said: 'The little rule for beginners describes a life of great earnestness and severity: to those of us who lead the life of ordinary mortals in the late twentieth century, a life of dedication and monotony beyond our dreams.'[4]

On his profession as a monk, the Rule lays down that the new member of the community must promise 'stability, conversion of his life, and obedience.' He must renounce personal property, 'knowing that thenceforward he will not have the disposition even of his own body.'[5] His life henceforth was to be one of self-denial, chastity, humility, and frequent prayer within the enclosure of the monastery, rendering absolute obedience to the abbot as Christ's representative there and subject to a strict discipline. He should practise silence at all times, and 'when he speaks, do so gently and without laughter, humbly and seriously, in few and sensible words, and without clamour.'[6] The most important activity of each day was participation in the Divine Office, the set round of prayers, lessons and psalms which brought the community together in the choir of their church for the night office after midnight and for the seven offices of the day. 'Let nothing', St Benedict decreed, 'be put before the Work of God.'[7] But liturgical prayer formed only one part of an ordered existence, in which meditative reading and manual labour (including domestic duties and crafts) were also prescribed.[8] There was necessary variety, then, even within an unchanging routine.

The monastery described by the Rule was a largely self-contained community, where the concept of the communal life embraced virtually all aspects of the monks' existence. They worshipped together, slept where practicable in a common dormitory, and in case of sickness were cared for in a special room provided as an infirmary. Property and the resources needed for the brethren's support were held in corporate ownership under the controlling hand of the abbot, himself elected by the community. Individual monks were strictly forbidden private possessions, 'this most

[3] J. McCann (trans.), *The Rule of St Benedict*, London, 1976 edition, p. 4. All quotations from the Rule that follow are taken from this edition.
[4] C. Brooke, *The Monastic World*, London, 1974, p. 47. For other short commentaries on the Rule, see E. Searle and B. Ross (ed.), *Accounts of the Cellarers of Battle Abbey 1275–1513*, Sydney University Press, 1967, Introduction; and D. Knowles, *The Monastic Order in England*, Cambridge, 1966, ch. I.
[5] Chapter 58.
[6] Chapter 7.
[7] Chapter 43. The seven offices of the day were Lauds, Prime, Terce, Sext, None, Vespers, and Compline.
[8] 'Idleness is the enemy of the soul. The brethren, therefore, must be occupied at stated hours in manual labour, and again at other hours in sacred reading.' (Chapter 48)

wicked vice',[9] though here as in other matters a certain discretion was left to the abbot. The corollary of this was that all necessities were to be supplied from the common store, and guidelines were laid down governing the quantity and quality of the food and clothing to be provided. Adequate but frugal fare, sufficient yet inexpensive clothing, was the aim. Whilst wine was allowed, if reluctantly, self-denial was enjoined in the matter of fleshmeat.[10] Meals were to be eaten in silence in the common refectory, with readings from suitably edifying books during their course. The abbot alone normally ate elsewhere, in order to entertain guests and pilgrims at his table. In the absence of guests, however, he might vary the routine of at least some of the monks by invitations to share his meal.

The abbot of the Rule was 'the father of the monastery', the head of the family of monks with ultimate control over all aspects of its life: 'let them look to the father of the monastery for all that they require'.[11] Decisions on all important matters were taken by him, though he must consider the counsel of the community. Appointments to all offices within the abbey were in his hands. As this last statement implies, however, the running of the monastery demanded delegation of responsibilities for its successful operation. In a large community the abbot would have a deputy, the prior, and deans to assist his supervision of the religious life; whilst a senior monk would be appointed to take charge of the novices during their period of probation and training. Supply was the province of the cellarer, 'in essence the housekeeper of a large, prosperous, frugal Roman country family, presiding over cooks and servants, giving special attention to the children, the sick and the old people of the household, and succouring, as far as family resources would allow, the poor at the gate and the traveller or guest.'[12] The guest-house was to be in the charge of another brother; its kitchen, which was separate from the community's and also served the abbot, was manned by two further monks. There are thus the beginnings in the Rule of the administrative structure which was to become highly organized in later medieval houses of any size.

Service of God enclosed from the distractions of the world, not service of a wider society as a welfare agency, was the primary objective of the monastic community. The Rule views excursions by the monks beyond the monastery's walls with disfavour and subjects them to the strict control of the abbot. Nonetheless, as previous references to visitors make clear, the world was expected to come to the abbey: 'guests ... are never lacking in a monastery.'[13] Suitable hospitality was to be provided, including accommo-

---

[9] Chapter 33.
[10] 'Except the sick who are very weak, let all abstain entirely from the flesh of four-footed animals.' (Chapter 39)
[11] Chapter 33.
[12] E. Searle and B. Ross (ed.), *Accounts of the Cellarers of Battle Abbey*, p.6.
[13] Chapter 53.

dation and meals at the abbot's table. As for the poor and pilgrims, 'special attention should be shown, because in them is Christ more truly welcomed; for the fear which the rich inspire is enough of itself to secure them honour.'[14] Charitable relief at the monastery's gate is implied in the instructions for the gatekeeper. Such charity necessarily placed some strain on the community's ability to live apart from the world, and attempts were made in the Rule to minimize contacts between monks and visitors. But the obligation itself was recognized and remained part of Benedictine monasticism throughout the medieval period.

Between the Italian monastery of St Benedict and late medieval Selby were more than eight centuries of change and development in Western Europe, during which the style of life in monasteries following the Rule also underwent a long process of change in response to different political, religious, and social conditions. Similarly the role and importance of monasticism within the Church did not remain static. We can do no more here than indicate some of the broad changes important to an understanding of fifteenth century Benedictine monasticism.[15]

'Nothing in the Rule forbids corporate wealth or magnificence of church and liturgical objects, so long as the monks themselves live simply and do not waste the monastery's substance.'[16] In worldly terms the success of early medieval monasticism meant that the monasteries attracted patrons, who endowed them with the wealth at their disposal in the expectation of spiritual gain; they became the owners of large estates, of manors and churches, an important part of society and its economy. Seclusion from the world had to be tempered by the demands of estate administration and the secular obligations attached to the ownership of land. Abbots of major houses became great magnates, subject to the demands of rulers for secular service, and increasingly separated from the communities of which they were spiritual fathers.

Within the monastic precincts the simple buildings of St Benedict's era were transformed into an extensive complex, whose layout came to have a generally standard basic form. A large church housing the relics of saints and precious objects of religious art was one universal feature; the other a quadrangular cloister, along three sides of which were ranged the principal monastic buildings. The cloister itself was a covered walk around an open court, providing easy access to the buildings grouped around it; but it was more than this, serving also as an area for study and writing. The nave of the church formed one side of the quadrangle; the dormitory and meeting-hall (chapter house) a second; the refectory and kitchens a third;

---

[14] Chapter 53.

[15] For a short discussion of developments, see D. Knowles, *Christian Monasticism*, London, 1969.

[16] E. Searle and B. Ross (ed.), *Accounts of the Cellarers of Battle Abbey*, p. 5.

and store-rooms and guest-rooms the fourth. The abbot's quarters, when these became separate from those of the rest of the community, were usually in this fourth range with the guest-rooms, on the side of the cloister that opened on to the outer court and contact with the outside world. The infirmary by contrast, for the peace and quiet of the sick, was located away from the cloister on the other side of the complex. The outer courtyard, generally placed west of the cloister, contained the various buildings needed for day-to-day maintenance of the community, such as stables, bakehouse, brewhouse, and barns. Finally, around the whole area there was a precinct wall entered by one or more gates, often themselves elaborate buildings in the later middle ages.[17]

Growth in the size and magnificence of the monastic church reflected changes of emphasis in observance of the Rule. Those patrons who provided the resources to build to the greater glory of God expected a return for their outlay, the prayers of the monks for the souls of themselves, their families, and society at large. The monasteries became the great centres of organized prayer and intercession for society, qualified for this role by the fact that the monastic life was regarded as the only clear way to salvation. The liturgy became increasingly elaborate, masses multiplied, and time spent in church on the Divine Office was markedly increased, so that at Cluny Abbey in the mid-eleventh century the monks normally spent more than eight hours a day in church and chapter.[18]

Under such a regime there could be little time for the other activities prescribed by the Rule, manual labour and sacred reading. But then manual labour as a regular part of monastic life had also been undermined by another development, in which communities became increasingly composed of priests, literate men for whom scholarly or artistic activities were deemed more suitable. With their facilities for study and writing the monasteries could develop as centres of learning as well as worship where the extreme Cluniac emphasis on the liturgy was not adopted. The leading scholars of the eleventh century, like Lanfranc and Anselm at the Norman abbey of Bec, were monks. 'As historians, as theologians, as biblical commentators and as writers of spiritual instruction they were supreme until 1100 and still notable in 1150.'[19] Thereafter the monks were to find themselves overtaken and eclipsed by the secular scholars of the universities and in the thirteenth century by the friars.

The splendours of the liturgy at Cluny or the scholarly excellence of Bec were accompanied in the eleventh century by a high level of devotion

[17] Plans, pictures, and descriptions of English monastic houses are conveniently brought together in R. Gilyard-Beer, *Abbeys. An illustrated guide to the abbeys of England and Wales,* HMSO, second edition 1976. At Selby Abbey only the church has survived, and the plan of the monastic buildings has not been recovered by archaeological excavation.

[18] D. Knowles, *Christian Monasticism*, p. 52.

[19] D. Knowles, *Christian Monasticism*, p. 60.

within the cloister; and both houses at their height were strong reforming influences in Western Europe. This was an age of achievement for Benedictine monasticism not merely in terms of expanding numbers and new foundations, of scholarship or influence within the Church, but also for its widespread revitalization of observance. Bec, founded in 1039, was itself part of a major revival of monasticism in Normandy, whose vigour was then transmitted to England by the Norman conquest of 1066 through an infusion of Norman superiors for English houses, new foundations, and a tightening of discipline.[20] One product was a revival of monasticism in the north of England, where the monastic life had been obliterated by the Viking invasions of the ninth century and had never recovered hitherto. Selby Abbey, founded in 1070 or thereabouts, has the distinction of being the first monastery established north of the Trent since the Viking catastrophe.[21]

Within a few years of the foundation of Selby Abbey, monasticism of this type came under challenge by more austere movements, most notably by the Cistercians for whom the north of England was to prove fruitful ground in the second quarter of the twelfth century. For the Cistercians, whose mother-house Cîteaux was founded in 1098, modification of the Rule had led to a deformation of the ideal; and they sought a return to its exact and rigorous observance in a life of extreme simplicity. Internally there was a return to the tripartite division of the day: manual labour and spiritual reading were returned to the timetable; liturgical elaboration was swept away. Externally they reacted against what they saw as excessive involvement with the world, seeking instead seclusion and freedom from secular ties. Manors and tithes were rejected as sources of revenue, in favour of land in little populated areas that could be cultivated by their own workforce of lay brothers. Moreover, in order to prevent growth from leading to relaxation of observance, a programme of uniformity of practice and discipline was inaugurated for all Cistercian foundations, and a constitutional framework developed which bound them into the first closely knit religious order.[22]

The expansion of the Cistercians in the twelfth century was phenomenal, so that by 1153 the order numbered three hundred and thirty-nine houses very widely spread in Europe.[23] Success in fact brought its own problems and an eventual falling-away from strict observance of early ideals; but maintenance of a high level of uniformity and discipline within a numerous and widespread family had meanwhile convinced reformers at the highest

---

[20] D. Knowles, *The Monastic Order in England*, chs V and VI.
[21] B. Dobson, 'The First Norman Abbey in Northern England. The Origins of Selby: a ninth centenary article', *The Ampleforth Journal*, 74, pt II, Summer 1969, pp. 161–176.
[22] D. Knowles, *The Monastic Order in England*, chs XII and XIII.
[23] D. Knowles, *Christian Monasticism*, p. 77. In England the Cistercians had some 70 houses in 1200, compared with 300 Benedictine houses (*Ibid.*, p. 97).

level of the Church that elements in the Cistercian constitution would benefit traditional monasticism. Two provisions of their fundamental constitution, the Charter of Love (*Carta Caritatis*), are of particular importance here. Under its terms each abbey was made subject to a yearly visitation, an inspection of its manner of life, by the abbot of the house from which it was founded. And secondly, all heads of Cistercian houses were instructed to attend an annual assembly, the general chapter at Cîteaux, which was the supreme disciplinary and legislative body of the order. Both these provisions were borrowed in an adapted form for all monastic houses by the Fourth Lateran Council of 1215. In every ecclesiastical province all houses were ordered to meet in general chapter every three years 'for careful consideration of the reform of the order and the observance of the rule, and what is decided ... is to be inviolably observed by all, without any excuse, opposition or appeal.' At the same time chapter visitors were to be appointed, charged with visiting every house in the province 'to correct and reform what in their view needs correction and reform.'[24]

Hitherto fully autonomous Benedictine monasteries like Selby Abbey were thus brought within a loose provincial organization of Black Monk houses for purposes of common discipline and legislation. At first in England there were two provincial chapters, for the provinces of York and Canterbury; then in 1336 Benedict XII replaced these with a single triennial chapter, which continued to meet until 1532 on the eve of the Dissolution and to appoint visitors.[25] In practice, however, these institutions never had for the English Black Monks, with their characteristic distaste for strong central authority, the power and efficiency of the early Cistercian model. There were intermittent attempts at comprehensive reform, most notably in the 1270s; but all failed to reverse the tendency towards less rigorous observance of the Rule. At the start of the fourteenth century the monks had not lost their ability to respond to the prevailing social and religious trends, as we can see by the general chapter's establishment and maintenance of a common house of studies at Oxford University. Yet even so the career of the university monk must be hard to reconcile with stringent adherence to St Benedict's injunctions.[26]

---

[24] Canon 12; H. Rothwell (ed.), *English Historical Documents*, III, 1189–1327, London, 1975, pp. 651–652. At the same time episcopal visitation of monasteries was encouraged: 'diocesan bishops shall make it their business so to reform the monasteries under their jurisdiction that when the said visitors come they find more in them worthy of commendation than of correction' (*Ibid.*, p. 652).

[25] D. Knowles, *The Religious Orders in England*, III, Cambridge, 1959, p. 10. For the records of the general chapters, see W. A. Pantin (ed.), *Documents illustrating the activities of the General and Provincial Chapters of the English Black Monks 1215–1540*, 3 vols, Camden Society, third series 45, 47, and 54, 1931–37.

[26] D. Knowles, *The Religious Orders in England*, I, Cambridge, 1948, ch. II, and vol. II, Cambridge, 1955, ch. I.

The presence of the Black Monks at Oxford was a belated response to thirteenth century developments: the high esteem in which university studies were held, and the challenge of the friars, who themselves had rapidly become intellectual orders with major centres at the universities. In the friars monasticism faced the competition of a new outgoing ideal of the religious life that swept Western Europe like other reforming movements before it. In place of the monastic concept of poverty the friars' ideal was a more absolute adherence to the poverty of the Gospels, involving renunciation of corporate wealth and dependence on alms. Preaching and teaching in the community replaced a life of liturgical worship secluded from the world in the cloister. Evangelization and a general raising of religious standards by pastoral work and example took the place of intercession on behalf of, but apart from, society. The success of the friars showed how well attuned to their age was their programme: 'For more than a century they attracted a majority of the most earnest and brilliant of successive generations of youth throughout Europe and became the preachers, confessors, spiritual directors and theological masters of their age.'[27] The monasteries, of course, continued to attract recruits and patrons; they remained important to their society as great landowners and purveyors of spiritual services. But they never recovered the powers of regeneration apparent in successive earlier movements of reform.

The level at which comprehensive reform of the Benedictines was now pitched is indicated by the legislation of Pope Benedict XII in 1336.[28] There was no question of a radical return to strict observance of the Rule. Rather the papal constitutions attempted to maintain respectability by control of current practices, and made general within the order the existing movement towards provision of facilities for higher studies. Thus each monastery with adequate resources was instructed to maintain a master to teach the monks grammar, logic and philosophy; and the ablest students were to proceed to the universities to study theology or canon law. Every house was obligated 'to send out of every twenty monks one who is fit to acquire the fruit of greater learning to a university and to provide each one so sent with the yearly pension underwritten.'[29] Whilst this blanket obligation proved impossible to enforce, particularly on small and impoverished houses, surviving evidence in England shows that substantial monasteries like Selby Abbey maintained a succession of student monks at Oxford and Cambridge. At Westminster more than one in ten of the monks between 1300 and the Dissolution went up to Oxford.[30]

[27] D. Knowles, *Christian Monasticism*, p. 116.
[28] For a discussion, see D. Knowles, *The Religious Orders in England*, II, pp. 3–4.
[29] A. R. Myers (ed.), *English Historical Documents*, IV, p. 780.
[30] D. Knowles, *The Religious Orders in England*, II, p. 19.

The university-monk may be seen as a positive adaptation to the values of an age that held learning in high regard. Another provision of 1336, however, is more readily characterized as official acceptance of a widespread relaxation of the Rule that might be controlled but not eradicated. At least since the end of the twelfth century St Benedict's prohibition against meat-eating had been increasingly disregarded.[31] Now the Black Monks were officially permitted to eat meat on a regular basis four days a week (Sunday, Monday, Tuesday and Thursday), except during the four weeks of Advent and the nine weeks between Septuagesima and Easter. That this was a breach of the Rule was underlined by the regulations governing its practice: meat was only to be eaten in a dining-room other than the refectory, and only half of the community was to be absent from the refectory at a time. But such restrictions did little more than preserve appearances; the reality of a distinctive abstinence had been abandoned.

Similarly difficult to restrain were other developments which eroded the fully common life of Benedictine monasteries and blurred the dividing-line between the monastic lifestyle and that of colleges of secular priests. Although Benedict XII recalled the Black Monks to observance of the Rule's ban on private possessions and its corollary, provision of all necessities from a common store, repeated regulations on the subject failed to halt practices which gave the monks control of private funds and more individual privacy. The abbot had long had his own private establishment, and with his external concerns and absences from the cloister had ceased to exercize the close paternal control over the monastic family envisaged by the Rule. Other members of the community then secured their own separate quarters in the house, beginning with the prior as the abbot's second-in-command, and continuing in the fourteenth century with returned graduates in theology and senior monastic officials. By the end of the century the monastic dormitory was being partitioned into private cells.

Concurrently the 'wage-system'[32] had been introduced. Despite the emphasis in the Rule on personal poverty, the period 1150–1250 had seen the establishment in some monasteries of the practice of paying small sums of money to each monk for expenditure on alms and small personal needs; and at the same time the system of providing clothing from a common store began to be replaced by payment of a fixed allowance of money.[33]

---

[31] D. Knowles, *The Religious Orders in England*, I, pp. 17–21.
[32] Professor Knowles' phrase in *The Religious Orders in England*, II, ch. XVIII, where these developments are discussed in detail.
[33] D. Knowles, *The Religious Orders in England*, I, pp. 287–289. The clothing-allowance was generally in the neighbourhood of £1 in the early fifteenth century, and this was the sum paid at contemporary Selby Abbey. The Selby pittance for personal expenditure was 13s.6d. in 1362, but had risen to £1 by the fifteenth century (see the translated rolls of pittancer and chamberlain below).

Both these payments became normal in the fourteenth century. In addition individual monks began to be paid for various services performed in the monastery, so that monastic officals might now receive fees for the offices they held and masses said at endowed chantries be rewarded at a fixed rate. How much personal income individual monks could acquire by these means is difficult to calculate, and no doubt varied from house to house; but some idea of the scale of payments is perhaps gained by comparing the £1 pittance paid to each monk of Selby Abbey annually in 1403–1404, or the 40s. paid to the two monk-bursars of 1398–1399, with the yearly wages of 20s. paid to the abbot's cook, and the 13s.4d. received by superior servants. The sums involved are certainly not trifling by the standards of the time.

In these and other ways[34] the English Benedictines had by 1400 moved a long distance from the reality of renunciation of the world that in earlier centuries had brought them admiration, patronage, and influence. Material comfort bulks larger in their lifestyle than fervour or asceticism. Evidence of a similar failure of reforming vigour and a preoccupation with secular concerns is not lacking in many areas of the contemporary English Church, leading one historian to find in the period 'a widespread sense of decline, a feeling that abuses were gaining ground instead of being overcome.'[35] One may note, for example, that Chaucer's portrait of the friar is decidedly more virulent than that of the monk, reflecting contemporary disenchantment at the friars' falling-away from primitive ideals in their practice of poverty and mendicancy. But richly endowed monasteries could not hope to escape hostile scrutiny when a vigorous anti-clericalism began to question the very title of ecclesiastics to their endowments in the last quarter of the fourteenth century.

For many of Chaucer's contemporaries the worldliness of the Church of their day was a commonplace, its wealth the object of repeated attacks in a time of heavy taxation.[36] A bill said to have been presented to parliament in 1410 suggested that 'these worldly clerks, bishops, abbots and priors, who are such worldly lords be put to live by their spiritualities; for they ... do not do the office of true curates as prelates should, nor do they help the poor commons with their lordship as true secular lords should, nor do they live in penance nor in bodily travail as true religious should, by means of

[34] See R.H.Snape, *English Monastic Finances in the later middle ages*, Cambridge, 1926, ch. VI.
[35] A.R.Myers, *England in the late middle ages*, Harmondsworth, 1952, p.60. Chapter IV of this book provides a summary of fourteenth century developments in the Church.
[36] For the anti-clericalism of the 1370s and 1380s, see M.McKisack, *The Fourteenth Century*, Oxford, 1959, pp.289–291. The chronicler Thomas Walsingham reports that in 1385 the Commons responded to opposition by the clergy to their plans for binding the Church to a specified level of taxation by proposing disendowment of the temporalities of the Church (*Thomae Walsingham, Historia Anglicana*, ed. H.T.Riley, II, Rolls Series, 1864, p.140).

their possessions.'[37] Criticism of the religious was notably virulent, so much so that an earlier parallel can only be found two hundred years previously in the reign of Henry II according to the great historian of English monasticism, Professor David Knowles.[38] If words did not break any monastic bones and the assault on monastic wealth proved generally ineffective,[39] disquiet about the standards of religious life maintained in the monasteries did penetrate to the highest levels of lay society and prompt efforts at reform by a ruler far from unsympathetic to the monks. In 1421 Henry V summoned a special assembly of representatives of the Benedictine Order to discuss a list of specific reforming proposals.[40]

Although no radical changes eventuated from this meeting, the articles put forward in the king's name indicate the aspects of contemporary Benedictine monasticism that were of particular concern to the moderate reformers of the day. They were not dealing here with scandal, but with developments in Benedictine houses that had eroded the distinctive features separating the lifestyle of monks from that of the secular clergy: with modifications to the traditional concept of the monk as a member of a community apart from the world, committed to personal poverty and deriving his necessities from a common store, dedicated to the maintenance of worship and intercession in the abbey church. Beginning at the top they sought to restore effective leadership to the monastery by restricting the length of absences of its head, the abbot; to curb his worldly display in travelling from place to place; and to give the community greater participation in the disposal of income and property. For the general body of the convent they proposed stricter regulation or even reversal of relaxations of the Rule. Whilst meat-eating was accepted as established fact, it was to be regulated. Personal poverty was to be more strictly enforced by abolishing the payment of clothing and other allowances in money to individual monks, who would receive their habits and other necessities instead from a designated monk-official, and by controlling permissible private possessions. As for the monks' dress itself, there was to be uniformity and greater simplicity. The communal life was to be strengthened by forbidding private cells and apartments within the monastery to all

---

[37] A. R. Myers, *English Historical Documents*, IV, p. 669.

[38] 'During the latter half of the fourteenth century the religious orders, and in particular the friars, were subjected to attacks both public and literary, to which an earlier parallel can only be found in the simultaneous assaults by a group of bishops and by the court circle of writers upon the monks in the last years of Henry II.' D. Knowles, *The Religious Orders in England*, II, p. 90.

[39] The exploitation and eventual dissolution of the alien priories in this period is a notable exception, but this appears to have resulted from xenophobia generated by the Hundred Years War rather than hostility to monasticism or its practitioners. See M. M. Morgan, 'The Suppression of the Alien Priories', *History*, 26, 1941–42, pp. 204–212.

[40] For a discussion of this assembly see D. Knowles, *The Religious Orders in England*, II, pp. 182–184.

except the abbot and the sick, forcing a return to the common dormitory where a more spartan regime was to be enforced. Separation from the world outside the cloister and its female temptations was to be stricter, with visits to parents or friends restricted to once a year and trips into the city forbidden unless adequately accompanied.[41]

That meat-eating, money payments to individual monks, personal rooms in the monastery, and trips outside the confines of the cloister, were all common and valued features of early fifteenth century Benedictine houses is indicated by the opposition of the monks' representatives to the proposed changes and restrictions.[42] There was a plain unwillingness to reverse the trend towards a less restricted, more comfortable and individualistic life within the monastery, which perhaps only conformed to the rising living standards in society generally. The accuracy of Chaucer's portrayal of the tone of late medieval monasticism is confirmed by evidence from a source that can by no stretch of the imagination be termed hostile. By the nature of their proceedings, however, the reformers of 1421 could only produce in their proposals a partial view of monasteries as functioning institutions in fifteenth century society. Their object was to identify widespread failings and correct them; they have nothing to say of virtues, nor of the balance between the two in the very individual houses of the Order.[43] What social utility helped to preserve the monasteries for another century virtually intact will only appear from the records of the abbeys and priories themselves, where they are seen in interaction with the people and institutions around them.

II

Account rolls from one such community, Selby Abbey in Yorkshire, are presented here, providing as they do an intimate view of the internal organization of the monastery and of its contacts with the secular and ecclesiastical world outside its walls. The object has been to reconstruct and illustrate, as fully as archival survival will allow, the structure of administration and its functioning in a moderately important house during

[41] The proceedings of the 1421 meeting are printed in W. A. Pantin, *Documents Illustrating the Activities of the General and Provincial Chapters of the English Black Monks, 1215–1540*, II, Camden Society, third series 47, 1933, pp. 98–134.

[42] For their criticisms of the king's proposals see *ibid.*, pp. 116–124.

[43] As Professor Searle has remarked in her excellent introduction to Benedictine monasticism at Battle Abbey, 'the atmosphere of each individual house has always been unique to itself, the atmosphere of a family, the result of traditions developed within the house rather than of regulations imposed upon the house by a superior authority.' E. Searle and B. Ross, *Accounts of the Cellarers of Battle Abbey 1275–1513*, Sydney University Press, 1967, p. 4.

this period of criticism and attempted reform. An abbey of substantial wealth but not in the first rank of English monastic foundations has been preferred because, with all the inadequacies and dispersal of evidence that exist in regard to Selby, it offers a better opportunity to see and understand the normal monastic life of the times than, for instance, the already much-studied cathedral priories, whose archives may be better preserved. Even the defects in its surviving evidence may, perhaps, have the one virtue that they illustrate a common enough problem for the student of monastic history.

Selby Abbey is situated close to the Ouse River some 22 kilometres south of York in the town which began to grow up around it during the twelfth century. In 1377 five hundred and eighty-six taxpayers were recorded as contributing in the town to the poll tax levied on all lay persons over the age of fourteen, suggesting a total population of under a thousand persons.[44] Even by medieval standards, then, Selby was an urban community of modest size; and it ranked sixth in the West Riding of Yorkshire behind Pontefract, Doncaster, Sheffield, Ripon, and Tickhill, in the poll tax returns of 1379.[45] Over the life of the town the abbey exercized an ever-present dominance. The abbot was its lord; his representatives held a court at the gates of the abbey which regulated its affairs;[46] and his officers collected rents, tithes, and other dues for the maintenance of the ecclesiastical corporation that affected in one form or another all inhabitants. Even the parish church was a dependent chapel served by a chaplain appointed and salaried by the abbey. No other religious foundation existed in Selby to challenge its position.

Inevitably much of Selby's population depended for their livelihood directly or indirectly on the monastery, with its demands for servants, goods, and services. But the town also served the local economy as a market centre and an inland port for the busy river traffic between the Humber mouth and York. The 1379 poll tax returns reveal a flourishing

---

[44] J. C. Russell, *British Medieval Population*, Albuquerque, New Mexico, 1948, p. 143. Attempts to use poll tax returns to estimate total population of towns and villages are fraught with difficulties. Professor Russell's multiplier of 1.5 does not command general acceptance (see J. Hatcher, *Plague, Population and the English Economy 1348–1530*, London, 1977, pp. 13–14). An idea of relative size can be obtained from the fact that in 1377 York, the realm's second city, recorded more than 7,000 taxpayers, and the town of Kingston-upon-Hull lower down the river from Selby 1,557 (J. C. Russell, *British Medieval Population*, pp. 142–143).

[45] Selby recorded 460 taxpayers in 1379, when markedly increased evasion seems to have accompanied collection of the poll tax compared with 1377. The returns for 1379 in the West Riding of Yorkshire have been printed in the *Yorkshire Archaeological Journal*, vols 5 (1879), 6 (1881), and 7 (1882), and record 914 taxpayers for Pontefract, 757 for Doncaster, about 530 for Sheffield, 483 for Ripon, and 461 for Tickhill.

[46] More than a hundred court rolls from Selby survive in the collections of documents at Hull University Library (HUL, DDLO 21/1–105) and in the Westminster Diocesan Archives (WDA, Se/CR/1–16). The series begins in 1322 and continues with gaps to the Dissolution.

group of six merchant families at Selby, assessed at a level of tax which placed them among the moderately prosperous members of society.[47] At the same time a wide variety of trades was carried on there, though none involved more than a handful of craftsmen.[48] The largest single group, engaged in textile production, comprised a chaloner, a draper, five weavers and five dyers, making Selby a small centre of an industry widely dispersed in the villages and townships across the river in the wapentakes of Ouse and Derwent and Howdenshire.[49] A further important activity is suggested by its five inn-keepers. With its great monastery bringing visitors to the town, its regular ferry-service across the Ouse on a major north-south route, and the river traffic, Selby was able to support several establishments serving the needs of travellers.[50]

In the ecclesiastical organization of the English Church the abbey belonged to the diocese of York, which with the dioceses of Carlisle and Durham made up the northern province under the archbishop of York as metropolitan. It was this archbishop, or his suffragans, who ordained the monks of Selby as priests; and it was he who exercized episcopal rights of visitation over the monastery. Similarly the abbot was regularly summoned to attend convocation at York, the provincial assembly of the clergy, whose main concern like its counterpart at Canterbury was grants of taxation to the crown.[51] Whilst Selby was an important house in the north, it was also only one substantial community in the midst of a rich diversity of religious foundations spread thickly over the countryside.[52] Within a day or two's journey from Selby were to be found representatives of all the major orders for men and women: other Benedictine houses like Monk Bretton or the great abbey of St Mary's York; a Cluniac priory at

---

[47] The tax was graded from a minimum of 4d. for all persons above the age of sixteen years to the £6 13s.4d. paid by the dukes of Lancaster and Brittany. Merchants and artificers paid a minimum of 6d. (*English Historical Documents*, IV, ed. A. R. Myers, pp. 125–126). Selby's six merchants each paid 3s.4d.; and the only comparable taxpayer in the town was a single esquire probably retained by the abbot in his household (*YAJ*, 6, 1881, p. 146).

[48] The following trades are recorded, the number in each category being given in brackets: butcher (2), inn-keeper (5), spicer (1), chaloner (1), draper (1), dyer (5), weaver (5), shoemaker (1), tailor (7), smith (5), carpenter (6), cooper (1), dauber (1), mason (1), slater (1), tanner (3), fletcher (1). See *YAJ*, 6, 1881, pp. 129–149.

[49] More than eighty weavers and three drapers are recorded in the poll tax returns for Howdenshire and the southern townships of Ouse and Derwent in 1379. See *YAJ*, 9, 1886, pp. 129–162.

[50] Medieval Selby is briefly discussed in R. B. Dobson, *Selby Abbey and Town*, Selby, 1969, pp. 21–23.

[51] See D. B. Weske, *The Convocation of the Clergy*, London, 1937, and E. W. Kemp, *Counsel and Consent*, London, 1961.

[52] This fact is best appreciated by consulting the two sheets of the *Map of Monastic Britain*, Ordnance Survey, Chessington, Surrey, second edition 1954 (south sheet) and 1955 (north sheet). There is also a useful ecclesiastical map of Yorkshire in *The Victoria History of the Counties of England*, Yorkshire, III, ed. W. Page, London, 1913, facing p. 1; and this volume also contains brief histories of the religious houses of Yorkshire, including Selby Abbey.

Pontefract; Cistercian monasteries at Kirkstall and Meaux; nunneries at Nunburneholme and Nun Appleton; Augustinian canons at Drax, Nostell, or Bridlington; Gilbertines at Watton; and the friars at York, Pontefract, or Hull. Over one of these houses, Bridlington Priory, the last Englishman canonized in the medieval period ruled as prior from 1361 to his death in 1379, lending a touch of distinction to the prevailing tone of mediocrity in northern monasticism. John Thwenge's reputation for holiness of life, and local veneration within a few years of his death, resulted in his canonization in 1401.[53]

By the fourteenth century successive waves of founding zeal had multiplied religious houses to saturation point, and with the dramatic fall in population after the arrival of bubonic plague in 1348 there was hardly need for more, even if fashion had not moved in other directions. Yet two new monastic foundations were made in Yorkshire at this time, the Carthusian houses at Kingston-upon-Hull and Mount Grace, founded respectively in 1378 and 1398.[54] The explanation lies mainly in the exceptional character of the Order. Carthusians were part hermits, part community monks, combining the self-denial and solitude of private cells with community worship in the monastery church and common meals on certain days.[55] Their reputation for undiminished austerity and observance made them still attractive to patrons even in a period critical of contemporary monasticism. More typical of popular piety than investment in new monastic houses, however, was the endowment of private chantries in churches great and small; or the employment of pious benefaction in enlarging and rebuilding parish churches.[56]

As we have seen, Selby Abbey was an old-established house in Chaucer's day. Its foundation dated to 1070 or soon thereafter.[57] It was one of five independent Benedictine monasteries in the province of York, two of which, the abbey of St Mary's York and the cathedral priory of Durham, were larger and wealthier.[58] Size and revenues alike place Selby in the second rank of monastic houses, though its head had the distinction of being one of the twenty-four Black Monk superiors regularly summoned

---

[53] See D. Knowles, *The Religious Orders in England*, II, pp. 118–119.

[54] *VCH*, Yorkshire, III, pp. 190–192.

[55] See D. Knowles, *The Monastic Order in England*, pp. 377–380, and *The Religious Orders in England*, II, pp. 129–138.

[56] See K. L. Wood-Legh, *Perpetual Chantries in Britain*, Cambridge, 1965, and *VCH*, Yorkshire, III, pp. 41–43.

[57] See R. B. Dobson, 'The First Norman Abbey in Northern England', *The Ampleforth Journal*, LXXIV, pt II, Summer 1969, pp. 161–176.

[58] The other two were Whitby Abbey and Monk Bretton Priory. St Mary's York had a net income of £1,650 in 1535, whilst Durham had one of £1,366 at the same date. The abbot and 50 monks surrendered St Mary's in 1539; and Durham had a community of about 70 monks in the fifteenth century, some 40 of them resident at the cathedral priory itself. D. Knowles and R. N. Hadcock, *Medieval Religious Houses. England and Wales*, 2nd edition, London, 1971, pp. 53, 58, and 82; R. B. Dobson, *Durham Priory*, Cambridge, 1973, p. 52.

as spiritual lords to parliament. Its income in the late fourteenth century was about £800 a year, exclusive of loans and other income anticipations,[59] a figure that did not change greatly between then and the dissolution of the abbey in 1539.[60]

The resources of the monastery divided basically into two groups, its landed endowment of manors and estates on the one hand, and its spiritual possessions, the appropriated churches with their tithes and other dues, on the other. The former provided the larger proportion of income. According to an assessment of the taxable income of the abbey included in a register of Abbot Shirburn's time (1369–1408) temporalities accounted for four sevenths of the total valuation of about £718.[61] The abbey's landed interests were concentrated in south-east Yorkshire and northern Lincolnshire around the Ouse, Aire, and Trent rivers. Close to Selby itself were Stainer, Brayton, Thorpe Willoughby, and Hambleton, with Monk Fryston and Hillam about 12 kilometres to the west. To the north was the manor of Acaster Selby and lands in Stillingfleet; to the east the small manor of Gunby and land in Holme upon Spalding Moor. Some 12 kilometres south-east of Selby was the manor of Rawcliffe, with parcels of land nearby in villages such as Cowick and Pollington; whilst further away on the old borders of Lincolnshire and near to the River Trent were Eastoft, Luddington, and Garthorpe. In Lincolnshire the chief estates were centred on Crowle and the west bank of the Trent; but there was also a manor at Stallingborough near to Grimsby and the mouth of the Humber. Right outside these areas and well to the south were the manors of Queniborough in Leicestershire and Stanford on Avon in Northamptonshire.[62] The manor-house at Stanford served as a guest-house for Selby monks and their officials travelling to or returning from the south, notably Oxford and London.[63]

By the later years of Abbot John de Shirburn Selby Abbey restricted its direct involvement in cultivation of its demesnes to a very few estates. Like other landowners in this period of contracting population, economic difficulties, and social changes, the monks of Selby were engaged in the

[59] See G.S.Haslop, 'The Abbot of Selby's Financial Statement for the Year Ending Michaelmas 1338', *Yorkshire Archaeological Journal*, 44, 1972, pp.168–169. Mr Haslop supplies a figure of about £795 in 1373, which is close to my own tentative estimate, based on the incomplete series of obedientiary accounts for the early fifteenth century.

[60] At the Dissolution in 1539 net income was about £733, gross income about £819. *Valor Ecclesiasticus temp. Henrici VIII, auctoritate regia institutus*, ed. J.Caley and J.Hunter, V, 1825, pp.12–14.

[61] See G.S.Haslop, 'The Abbot of Selby's Financial Statement for the Year Ending Michaelmas 1338', pp.161 and 168.

[62] For a full description of Selby's estates, see *ibid*. pp.159–161. The distribution of the abbey's estates is shown on Maps A and B.

[63] See, for examples, the bursars' account for 1398–1399 translated below under 'Small expenses'.

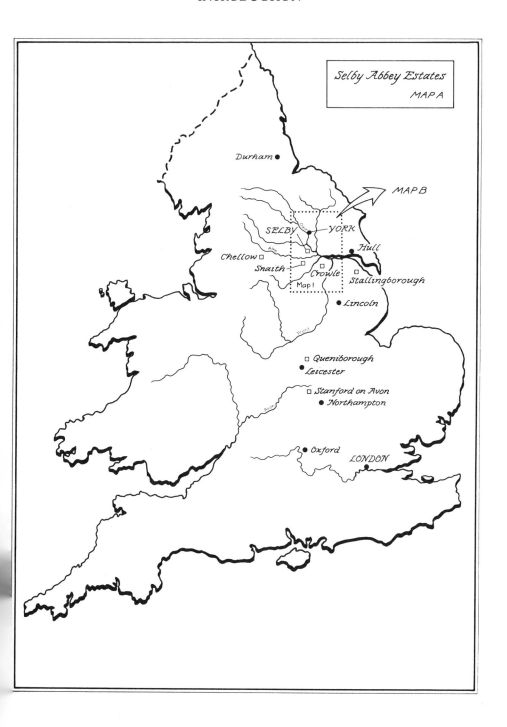

Selby Abbey Estates
MAP A

later fourteenth century in leasing the bulk of their demesnes for money rents.[64] Lack of manorial and obedientiary accounts for these years hampers detailed analysis of changes in policy at Selby towards its manors; but surviving registers show leasing underway from shortly after the middle of the century.[65] As might be expected the outlying manors of Queniborough and Stanford on Avon provide early evidence of this new regime; the abbey's interest in them was now money rents, not agricultural production for the market.[66] When bursars' accounts become available to provide a wider view of abbey finances, they confirm the extensive and permanent leasing of demesnes all over Selby's estates.[67] Nonetheless, the monks did not entirely abandon agricultural production. They continued to need large supplies of food stuffs, particularly grain, for the support of the community; and for these they still looked partly to a handful of manors, as well as to their tithe-barns and the market. Their officers on these manors were the *servientes* or serjeants,[68] salaried estate-managers responsible for the cultivation of the demesne land still in hand and accountable for the disposal of its yields to the central auditor of the house.[69]

---

[64] For discussions of the problems of landowners in the fourteenth century and their responses, see M. M. Postan, *The Medieval Economy and Society*, London, 1972, ch. 6; and D. Knowles, *The Religious Orders in England*, II, pp. 322–324. Durham Cathedral Priory established a thoroughgoing leasehold system early in the fifteenth century (see B. Dobson, *Durham Priory*, p. 272).

[65] For an analysis of the evidence, see G. S. Haslop, 'The Abbot of Selby's Financial Statement for the Year Ending Michaelmas 1338', pp. 166–168.

[66] The manor and demesnes of Stanford on Avon had been leased for 21 years in 1377 at £7 p.a., and the services of bond tenants granted to the lessees during the period of their lease for £6 17s.10d. a year (British Library, Cotton Vitellius E.XVI, fos 152v–153). Queniborough manor and the services of its villeins had been leased for 15 years about 1355 at a rent that rose by stages to £10 p.a. in the last five years (Leeds City Libraries, Towneley Manuscript, fos 32–33, no. 149).

[67] For a list of demesnes leased in whole or part in 1398–1399, see the bursars' account translated below under 'New farms, with mills, customary services, and courts'. In 1416–1417 the bursar recorded the following demesnes as so leased: Stanford on Avon, Queniborough, Crowle, Rawcliffe, Holme upon Spalding Moor, Gunby, Chellow, Stallingborough, Acaster Selby, and Thorpe Willoughby (WDA, Se/Ac/9, s.v. *Nove firme cum molendinis et operibus*).

[68] The translation 'serjeant' has been preferred to the alternative 'servant' in order to differentiate these officers clearly from other employees of the abbey, notably at the monastery itself. The same word 'serviens' is also used to describe the officials responsible for collecting, storing, and disposing of tithes belonging to the abbey in certain areas; and since serjeants in charge of demesnes also account for tithes in some cases, the same translation has been employed. The word 'bailiff' was used as an alternative to serjeant in one account of the period (*ballivus vel serviens*), HUL, DDLO 20/48.

[69] Their accounts have survived from only four estates for the late fourteenth and early fifteenth centuries. At Eastoft there is a damaged bundle of five accounts, in several cases covering part of the year only, from c.1358–c.1360, and a single account for the year 1424–25 (HUL, DDLO 4/2 and 4/3). Garthorpe provides dated accounts for 1389–90, 1390–91, and an undated account of about 1390 (HUL, DDLO 20/62, 63, 64); and Monk Fryston a single account for 1393–94 (WDA, Se/Ac/4). A description of the manor of Monk Fryston in 1320 can be found in the Extent translated in YAS, Misc. IV, RS 94, 1937, pp. 39–53. For the

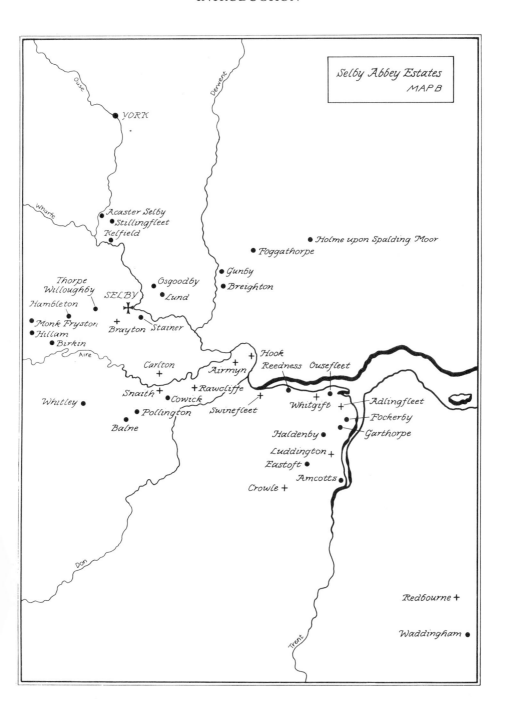

Selby Abbey Estates
MAP B

INTRODUCTION

Whilst the larger proportion of Selby's income and resources came from its landed endowments, a substantial part was derived from the spiritual possessions of the house, its several appropriated parish churches, whose revenues of tithes and various offerings were paid to the monks as perpetual rector. Appropriation of churches had been a favourite method of augmenting the income of monasteries[70] since the twelfth century. In return for enjoying the revenues of the benefice, the appropriator had the obligation of providing for the cure of souls in the church, usually by means of an endowed vicar or stipendiary chaplain, and of supporting charity and hospitality in the parish. The expected surplus of receipts over expenditure went to support the appropriating house.

By the late fourteenth century Selby Abbey was receiving tithes and other income from numerous churches and chapels in the dioceses of York and Lincoln.[71] Selby, Snaith, Brayton, and Adlingfleet, had been appropriated in the diocese of York, with a variety of arrangements for the cure of souls. At Selby there was a parish church served by a salaried chaplain, whereas the church at Snaith was cared for by two resident Selby monks, one of whom was known as the prior. Snaith, however, had an extensive parish; and dependent chapels served by chaplains had been created at Carlton, Whitgift, Hook, and Airmyn, to look after the needs of their inhabitants. In 1370 the parishioners of Whitgift living in Swinefleet were also given permission to build themselves a chapel,[72] and another was established at Rawcliffe about this time. Brayton and Adlingfleet both had vicarages, whose vicars received a fixed part of the revenues of their livings;[73] and vicarages had also been ordained in all Selby's appropriated churches in the diocese of Lincoln. These were at Crowle, Luddington, Redbourne, and Stallingborough. The only addition to this list in the

---

monastery's home farm at Stainer, less than two kilometres from the abbey, there are two serjeants' rolls of 1421–22 and 1423–24 (WDA, Se/Ac/12; and HUL, DDLO 20/66). An account also survives for 1523–24 (HUL, DDLO 20/74), the account of the keeper (*Custos*) of Stainer, by then a stock-keeper for the abbey's meat supplies without responsibility for domestic cultivation.

[70] But also other corporate bodies such as colleges and cathedral chapters, and even the personal incomes of bishops. See R. A. R. Hartridge, *A History of Vicarages in the Middle Ages*, Cambridge, 1930, p. 29. The *Taxatio* of 1291–92 shows that there were then some 1,500 vicarages out of a total of about 8,100 churches. In 1535 the *Valor Ecclesiasticus* shows that out of 8,838 rectories, 3,307 had been appropriated with vicarages, or over 37 per cent of the total. *Ibid.* pp. 79 and 214.

[71] This paragraph is based on Mr Haslop's discussion of the subject in his article 'The Abbot of Selby's Financial Statement for the Year Ending Michaelmas 1338', p. 161.

[72] British Library, Cotton Vitellius E.XVI, f. 100r.

[73] The ordination of the vicarage at Adlingfleet in 1307 is printed in *The Coucher Book of Selby*, ed. J. T. Fowler, I, Yorkshire Archaeological Society, Record Series 10, 1891, pp. 344–345, whilst that at Brayton in 1348 is recorded in the register of Archbishop Zouche (Borthwick Institute of Historical Research, Archbishop's Register 10, fos xxi verso–xxii). The annual value of Brayton was then assessed at £33 6s.8d. and the vicar's portion at £14 13s.4d.

fifteenth century was the appropriation of the rectory of Stanford on Avon, licenced by the crown in 1441 and confirmed by the pope in 1453.[74]

More than £300 a year was calculated to be derived from these churches in Abbot John de Shirburn's time; and when the Dissolution was imminent in 1535, spiritual revenues accounted for a third of the gross income of about £819.[75] Such revenues could be extracted basically by two alternative methods, both of which were used at Selby in the late fourteenth and early fifteenth centuries. The monks could collect their tithes and offerings for themselves, employing members of the community or salaried officials to supervize their exaction and account for the proceeds; or they could lease the expected revenues to a farmer and settle for a fixed income. Leasing was permitted by an archiepiscopal licence of 1382;[76] and a document entered in Shirburn's register, dated 1401, records the terms of one such agreement. William de Croft, chaplain at Hook, was given the right to collect from Airmyn, Hook, *Morham*, and *Loune*, all offerings and dues except mortuaries, lesser tithes, and tithe hay from the first three places, for ten years. In return he was to serve the chapel, provide bread and wine for masses, candles and incense for the church, and pay £10 through the kitchener to the abbey yearly. As the monk's proctor there he also had a residence in Hook and the right to obtain fuel from the monastic turbary.[77] Other farmers of Selby's tithes and offerings were clearly laymen, as a later papal licence of 1412 specifically permitted.[78]

At the same time the abbot and convent of Selby looked to officials accounting to their central auditors for the exaction of their rights in other areas. A monk was regularly appointed to the office of keeper of the spirituality of Snaith, two-thirds of whose assessed revenues of £38 p.a. were derived from spiritual sources in 1535 including the profits of the ecclesiastical court there.[79] No accounts have survived from this office. At Garthorpe, Eastoft, and no doubt elsewhere, salaried servants of the abbey combined responsibility for cultivation of the demesne with the task of accounting for local tithes.[80] Lastly, the abbot appointed officers charged with managing particular tithe-barns belonging to the abbey or responsible for both revenues and expenses of its dependent chapels; and a handful of

---

[74] *CPR*, 1436–41, p. 496 and *CPL*, X, 1447–55, pp. 246–49.

[75] See British Library, Cotton Vitellius E.XVI, f. 153v for the assessment of Abbot John de Shirburn's time and HUL DDLO 20/60 for that of 1535. The proportion of Selby's income derived from spiritual sources is very comparable to that calculated for Bolton Priory, another northern house, in its last days (I. Kershaw, *Bolton Priory: the economy of a northern monastery, 1286–1325*, p. 71).

[76] British Library, Cotton Vitellius E.XVI, f. 123v.

[77] British Library, Cotton Vitellius E.XVI, f. 146r.

[78] *CPL*, VI, 1404–1415, p. 393.

[79] HUL, DDLO 20/60.

[80] See the serjeants' accounts for these manors, HUL, DDLO 4/3 and 20/62.

accounts for parts of the parish of Snaith survive to illustrate their responsibilities.[81]

Since the purpose of a monastic appropriation was to divert revenues from the parish church and its priest to other purposes, often on the basis of a claim of financial difficulties by the monastery concerned, neglect of parochial responsibilities had long been a problem within the system[82] and in the critical atmosphere of the later fourteenth century its alleged abuses and evil consequences aroused sharp concern in parliament. In 1391 the Commons claimed that appropriators knocked down and removed buildings, and brought to an end divine service, hospitality, and other works of charity customarily performed there for the poor and unfortunate.[83] They sought a virtual end of further appropriations in 1401;[84] and failing to secure this from the king, pressed in the next year for restrictions and regulation in the interests of the spiritual welfare of parishioners.[85] The result was statutory provisos for the endowment of a vicarage and provision of a suitable sum of money for yearly distribution as alms in all future appropriations, terms which we find implemented in Selby's appropriation of Stanford on Avon.[86]

There is a little evidence that the parishioners of Selby's appropriated churches might have shared some of the sentiments expressed in parliament, whose causes may partly have lain in attempts to adjust to a falling population and reduced incomes from tithes and offerings. A petition to the archbishop of York from the men of Whitgift, entered without date in the Shirburn register, complains that Whitgift church used to have two chaplains to serve the needs of parishioners, but that the abbot of Selby had reduced the number to one for forty years past. The Whitgift petitioners

---

[81] Just seven such accounts remain. Four are records of the tithe-barns at Hook and Carlton 1425–28 and 1430–31 (HUL, DDLO 20/67–70), and the others compiled by the abbot's proctor at Whitgift and Reedness for the years 1377–78, 1397–98, and 1420–21 (WDA, Se/Ac/3; HUL, DDLO 20/65; and *Two Obedientiary Rolls of Selby Abbey*, ed. B. Holt, YAS, Misc. VI, Record Series 118, 1953, pp. 41–52). The accountants at Hook and Carlton had a restricted responsibility, dealing only with tithes of grain, its collection, storage, sale, and transport to the abbey. The dues and offerings coming to the two chapels were separately accounted for, in 1416–17 to the kitchener. The proctor at Whitgift and Reedness, however, answered not only for all kinds of tithes, but also for mortuaries and offerings at the chapels within his area, for whose general running-costs he provided.

[82] See R. H. Snape, *English Monastic Finances in the later middle ages*, ch. III.

[83] J. Strachey and others (ed.), *Rotuli Parliamentorum; ut et Petitiones, et Placita in Parliamento*, 6 vols, 1783, III, pp. 293–294. The king granted legislation enacting that in each royal licence for the appropriation of a parish church in future provisos would be included that the vicar be properly endowed and a suitable sum of money ordained for distribution among the poor parishioners of the church annually.

[84] *RP*, III, p. 468.

[85] *RP*, III, pp. 499–500.

[86] A perpetual vicarage was instituted with a yearly portion of £10 and a suitable house for the vicar. In 1535 we find that the abbey distributed 3s. 4d. annually in alms, whilst the bursar was then receiving £20 a year from tithes of grains and hay in the parish. *CPR*, 1436–1441, p. 496; *CPL*, X, 1447–1455, pp. 246–249; and HUL, DDLO 20/60.

asked for redress, alleging that people were dying without the last rites of confession and communion.[87] They appear to have achieved their objectives. For whereas the proctor's account for 1377–1378 records the payment of £5 6s.8d. salary to only one parish chaplain of Whitgift, the account of 1420–1421 shows £10 paid to two chaplains.[88]

The income derived by Selby Abbey from its manors and churches supported a large house by late medieval standards, though not one of the largest. The community in 1362 numbered 27 monks, and can be shown to have remained close to that level throughout the fifteenth century. In 1496–1497, for example, there were 29 monks at Selby.[89] Whilst the average size of the fifty largest English Black Monk abbeys and priories was also about 30 in 1500, some houses were considerably larger. Canterbury had 70 monks about the same time, Bury 60, St Albans 57, Gloucester 50, Westminster 46, Ely 42, and Reading 40.[90] In the northern province St Mary's abbey at York and Durham cathedral priory again housed substantially larger communities than Selby. The stability of Selby's numbers is, however, worth noting as some evidence of continuing vitality. If ability to secure recruits necessary to maintain a community at a stable size, presumably commensurate with its income, is any guide to the health of a monastic institution, then the abbey's state was sound enough in its last century and a half of existence.

Where these recruits to the monastic life came from, and the social classes from which they were drawn, are questions to which it is difficult to provide satisfactory answers. Very many of the Selby monks are identified in its records, not by surnames, but by a placename used with the preposition 'de' between it and the Christian name (John de Seleby, Nicholas de Rouclif, for example). Indeed all except one of the names in the 1362 pittancer's roll are of this type. Whilst it is not certain that such names necessarily indicate the place of origin of each individual monk,[91] it seems likely that this is so; and the results of an analysis are interesting if not surprising. Of the 26 monks named or identifiable in the pittancer's roll for 1362,[92] more than two-thirds had the names of places within a radius of 50 kilometres of the abbey, and twelve of places within a radius half that distance. Many obviously came from villages and parishes in which Selby Abbey had a financial interest as landlord or appropriator, like

---

[87] British Library, Cotton Vitellius E.XVI, f. 115v.
[88] WDA, Se/Ac/3, s.v. Res' Capelle (1377–78); Two Obedientiary Rolls of Selby Abbey, ed. B. Holt, p. 45 (1420–21).
[89] WDA, Se/Ac/2 and 21, pittancer's rolls for 1362 and 1496–97.
[90] D. Knowles, The Religious Orders in England, II, p. 258.
[91] For a discussion of the question in relation to Durham Cathedral Priory, see R. B. Dobson, Durham Priory 1400–1450, pp. 56–58.
[92] Neither abbot nor prior is named in the roll, but the former is known to have been Geoffrey de Gaddesby (1342–68).

Walter de Stallingborough who took his name from a manor near Grimsby in Lincolnshire. In general the monastery's main area of recruitment was evidently where one might expect it to be, in and around south-east Yorkshire and northern Lincolnshire where the bulk of its possessions lay.

Evidence of the social origins of the monks is very sparse. The likeliest conclusion is 'that most late mediaeval Selby monks derived from the middle, rather than the lower or upper, ranks of urban and village society';[93] but the strongest indication of the relative obscurity of the families of most recruits is simply the paucity of information on the subject. Among the abbots under whose rule the present account rolls were compiled, William Pygot (1408–1429) appears quite exceptional in the amount of evidence we have about his family. In Pygot's case we know that he was related to the gentry family of Pygot of Butley, county Chester; that his brother, John Pygot, was rector of Roos in Holderness, some 70 kilometres east of Selby; and that another possible relative had been prioress of Gokewell in Lincolnshire sometime before 1431, when she was in receipt of a pension at Selby.[94] Yet even in Pygot's case it has not proved possible to trace his parents.

Hardly less difficult to estimate is the quality of monastic life and fidelity to the Rule of these monks. After the time of Archbishop William Melton (1316–40) the records of episcopal visitations at Selby, which provide the only extensive evidence for such judgements, are no longer entered in the registers of the archbishops of York. What other bits and pieces do remain suggest that Selby in the fifteenth century may have sustained a higher standard than it had in the late thirteenth or early fourteenth centuries. Then the women of the town were a persistent source of temptation and difficulty to the monks and, in 1280, to their abbot, who was deposed by Archbishop Wickwane for immorality among other offences. Late in 1335 six of the monks were found at the archbishop's visitation to be seriously compromised by relations with townswomen. Brother Adam de la Breuer, whose offences were evidently the most blatant, had a liking for female company that showed itself in conversations with women even in the monastic cloister. Drink-loving, lecherous, and the cause of contention within the community, so it was reported, he had been involved in sexual relations with two sisters, the daughters of Roger, a Selby smith. His duties in church may well have bored him, for he was accustomed to leave the choir before the end of services without leave. His punishment as laid down by the archbishop seems designed to make him a warning to others:

---

[93] R. B. Dobson, *Selby Abbey and Town*, p. 24.
[94] See W. W. Morrell, *The History and Antiquities of Selby*, Selby, 1867, pp. 94 and 97; WDA, Se/Ac/9, s.v. *Forinsece expense*; F. Renaud, *Contributions towards a history of the ancient parish of Prestbury, in Cheshire*, Chetham Society Publications, Old Series 97, 1876, pp. 66–70; Durham Dean and Chapter Muniments, Loc. XXV, no. 74; and HUL, DDLO 20/1, s.v. *Pensiones*.

imprisonment for a year, well away from the possiblility of female access and deprived of culinary delicacies, with regular floggings administered in chapter and days of fasting on bread and weak ale.[95]

Twenty or so years later, in 1359, there was scandal of a different kind, when Abbot Geoffrey de Gaddesby sought the aid of the crown and its officers in securing the person of an apostate monk, who had abandoned his religious habit and left the house without licence. A royal commission was duly issued to the sheriff of York and certain local landowners.[96] The monk in question, Brother John de Hemmyngburgh, was no obscure or recently acquired member of the community, but a former proctor of the abbot to parliament in 1346 and prior of Selby in 1351.[97] The background to this affair is obscure, but it is unlikely that it was permanently settled by the return of Brother John to the abbey as a result of the royal mandate for the seizure of his person. In 1372 he was in London seeking to leave the realm for the court of Rome, an objective that he was eventually able to achieve 'for the furtherance of certain business which concerns his soul's health'. An undated document in an abbey register suggests that he then proceeded to the papal court, where his activities alarmed the abbey into appointing a proctor to protect its interests.[98]

Neither the incontinent nor the apostate monk was an uncommon phenomenon,[99] and at Selby on at least two earlier occasions in 1280 and 1317 the abbot sought the aid of the secular arm in returning fugitive monks to the house.[100] After Hemmyngburgh, however, there is no evidence of further such cases, whether as a result of the accidents of record survival or greater commitment to the monastic profession we cannot be certain.[101] Certainly by comparison with the surviving reports of the archbishops' visitations, what little visitation material is available for fifteenth century Selby Abbey presents a striking contrast. In 1423 the proctor of the abbot of Burton on Trent, who visited the abbey on behalf of the Benedictines' own provincial chapter, reported to this assembly that at Selby 'by the will of God the highest peace is found, charity is

---

[95] See *The Victoria History of the Counties of England*, Yorkshire, III, London, 1913, p. 98, and Borthwick Institute of Historical Research, University of York, Archbishop's Register 9A, William Melton, fos 206–207.

[96] PRO, C. 81/1786, no. 45 and British Library, Cotton Vitellius E.XVI, f. 162v; *CPR*, 1358–61, p. 224.

[97] PRO, D.L. 42/8, fos 11v–12r, and Borthwick Institute of Historical Research, Archbishop's Register 10, William Zouche, f. 210.

[98] British Library, Cotton Vitellius E.XVI, f. 113v and 147v; *CCR*, 1369–74, p. 471.

[99] See R.B. Dobson, *Durham Priory 1400–1450*, pp. 74–77 and C. Harper-Bill, 'Monastic Apostasy in late medieval England', *Journal of Ecclesiastical History*, 32, 1981, pp. 1–18. There are 55 requests for secular aid against Benedictine apostates in the surviving Chancery file PRO, C. 81/1786.

[100] PRO, C. 81/1786, nos 43 and 44.

[101] No Selby Abbey register survives for any abbacy after that of John de Shirburn (1369–1408).

nourished, and the other virtues belonging to men of religion are daily augmented.'[102] It is true that at this same meeting of the provincial chapter the abbot of Selby reported a similar inability to find any flaws in the religious life of the other Benedictine houses in the dioceses of Durham and York, which may suggest a lack of penetrating inquiry in these visits by monastic prelates to brother houses.[103] But we can assume that the Selby visitor would not have been so fulsome if there had been any obvious and serious problems.

The peace and charity praised by the abbot of Burton on Trent had been less evident a decade previously, as one of the members of the community in 1423, Brother Thomas Allerton, could have testified. In 1410 he and Brother Adam Crosseby had complained to the archbishop of York, Henry Bowet, about the actions of fellow-monks against them. For reasons that are not revealed by the entry in Bowet's register, Brother Thomas Allerton was sufficiently unpopular with certain unnamed Selby monks for them to post up a document about him in the infirmary making slanderous accusations. In order to do this secretly and unimpeded, Brother Adam Crosseby had been prevented from leaving his cell in the infirmary to attend matins in the monastery church, the door being secured from the outside.[104] Perhaps we have here no more than a malicious prank producing an excessive reaction; there is no further evidence to shed more light on the incident. It does, however, indicate the tensions and backbiting of a small enclosed community, which could lead in extreme cases to serious physical assault. Selby Abbey did not, it appears, suffer the scandals of contemporary Durham, where monks were wounded with knives by other monks.[105]

Although Selby Abbey may not have had the problem of apostasy in the early fifteenth century, there is other occasional evidence to suggest that a few recruits lacked genuine commitment to the monastic life. Two of the novices who came to Selby in Abbot William Pygot's time (1408–29) seem to have ended their careers there under his successor John Ousthorpe (1436–66) by securing papal dispensations to hold benefices with cure of souls, such as a parish church or perpetual vicarage. Brother Thomas Duffeld, who had entered the house about 1427, was one of the select group of university monks from which Abbots Pygot and Ousthorpe had

---

[102] *Dei nutu pax summa reperitur, caritas enutritur, cetereque virtutes religiosis viris pertinentes indies augmentantur.* W. A. Pantin, *Documents Illustrating the Activities of the General and Provincial Chapters of the English Black Monks, 1215–1540*, II, p. 144.

[103] *Ibid.* R. B. Dobson expresses similar doubts in *Durham Priory 1400–1450*, p. 248.

[104] Borthwick Institute of Historical Research, Archbishop's Register 18, Henry Bowet, fos 274v–275. Brother Adam de Crosseby's cell in the infirmary would be a concession to his age; he was already a member of the house forty-eight years earlier in 1362 (WDA, Se/Ac/2. Pittancer's roll).

[105] Shortly before 1400 and again in 1407 monks of Durham were wounded by other monks. See R. B. Dobson, *Durham Priory 1400–1450*, p. 74.

been drawn for leadership of the house. He was being supported by Selby Abbey at Oxford in 1431–32.[106] In 1438–39 he is found serving as pittancer and chamberlain; but three years later he obtained his papal dispensation and immediately disappears from the Selby records.[107] Similarly, Brother Thomas Normanton, 'of noble race' according to his papal grant, received permission to hold a benefice in 1443, after a career of nearly twenty years at Selby that included tenure of the office of pittancer and chamberlain 1433–35 and 1436–38.[108] He too does not figure again in the abbey's records.

III

Both Duffeld and Normanton are typical of Selby monks in one respect. Whilst service of God through worship and prayer was the objective of their lives, few of them could expect to avoid the mundane responsibilities of office within the abbey. Perhaps many of them did not wish to evade these duties at all, for they offered release from the normal routine of monastic life and an opening for the exercise of talents that were essential to the welfare of the abbey and its religious purposes, but quite different from those that distinguished the spiritual athlete.[109] At the very least office offered variety of occupation and the satisfactions of successful administration. In practice the management of the affairs of a community of some one hundred persons,[110] both for the maintenance of divine worship within the

---

[106] Borthwick Institute of Historical Research, Archbishop's Register 19, John Kempe, f. 228v, for his ordination as a sub-deacon; and HUL, DDLO 20/1, s.v. *Pensiones*, for payment of his pension of £10 p.a.

[107] His account as pittancer and chamberlain in 1438–39 survives (HUL, DDLO 20/20). For his dispensation see *CPL*, 1431–47, p. 261. In the pittancer's roll for 1441–42 he received a pittance only for the first half of the year (HUL, DDLO 20/21, s.v. *Liberationes denariorum*). In March 1446 he was instituted to the vicarage of the church of East Cowton, Yorkshire, at the presentation of the prior and convent of Bridlington (A. Hamilton Thompson (ed.), 'The Register of the Archdeacons of Richmond, 1442–1477, pt I 1442–1465', *YAJ*, 30, 1932, p. 116 no. 134).

[108] His accounts for 1433–34 and 1437–38 survive (HUL, DDLO 20/18 and 19). His dispensation is printed in *CPL*, 1431–47, p. 264. Later in the century in 1476 Brother Edward Wakefield obtained a similar grant (*CPL*, 1471–84, p. 527). For a brief discussion of the 'spate of privileges issued from c. 1390 onwards to members of all orders, friars included and Carthusians not excepted, to hold benefices', see D. Knowles, *The Religious Orders in England*, II, p. 293.

[109] 'When once the system had developed the obedientiaries, great and small, became a definite class, exempted by their duties from the normal life of silence, reading, and writing in the cloister, and often excused from attendance at the liturgical offices in the church and absent for a number of days on a journey.' (D. Knowles, *The Monastic Order in England*, p. 438)

[110] The figure includes servants, guests, and corrodarians. For a discussion of the size of the community at Selby, see the introduction to the granger's account translated below.

abbey church and for the tasks of supplying the material needs of abbot and convent or conducting its relations with the world outside the cloister, occupied the attentions of half or more of the monks in any year. As in other great monastic houses there was at Selby a system of offices known as 'obediences' held by the monks, many of which had independent sources of revenue to administer.[111] It is their accounts that form the bulk of the documents translated in this collection. Obedientiary systems in late mediaeval houses were not static, but subject to change and modification; and the general remarks that follow on Selby Abbey are not intended to suggest a rigidly established structure. At this point individual offices will not be described, because they are discussed in the introductory remarks preceding each translated document.

In all there were more than twenty established offices at Selby Abbey at the time of John Ousthorpe's election as abbot in 1436. A catalogue of Selby monks and their offices has survived among the records of his election, and provides the following list of obediences:[112]

prior	keeper of the store-	precentor
sub-prior	room	succentor
third prior	pittancer	sub-sacrist
prior of Snaith	chamberlain	keeper of the choir of
bursar	almoner	the blessed Mary
kitchener	keeper of the guest	keeper of the spiritu-
granger	house	ality
extern cellarer	refectorer	

This is not, however, a complete list of Selby offices, as surviving account rolls show; and we may add to it the sacrist, infirmarer, keeper of the chantry of the bishop of Durham, keeper of the fabric, and abbot's chaplain. At the same time it should be noted that a number of offices had become permanently united to another office by about this time: pittancer and chamberlain; almoner and keeper of the chantry of the bishop of Durham; sacrist and fabric keeper. And in any year some monks would hold more than one office, as Brother Robert Schipwyth was both bursar and extern cellarer, and Brother John Haldynby keeper of the spirituality and granger in 1436. The nineteen offices listed in that year were shared amongst sixteen members of the community, just about half the total number of monks (including novices) in the house.

---

[111] For a discussion of the system and the wide variety of practice in different houses, see E. Searle and B. Ross (ed.), *Accounts of the Cellarers of Battle Abbey 1275–1513*. For the various financial systems adopted by English houses, see R. A. L. Smith, *Collected Papers*, London, 1947, pp. 23–73.
[112] B. Dobson, 'The Election of John Ousthorp as Abbot of Selby in 1436', *Yorkshire Archaeological Journal*, 42, 1967, p. 38.

Several of these offices had no independent revenues attached to them and thus have left no accounts to provide evidence of their activities. The prior, the abbot's deputy, and his lieutenants the sub-prior and third prior, fall into this category; whilst the keeper of the storeroom, who recorded the monastery's daily consumption of food, was paid a fee by the bursar for his work. The only complete analysis of Selby's income identifying the various obediences whose revenues made up the total, is that prepared for the *Valor Ecclesiasticus* in 1535; and it lists just eleven officers (given here in order of size of income):[113]

bursar	(£616 12s.10d.)
kitchener	(£74 15s.3¾d.)
pittancer	(£44 4s.7d.)
keeper of the spirituality of Snaith	(£38 3s.0½d.)
sacrist	(£20 12s.10d.)
almoner	(£15 16s.7d.)
keeper of the guest house	(£3 6s.6d.)
keeper of the choir of the blessed Mary	(£2 4s.1½d.)
keeper of the infirmary	(£2 1s.8d.)
keeper of the refectory	(£1 0s.4d.)
precentor	(4s.9d.)

From surviving accounts, however, it is plain that this does not include the offices of all monk-accountants active circa 1400; there had been unifications of some obediences to form joint offices, and the disappearance of others, during the last hundred or so years of the abbey's history. Granger, extern cellarer, chamberlain, keeper of the fabric, and keeper of the chantry of the bishop of Durham, all need to be added to a list for the earlier period and are represented in the translated documents that follow.

Within this obedientiary system the dominating figure in terms of command of financial resources was undoubtedly the bursar or bursars,[114] with close to two-thirds of the abbey's income passing through this office at the end of the fourteenth century and three quarters at the time of the Dissolution. At Selby the separation that occurred elsewhere of the revenues of the head, the abbot, from those of the convent never took place,[115] and his expenditure on maintaining his household and estate as a local lord is recorded in the accounts of the bursary. The breadth of concerns that received the attention of this department marks it off from all

---

[113] *Valor Ecclesiasticus*, V, 1825, pp. 12–14.
[114] Only the account roll for 1398–99 translated below (WDA, Se/Ac/5) has two accounting bursars, but there is sporadic evidence dating back as far as visitation articles of Archbishop Gray in 1233 (*VCH*, Yorkshire, III, p. 96) that two bursars might be appointed.
[115] See D. Knowles, *The Monastic Order in England*, pp. 612–615, for this separation of endowments and the reasons for it. Battle Abbey was another major Benedictine house that had not made such a separation (see E. Searle and B. Ross, *Accounts of the Cellarers of Battle Abbey 1275–1513*, p. 13).

the others, whose functions were to perform a specific task or care for one part of the monastic complex.

A particularly important group of monk-officials was concerned with provisioning the abbey, the granger and extern cellarer supplying stock, the kitchener supervising its preparation for the table, and the keeper of the refectory maintaining the dining-hall in which the food was eaten by the convent. Another group of officials looked after the services in the monastic church, the sacrist in charge of general maintenance, the precentor of singing, and the keepers of the chantry of the bishop of Durham and of the choir of the blessed Mary entrusted with particular altars and their endowments. Hospitality and alms were the responsiblility of the keeper of the guest house and the almoner respectively, though neither had an exclusive charge in these areas; whilst the keeper of the fabric kept an eye on the state of the community's buildings. Other needs were met by yet other officers: clothing by the chamberlain; care of the sick by the keeper of the infirmary; money for small private expenses by the pittancer. Only the keeper of the spirituality of Snaith does not fit into this neat pattern, as his duties were obviously not directly concerned with the smooth running of the community at Selby. Without the aid of any extant accounts his precise functions can only be guessed, but it seems likely that he attended to the ordinary needs of the appropriated church of Snaith and administration of its court, whose revenues after deduction of necessary expenses came to the abbey.[116]

All these obedientiaries produced accounts at the end of each year of office for presentation to the abbey's auditors, recording revenues received and expended in pursuance of their duties; but only a small fraction of the total number that must once have been kept in the monks' archives has come down to the present day. In 1953 just six account rolls were known to the editor of two Selby obedientiary accounts, who wrote:[117]

> 'Selby Abbey is not as rich in records as many other abbeys. The surviving records of this Benedictine abbey, which are scattered over a long period, comprise a cartulary, a chronicle, six account rolls, two sixteenth-century surveys and the register of a fourteenth-century abbot.'

---

[116] The keeper of the spirituality of Snaith did not receive all the revenues from these sources, at least in 1535. The survey of that year allocates tithes worth £12 6s.8d. to the bursar, whilst the keeper received £25 7s.11½d. from spiritual revenues. *Valor Ecclesiasticus*, V, 1825, pp. 12–14.

[117] B. Holt (ed.), *Two Obedientiary Rolls of Selby Abbey*, Yorkshire Archaeological Society, Record Series 118, 1953, p. 31. At the beginning of the century another Selby Abbey account roll had appeared in the *Yorkshire Archaeological Journal* (Rev. Canon Atkinson, 'Account Roll of Selby Abbey, 1397–8', *YAJ*, 15, 1900, pp. 408–419.)

Snaith parish church from the south-east (photograph by Dianne Tillotson)

31

Subsequently the position has been substantially improved. Already in 1951 a large collection of medieval court rolls and a number of rentals for the manor of Crowle in Lincolnshire had been acquired by the Lincolnshire Archives Committee;[118] and during the next decade two separate collections of documents from the medieval abbey were discovered, which with a few records scattered in various archives brought the total of accounts known for Selby to 132. Two-thirds are in the Hull University Library and form part of the Londesborough collection;[119] whilst another 38 were found with other documents among the archives of the archdiocese of Westminster, and are preserved at Archbishop's House.[120] The rest are widely dispersed between York, Sheffield, Lincoln, and the British Library in London.[121]

The extant account rolls divide into two groups of unequal size. By far the major proportion are records of the various monk-obedientiaries; the remainder are the rolls of the abbey's servants on its manors or in charge of collecting the tithes and offerings from its appropriated churches. A total of 110 fall into the former group, ranging in date from a kitchener's roll of Abbot John de Heslyngton's time (1335–42) to an account of the sacrist and fabric keeper for 1537–38.[122] More than four-fifths belong to the fifteenth century, whilst just seven date from the previous century. The twenty-two accounts prepared by the abbey's manorial servants and proctors cover a very similar span of time to the other rolls, the earliest account being one from Eastoft in 1358–59 and the latest one from Acaster in 1535.[123] In this case twelve are from the fifteenth century, whilst seven were compiled in the previous fifty years. The net result is that one hundred of Selby Abbey's surviving account rolls belong to the fifteenth century, fifty of them to its first four decades where the most complete range of obedientiary records is also to be found.

---

[118] For a discussion of these Crowle manorial records and the descent of the manor, see Lincolnshire Archives Committee, *Archivists' Report* No. 4, 1952–53, pp. 13–20.

[119] They were originally in the East Riding County Record Office at Beverley, and moved to Hull University Library in 1973. See *Brief Guide to the Contents of the East Riding County Record Office*, Beverley, 3rd edition 1966, p. 33. In 1854 Lord Londesborough purchased the properties of the Petre family around Selby, including the lordship of the manor (see R. B. Dobson, *Selby Abbey and Town*, pp. 30–31).

[120] The collection comprises 60 manuscripts in all. It is not known how the collection came to be at Westminster, but possibly it was through the Catholic Petre family who held the manor of Selby during the eighteenth and early nineteenth century (see K. G. T. McDonnell, 'The Archives of Selby Abbey', *YAJ*, 44, 1972, pp. 170–172).

[121] The York Minster Library has two pittancer's rolls, part of a collection bequeathed by Edward Hailstone in 1890 (HH 21.3a–b). Sheffield City Libraries, Department of Local History and Archives, has an incomplete bursar's roll of 1459 and another document in its Bacon Frank collection (BFM 30–31). Lincolnshire Archives Committee have part of a bursar's roll of 1481 as well as Crowle Manor records (CM 8/7); and the British Library has a sacrist and fabric keeper's account of 1448 (Add. Charter 45854).

[122] WDA, Se/Ac/6 (kitchener's roll); HUL, DDLO 20/42 (sacrist and fabric keeper).

[123] HUL, DDLO 4/2 (Eastoft); HUL, DDLO 20/75 (Acaster).

Necessarily the accidents of loss and survival of documents have imposed certain constraints and limitations on the composition of this collection. In the first place for two of the sixteen monk-officials discussed earlier, the precentor and the keeper of the spirituality of Snaith, there are no extant records and hence they could not be represented. The precentor at least handled an income of but a few shillings, by far the smallest of any obedientiary; but the keeper of the spirituality ranked fourth in income in 1535 and was obviously a more important figure.[124] Secondly, the time-span over which the documents in the collection extend has had to be very broad, in order to secure a fully comprehensive selection from the remaining offices. The sole surviving account rolls from the offices of infirmarer, almoner, and keeper of the choir of the blessed Mary, for instance, are dated respectively 1399–1403, 1434–35, and 1536–37.[125] Finally, so few accounts remain from the manors and tithe-barns of the abbey, widely dispersed in time and representing only a fraction of its properties, that no full treatment of Selby's management of its estates and resources at the local level is possible. This fact coupled with the need to restrict the edition to manageable proportions has meant that examples of these last types of document have not been included.

Despite the deviations imposed by gaps in the surviving evidence, this is essentially a study of two abbacies, the later years of Abbot John de Shirburn (1369–1408)[126] and the rule of his successor Abbot William de Pygot (1408–29), who between them cover the 'Chaucerian' period of intense criticism and attempted reform of the religious. Nine out of the thirteen documents translated here fall within the years 1398–1422 and the centre-piece is the particularly fine bursars' roll of 1398–99, which is supported by an extant register of Shirburn's time providing complementary evidence lacking for all abbacies thereafter.[127] The only account roll included that is later than 1450 in date is that of the keeper of the choir of the blessed Mary, 1536–37, whose inclusion results from the fact that it is the only record of this office's activities. If it is an unreliable guide to fifteenth century practice, it is the only guide available.

---

124 *Valor Ecclesiasticus*, V, 1825, pp. 12–14.
125 HUL, DDLO 20/53 (infirmarer); HUL, DDLO 20/55 (almoner); HUL, DDLO 20/61 (keeper of the choir of the blessed Mary).
126 On Shirburn, see G.S.Haslop, 'Two Entries from the Register of John de Shirburn, Abbot of Selby 1369–1408', *YAJ*, 41, 1964, pp. 287–296, and 'The Creation of Brother John Sherburn as Abbot of Selby', *YAJ*, 42, 1967, pp. 25–30.
127 The register, which is not complete, is now in two parts (British Library, Cotton Vitellius E.XVI, fos 97–162, and Cotton Cleopatra D.III, fos 184–202). A register from the time of Geoffrey de Gaddesby (1342–68) is in the Public Record Office, London (PRO, DL 42/8. Duchy of Lancaster Records, Miscellaneous Books 8); and two leaves from another register are in the Bodleian Library, Oxford (Top.Yorks. d.2 (SC.35210)). The cartulary of the abbey has been printed by the Yorkshire Archaeological Society (J.T.Fowler (ed.), *The Coucher Book of Selby*, 2 vols, YAS, Record Series 10 and 13, 1891–93).

INTRODUCTION

The account rolls themselves, in all except one case written on parchment,[128] are the final reckonings for the year as presented for audit; and there are occasional alterations, additions, and marginal comments in a different hand to the main body of the document indicating the auditing process. We have no details for Selby of the procedure itself or the auditing committee, but presumably a panel of senior monks examined the accountants here as elsewhere, and a professional auditor of the accounts of the monastery is recorded as receiving a fee of 26s.8d. in 1413–1414.[129] There are two basic types of account: the money account only, which records the receipts and disbursements of offices not responsible for maintaining storerooms or livestock herds; and the money and stock account, whose accountant had responsibility for both money and goods. In the second case the account is divided into two parts, with a record of the incomings and outgoings of animals, grain, etc. written on the dorse or back of the roll after the money account. The bursars' roll is the most extensive instance of the first type of documents, whilst extern cellarer, granger, and kitchener supply the examples of the other kind.

All the accounts follow a standardized form typical of medieval accountancy and basically a process of charge and discharge.[130] The accountant set out the items of money, goods, or livestock for which his office acknowledged responsibility; then he claimed his expenditures and recognized deductions, and a final balance was reached. The stock accounts go through this procedure in turn for each category of livestock, grain, etc. in the accountant's care. A Selby Abbey money account was divided into two sections. First came a statement of potential receipts from rents, sales, and other sources, totalled together to form the possible revenues for which the accountant answered that year. Next followed a list of actual outgoings on wages, purchases, and other expenses, which were combined with various allowances to form the total deductions claimed by the accountant. Lastly at the foot of the roll the final balance was calculated.

The account invariably began with the item 'Arrears' (*Arreragia*), which referred back to the final balance of the previous account roll of the office. If total expenditures and allowances in that previous account had been less than the sum recorded in the Receipts section, then the balance was carried

---

[128] The exception is the account of the keeper of the choir of the blessed Mary 1536–37 (HUL, DDLO 20/61).

[129] See R. A. L. Smith, 'The Regimen Scaccarii in English Monasteries', *Collected Papers*, pp. 54–73; and HUL, DDLO 20/54b. Archbishop Melton ordered that the bursars should render yearly accounts to the abbot or his deputy, and certain of the more prudent members of the community, at his visitation in 1335 (Borthwick Institute of Historical Research, Archbishop's Register 9A, William Melton, fos clxiv verso–clxv).

[130] For medieval accounting practice, see J. S. Drew, 'Manorial Accounts of St Swithun's Priory, Winchester', *Essays in Economic History*, II, ed. E. M. Carus-Wilson, London, 1962, pp. 12–30; D. Oschinsky, *Walter of Henley and other treatises on estate management and accounting*, Oxford, 1971, ch. V.

forward to the next account and recorded under 'Arrears' as part of anticipated revenue for the current year. When income had been exceeded by expenses and deductions, the fact was recorded under 'Arrears' but the sum in question became the first item charged against receipts in the new account. Thus the first item on the Expenditure and Allowances side of an account is invariably 'Excess' (*Excessus*).

It has to be stressed that the Receipts side of the obedientiary accounts most often record a notional or expected income, and that not all of the revenue recorded there was necessarily obtained by the officer that compiled it. Rents reflected the rental, which might not be up to date; assignments of expected income might not be wholly realized for reasons that were not anticipated when they were made. The mechanism to correct this disparity between expectation and reality was not the simple one of recording what was received, with an explanation of why it was less than expected. Instead the full sum was recorded on the Receipts side, and the difference between this and actual income had to be claimed on the expenditure side of the account. This was the function of the 'Allowances' (*Allocationes*) section, which immediately preceded the final totalling of deductions and the calculation of the accountant's standing.

In preparing the account rolls for this edition the principal concern has been to make the information they contain readily accessible to those not expert in the Latin, accountancy, and monasticism of the later middle ages, whilst remaining as faithful as this allows to the form of the documents and to the strict meaning of the texts. The Latin rolls are presented in English translation, but consistency and accuracy have been preferred to elegance in rendering of entries. The structure of the accounts, with their marginal headings to each section, has been retained generally intact apart from one significant alteration. The entries in each section of the original rolls follow straight on from each other, ultimately forming in the case of the longer sections a solid block of text that would extend over whole pages of a printed version. In the interests of greater clarity and a less discouraging appearance the entries have been separated out and arranged as individual items with vertical spaces between each.

The practice followed in regard to personal names has been to translate Latin Christian names, but to give the rest of the name in its original form. This is true even where the surname is obviously taken from a local town or village, so that, for example, Brother Peter de Rouclif is not transformed into Brother Peter de Rawcliffe. Place-names have all been modernized where they could be identified; and if this proved impossible, they have been transcribed exactly and italicized in the text, as in the cases of *Eluesthwayt* or *Loune*. The more uncommon or unusual are given their modern form, but are followed by the original form italicized and within round brackets thus, Wheel Hall (*le Welehall*) or Reading Gate (*le Riddingate*). Uncertainties in the translation, unusual words, and the appearance of vernacular words in the text, have all been dealt with by the same method. Thus the rendering of the odd occupational description 'ministrallo pessimo' is 'lowest grade minstrel (*ministrallo pessimo*)'; whilst two English words for nails are modernized as 'spike-nails (*spikyng*)' and 'lead-nails (*leednayl*)'. In addition it has been thought desirable to provide the manuscript version of sectional headings in the accounts, as in 'Arrears (*Arreragia*)'.

When no suitable translation for a word, Latin or English, could be found, it has been italicized in the text, as in the entry 'And to John de Sutton, *adulator*, 6d.' Words added to the translation by the editor for the sake of clarity are enclosed in round brackets, as shown in this sentence: 'From customary services remitted at Crowle this year nothing (is answered for) here.' And doubtful translations caused by damage to the manuscript or other difficulties are indicated by enclosing the suspect words in round brackets and adding a question mark thus: 'from tithe-hay of the township of Waterton sold wholesale after (?drying)'. Where the text is totally illegible, the lost words are indicated by three adjacent points, as in 'And for ... 4 of the lord's oxen'. Very occasionally an accountant has failed to complete an entry in his account roll, leaving a blank in the text. The occurrence is noted by placing empty round brackets in the text: 'And for ()'. In all these cases, of course, further clarification is given in footnotes if necessary or advantageous.

Scattered through the documents are occasional alterations and additions made by the scribe or by a different hand. Words are crossed out, and replaced by others written between the lines; comments on the account are added in the margin of the roll; errors are corrected. All such amendments, however minor, have been noted in a footnote. In dealing with corrections the practice has been to make the translated text conform to the corrected version intended by the accountant, incorporating interlineations into the translation and omitting deletions. The Latin words interlined have been noted, and the deletions translated and transcribed, in footnotes. Entries in the margin of the roll, with the exception of the headings for sections provided by the scribe, have not been included in the translated text but have been treated in the same fashion as deletions.

The Roman numerals used throughout these rolls by the Selby Abbey accountants have been converted to Arabic figures for this translation. One small problem is the use of the long hundred of six score, (where $C = 120$, $D = 600$, and $M = 1200$), which may be employed anywhere except to denote sums of money.[131] Many, but not all, of the Selby accountants did use the long hundred, a common indicator being the use of V^{XX} (i.e. 5 × 20) to indicate 100. Where it has been employed in an account, this is noted

---

[131] The long hundred was consistently used at another northern house, Bolton Priory, in the thirteenth and fourteenth centuries (see I. Kershaw, *Bolton Priory*, Oxford, 1973, p. xiii).

in a footnote on the first occasion that a sum is affected; and the figure is translated to accord with modern conventions. All intermediate and final totals in the accounts have been checked and errors pointed out in footnotes. In calculating final totals the intermediate totals provided by the accountants have been used, even if one or more were incorrect. There are in fact surprisingly few errors to be found. No attempt has been made to express money figures in modern terms, and these conform to the pre-decimal system in which four farthings (¼d.) or two halfpennies (½d.) equal one penny (1d.), twelve pennies (12d.) make one shilling (1s.) and twenty shillings equal one pound (£1).

Like so many of their contemporaries the Selby monks dated their documents and the events recorded in them by the nearest festival of the Church.[132] Their account rolls ran from the festival of St Michael the Archangel or St Martin to the same festival in the following year. Except in the case of the most commonly known festivals such as Christmas, the day and month intended have been supplied in brackets immediately after the dating clause in the account thus: the festival of St Michael the Archangel (29 September) and of St Martin (11 November). A final point is that the punctuation throughout the accounts which follow is the editor's.

This discussion began by asking questions about the monasticism of Geoffrey Chaucer's day, its condition and the role of the monks in the late medieval Church and society, where their importance as landowners and patrons, consumers and builders, is readily discernible from their surviving records. It has not set out to provide definitive answers, because the editor's primary intention throughout has been to make accessible to non-expert students of the period a significant body of evidence from a single house, and to provide them with the means to seek answers to their own questions. As just one amongst so many monastic foundations,[133] Selby Abbey will not, of course, provide incontrovertible solutions to general problems in late medieval history. All that is claimed for the account rolls which follow is that they reveal one living institution, its corporate life and its relations with the world around it, through the unselfconscious evidence of its financial administration.

---

[132] For a discussion and a list of saints' days and festivals used in dating, see C. R. Cheney (ed.), *Handbook of Dates for Students of English History*, London, 1970, pp. 40–64.
[133] Perhaps 1,000 houses of monks, canons, friars, nuns and canonesses, containing 8–10,000 persons in the late fourteenth century (D. Knowles and R. Neville Hadcock, *Medieval Religious Houses, England and Wales*, p. 494).

THE ACCOUNT ROLLS

I

THE ABBOT AND THE WORLD
OUTSIDE THE CLOISTER

The office of the Bursary

The office of the bursary at Selby Abbey dominated the finances of the house, and at no time more so, it appears, than the period of the account of 1398–99.[1] Close to two-thirds of the normal income of the abbey passed through the bursars' hands at this time. The bursars' income for the year was £774 7s.8d. gross, or rather more than £520 if loans and payments for pensions and corrodies are deducted to arrive at the expected ordinary revenue from temporal and spiritual sources.[2] This compares with a total expected income for the abbey in 1373 of £795, exclusive of loans and other income anticipations.[3] No other Selby monk-official could approach the bursar in terms of income at his disposal; and the importance of the office makes entirely comprehensible the fact that most unusually among the Selby obediences two monks are appointed to act together as accountants.[4]

With so large a proportion of the abbey's income at their disposal, the bursars inevitably ranged widely in their activities and types of expenditure; and their records are central to the study of the affairs of the house. They were not, like other monk-officials at Selby, confined to a single sphere of duty such as provision of food (the kitchener's task) or clothing (the chamberlain's), or running one part of the monastic complex (like the

---

[1] In 1416–17 and 1431–32 the bursars' gross receipts were just over £586 and £713 respectively; and immediately before the Dissolution in 1535 the assessed income of the office was some £616. Other 15th century accounts, however, show the bursary income as between £300 and £400. (See HUL, DDLO 20/1, 4, 6, 7, 9, and 60; WDA, Se/Ac/9).

[2] The 'Allowances' section at the end of the account shows that about £15 of rents could not actually be collected, though charged as income earlier.

[3] See G. S. Haslop, 'The Abbot of Selby's Financial Statement for the Year ending Michaelmas 1338', *YAJ*, 44, 1972, pp. 168–169. The figure agrees with my own tentative calculations based on the incomplete series of obedientiary accounts for the early 15th century.

[4] The account roll of 1398–99 is the only surviving example of two bursars accounting; but stray references elsewhere in the records make it apparent that this year was not unique. See above p. 29 n. 114.

keeper of the refectory). So that whilst one does indeed find in their accounts much detail of the monastic lifestyle within the abbey walls, they also provide the basis for a broader view of the functioning of the community within the context of late medieval society, both at the local level and on a more national scale.

For his personal expenses and the maintenance of his household the abbot of Selby drew on the resources of the bursars' office, and in the account which follows there is abundant petty detail of his lifestyle: his furs, his food, his wine, and even his hunting dogs. But it is also here that the record of expenditures will reveal something of his role as a major ecclesiastical figure in the north of England: his participation in the York convocation; his appointment of proctors to parliament; his contacts with the politics of the period through his links with magnates and local gentry. By 1398 Abbot John de Shirburn was an old man, with nearly thirty years as the head of the Selby community behind him;[5] and his bodily infirmity is a much-used excuse for escaping unwanted responsibilities.[6] In this year of dramatic political changes, however, which saw Richard II replaced by his cousin on the throne, Selby Abbey could not avoid involvement altogether nor its abbot afford to become too much out of touch with events. The major participants in the political drama of 1399 make tantalizing appearances in this account, whilst the abbot's efforts to secure reliable information through established contacts and agents is plainly discernible.

Both as an important landowner in Yorkshire and Lincolnshire and as a major religious community drawing for goods, services, and finance on the countryside around it, Selby Abbey was necessarily involved in a network of relations with local society. Here too the detailed evidence is to be found in the accounts of the bursars, the officials who paid the fees and pensions, rewarded the servants of others with small gifts, and negotiated the important financial transactions. The subject has a particular interest in the late fourteenth and early fifteenth centuries for reasons already noted;[7] this was a period when the religious orders were the subject of much criticism, and proposals were made in parliament for secularization of the Church's temporal revenues. The knights and burgesses of parliament were representatives of classes who figure frequently in the account which

[5] He was elected abbot in 1369 and died in 1408. For some details of his rule, see G.S. Haslop, 'The Creation of Brother John Sherburn as Abbot of Selby', *YAJ*, 42, 1967, pp.25–30, and 'Two Entries from the Register of John de Shirburn, Abbot of Selby, 1369–1408', *YAJ*, 41, 1964, pp.287–296.

[6] As, for example, in excusing himself from the Benedictine Provincial Chapter c.1393 (W.A. Pantin, *Documents Illustrating the Activities of the General and Provincial Chapters of the Black Monks*, II, pp.92–93), or from the parliaments of 1391, 1392, 1394, 1395, and 1397 (PRO, SC 10/File 37/1847, 38/1872, 39/1916, 40/1952, and 40/1964).

[7] See above pp.10–11.

follows: the wealthy York merchants who supplied many of Selby's goods, made loans, and purchased corrodies and pensions; the gentry who received fees and served as the stewards of its manors; and the lawyers who acted as its advisers in the monks' frequent legal entanglements. The magnates as a class seem altogether more remote in Selby's affairs.

Similarly it is to the bursars' rolls that one must go for solid evidence on the financial health of the community and the basic material for generalization about its financial policies. Here is the record of loans raised, pensions and corrodies sold, repayment of debts, and the burden of taxation and royal demands. By 1410 his successor as abbot was complaining that John de Shirburn had burdened the house with annuities, corrodies, and other payments to the value of £200 yearly, and that the level of debt had reached £1040.[8] Selby, it would seem from this, was a classic instance of monastic financial mismanagement and extravagance under Abbot John. Whilst one account roll alone cannot be expected to confirm or disprove this, the account of 1398–99 does allow us to see a substantial Benedictine community operating under financial strains and to form hypotheses about their causes and actual severity.

The two monks who had the onerous task of managing Selby's problematical finances in 1398–99 illustrate in their careers the administrative responsibilities that were a substantial part of the monastic lives of many late medieval monks. Brother Peter de Rouclif became a full member of the community in 1377 and was an obedientiary by 1386.[9] His activity as an official spanned a range of offices, culminating in his appointment as prior sometime before 1407.[10] Whilst bursar in 1398–99 he was also extern cellarer; and he is known to have held these two offices together in 1386–87, 1391, and 1396–97.[11] As well he was extern cellarer 1387–88; master of the court at Crowle 1390–91; granger 1404–05, and apparently for the six years previously; and chamberlain at an uncertain later date.[12] In 1388 he is found representing the abbot in the duke of Lancaster's court at Snaith.[13]

His business dealings with York merchants brought de Rouclif into a closer relationship with at least one family than the purely commercial, and resulted in legacies for him from husband and wife. In 1406 Alan de Hamerton left him 100s. in his will; and in 1432 Alan's wife Isabella bequeathed him her best gold ring and one Veronica of Rome.[14] The

[8] *CPR*, 1408–13, p. 244.

[9] Borthwick Institute of Historical Research, Archbishop's Register 12, Alexander Neville, f.130; Lincolnshire Archives Office, CM 1/39.

[10] He is named as prior in a document dated 18 October, 1407 (British Library, Cotton Vitellius E.XVI, f.132v). By 1410 Brother John de Cave was prior (HUL, DDLO 18/1).

[11] Lincolnshire Archives Office, CM 1/39 and 1/47; HUL, DDLO 20/52; WDA, Se/Ac/5.

[12] Lincolnshire Archives Office, CM 1/40 and 43; HUL, DDLO 20/44 and 45.

[13] British Library, Cotton Vitellius E.XVI, f.127v.

[14] *Testamenta Eboracensia*, ed. J. Raine and J. Raine, II, Surtees Society 30, 1855, pp. 22–23.

Hamertons had purchased a corrody and pension from Selby Abbey in 1399 whilst he was bursar.[15] In January 1408 he may also have been the recipient of another legacy, this time of 6s.8d., when William son of John Escryk, priest of Selby, left the prior of the abbey a legacy of that sum in his will.[16] Brother Peter de Rouclif died either late in 1432 or early in 1433,[17] leaving behind him accounts that suggest both his administrative efficiency and a strong desire for self-justification.

His partner as bursar in 1398–99, Brother Robert de Selby, has a less well-documented career but one which also indicates regular employment as an obedientiary. He entered the house about 1377.[18] When he appears in the Selby Abbey records in 1391, it is as kitchener, an office that he also held in 1398–99 whilst serving as bursar.[19] He is known to have been kitchener also in 1397, granger for 4 years 1410–14, and for a further year 1416–17.[20] He last appears in the Selby records, so far as has been discovered, in 1418 when he was the abbot's representative in the court of Selby.[21]

In view of the importance of the office regrettably few bursar's account rolls have survived the ravages of the centuries. The one which follows is the earliest to have come down to us at all complete;[22] and in all less than a dozen such accounts have survived in any completeness for the whole period from 1398 to the dissolution of the house in 1539.[23] One of the factors that makes this particular roll so suitable for inclusion here is, indeed, the unusually excellent condition in which it is preserved. Apart from a tear that has damaged the heading and a little staining on the early part of the roll, it is in excellent order throughout its length of approximately 200 cm. The roll is in fact four pieces of parchment sewn together; and the account covers the whole of one side and half the dorse. With the possible exception of the account of 1431–32,[24] no other surviving bursar's roll is so wide-ranging in its contents and none so well preserved.

[15] British Library, Cotton Vitellius E.XVI, f.137.

[16] *North Country Wills*, ed. J. W. Clay, Surtees Society 116, 1908, p. 2.

[17] HUL, DDLO 20/17, pittancer's roll.

[18] Borthwick Institute of Historical Research, Archbishop's Register 12, Alexander Neville, f.129v.

[19] HUL, DDLO 21/14; WDA, Se/Ac/5.

[20] HUL, DDLO 21/16; 20/54 and 18/1; WDA, Se/Ac/9 and 10.

[21] HUL, DDLO 21/20. My thanks are due to Mr G. S. Haslop for generous help in compiling the details of the careers of the bursars of 1398–99.

[22] A fragment of an account roll, which can be dated 1397–98 on internal evidence, has been printed in *YAJ*, 15, 1900, pp. 408–419. It appears to be part of the bursars' account for that year.

[23] Complete accounts for 1416–17, 1431–32, 1527–28, and 1531–32 (WDA, Se/Ac/9; HUL, DDLO 20/1, 12, 13). Large fragments for 1459, 1480–81, and c.1531 (Sheffield City Libraries, Bacon Frank MS 30; Lincolnshire Archives Office, CM 8/7; WDA, Se/Ac/23); and portions of varying size for c.1454, c.1452–55, 1479–80, 1480–81, 1483–84, c.1490, 1496–97, and 1526 (HUL, DDLO 20/2, 7, 4, 6, 10, 8, 9, 11).

[24] HUL, DDLO 20/1.

The Bursars' account of 1398–99

Table of Contents

The account of Brothers Peter de Rouclif and Robert de Selby ...[25]
Martin A.D. 1398 to ...1399

Arrears[26] *(Arreragia)*	No arrears (from the previous account) because (the expenditure and allowances of) these same account-ants in their last account exceeded income.
Fixed rent *(Redditus assisus)*	The same persons answer for £48 17s.4d. from the fixed rent of Stanford on Avon yearly, with 4 marks from the farm[27] of 2 water mills yearly, according to the new rental.

And for £31 4s.3d. from Queniborough yearly, in addition to the mill, according to the new rental.

And for 20s. from Carlton by Lincoln yearly.

And for 9s. from Stainton Waddingham yearly.

And for 3s.4d. from Redbourne yearly.

And for £8 17s. from Stallingborough yearly, with 2 marks from the farm of the mill, according to the rental.

And for £31 2s.6d. from Crowle, in addition to the mills, yearly.

And for 113s.2d. from *Eluesthwayt*[28] yearly.

And for £6 19s.10½d. from Eastoft in county Lincoln yearly.

And for £26 5s.7¼d. from Luddington yearly, in addition to the mill.

And for £16 3s.11¼d. from Amcotts yearly, in addition to 40d. for the toft formerly John Skynner's in the hands of the heir of Robert Wacelyn.

And for £37 15s.6d. from Garthorpe yearly, in addition to the mill.

And for 57s.1d. from Eastoft in county York yearly.

And for 30s. from Haldenby yearly.

And for 33s.4d. from Fockerby yearly, with the farm of *les Intakes*.[29]

And for 14s.8d. from Adlingfleet yearly.

And for 16d. from 1 acre of land in Reedness yearly.

---

[25] Heading damaged by a tear. The account ran from the festival of St Martin (11 November) 1398 presumably to the same feast 1399.

[26] For 'Arrears' see above, pp. 34–35.

[27] The word 'farm' *(firma)* is used to denote rent from properties held under leases, as distinct from that received from holdings held by customary tenure.

[28] 'WODDEHOUSE ALITER DICTA ELUESTUATHE' in *The Coucher Book of Selby*, II, p. 276. There is a Woodhouse, co. Lincoln, about 5 kilometres south of Crowle.

[29] i.e. enclosures.

And for 18s. from the abbot of Thornton for his tithes yearly at Swinefleet on the eastern side of the quay (*le kay*).[30]

And for 6s.8d. from the tithes of the mill and fishery of Hook yearly.

And for £9 7s.11¼d. from Rawcliffe yearly, in addition to the mill, with 5s. from increased value of the holding (*de incremento tenementi*) formerly (in the possession) of Master John de Petreburgh.

And for £4 17s.7½d. from Snaith, Cowick, and Pollington yearly.

And for 36s.6d. from the houses lately acquired in Snaith yearly.

And for 4d. from the lord of Birkin yearly.

And for £25 6s. from the old farm of Hillam, with the farm of the tenement lately leased at penny farm (*Peniferm*), and with the farm of the pastures of the Bowers (*les Boures*) and the Stocking (*le Stokking*) yearly.

And for 69s.4¼d. from the new farm there yearly.

And for £13 8s.6d. from the old farm of Monk Fryston, with the farm of the holding lately leased at penny farm and with the farm of the Breck (*del Breck*) and the Ox pasture (*del Oxpastour*) yearly.

And for 77s.2d. from the new farm there yearly.

And for £2. . . . . . 4d.[31] from the old farm of Hambleton yearly.

And for 44s. from the new farm there yearly.

And for 66s.8d. from Thorpe Willoughby yearly.

And for 8s. from Lund yearly.

And for 37s.1½d. from Brayton yearly.

And for £13 15s.6½d. from Acaster Selby yearly.

And for 42s.6d. from Stillingfleet yearly, in addition to 10s. paid to the heir of John, lord Gray,[32] annually.

And for 40s. from the houses in York yearly.

And for 13s.4d. from Holme upon Spalding Moor yearly.

And for 13s.4d. from Foggathorpe yearly.

---

[30] For the agreement (1306) between the abbeys of Thornton and Selby concerning these tithes, see *The Coucher Book of Selby*, II, pp. 131–132.

[31] Part of the entry is illegible at this point. Assuming that the total for this section is correct, the entry should read £20 5s.4d.

[32] Robert de Grey, lord Grey of Rotherfield, who died in 1387, had as his sole heiress Joan, wife of John lord Deincourt. She held the manor of Stillingfleet in demesne as of fee, according to the inquisition *post mortem* taken in 1409 after her death (*Inquisitions post mortem relating to Yorkshire of the reigns of Henry IV and Henry V*, ed. W. P. Baildon and J. W. Clay, YAS, Record Series 59, 1918, pp. 78–79).

And for 13s. from Breighton yearly.

And for 5s. from Osgodby yearly.

Total £332 19s.10d.

New farms, with mills, customary services, and courts (*Nove firme cum molendinis operibus et curiis*)

Likewise the same persons answer for £6 6s.8d. from the farm of the demesnes of Stanford on Avon yearly.

And for 106s.8d., from the farm of the demesnes of Queniborough yearly.

And for £10 from the farm of 11 bovates of the demesne of Stallingborough yearly.

And for 67s.4d. from the farm of the demesnes of Crowle yearly.

And for 14s. from *les Intakes* of Amcotts yearly.

And for £14 14s. from the farm of the demesnes of Rawcliffe, the tithe of corn sheaves and hay there, and the most part of the tithe hay of Snaith yearly.

And for 40s. from the farm of the demesnes of *Nesse*[33] yearly.

And for £10 from the farm of the demesnes of Thorpe Willoughby yearly.

And for £15 from the farm of the demesnes of Stainer yearly, in addition to the meadowland of Roscarrs and 4 furlongs in Roscarrs in the hands of the kitchener for pasturing the sheep of the office.

And for 56s. from the farm of the demesnes of Acaster Selby yearly.

And for 33s.4d. from the farm of the demesnes of Holme upon Spalding Moor yearly.

And for £6 from the farm of the demesnes of Gunby yearly.

And for 33s.4d. from the farm of the demesnes of Chellow yearly.

From Queniborough mill nothing, because (it is) empty.

And for 40s. from the Crowle mills yearly.

And for 20s. from the Luddington mill yearly.

And for 16s. from the Garthorpe mill this year.

And for 24s. from the Rawcliffe mill yearly.

---

[33] Called *Rouclifnesse* in the bursar's account for 1416–17 (WDA, Se/Ac/9, s.v. *Nove firme cum molendinis et operibus*), i.e. Rawcliffe Ness.

From customary services remitted at Stanford on Avon this year nothing, because of the poverty of the tenants there.

From customary services remitted at Crowle this year nothing (is answered for) here, because the serjeant there accounts for them.[34]

From customary services remitted at Monk Fryston, Hillam, and Hambleton this year nothing (is answered for) here, because the serjeant there accounts for them.

And for 6s.8d. from the profits of the court of Stanford on Avon[35] this year, namely from the fine of John Hichecok, the lord's villein, in payment of 33s.4d. for having manumission.

From the court of Queniborough this year nothing, because no fines or amercements are had.

From the court of Stallingborough this year nothing, for the aforesaid reason.

And for 50s. from the court of Crowle this year.

And for 6s.8d.[36] from the court of Rawcliffe this year.

And for 43s.4d. from the court of Monk Fryston, Hillam, and Hambleton this year.

From the court of Thorpe Willoughby, Brayton, and Acaster Selby nothing this year, because there were no fines or amercements.

From pannage[37] of the pigs of the tenants of Monk Fryston, Hillam, and Hambleton this year nothing, on account of the poverty of the tenants there, and many holdings are let at penny farm and the tenants for the most part would refuse to hold their holdings in another way.

Total £89 18s.

Foreign receipts (*Forinsecum receptum*)   Likewise the same persons answer for £20 from 3 sacks of wool sold at Stallingborough this year.

---

[34] The serjeant (*serviens*) was a salaried estate manager. No serjeant's account appears to have survived for Crowle. For a discussion of surviving accounts, see above p. 32.

[35] No court rolls for the court of Stanford on Avon or for the courts of Queniborough, Stallingborough, and Rawcliffe, have been located. The record office at Lincoln has a collection of 201 court rolls from Crowle for the years between 1310 and the Dissolution (Lincolnshire Archives Office, CM 1/1–201); and the courts of Brayton and Thorpe Willoughby, and Monk Fryston and Hillam, are represented in the collection of abbey court rolls at Hull University (DDLO 2 and 14).

[36] *viii* interlined.

[37] Pannage is the payment made to the owner of woodland for the right of pasturing pigs there. See *OED*.

From wool from Redbourne this year nothing, but it is hoped for next year if the stock have remained healthy.

And for 36s. from 12 stones of wool coming from two thirds[38] of the tithe of the parish of Brayton this year.

From the rents of Amcotts in wheat this year nothing, because the serjeant at Eastoft accounts for them.

And for £10 from the altar-dues of the chapel of Whitgift this year, with the tithe of the corn sheaves etc. of the aforesaid township, and with the tithe of the corn sheaves of Swinefleet between Reading Gate (le Riddingate) and the quay (la kay), in addition to £9 9s.1d. deducted for (in reprisis) the new barn, gates, and wharf there.

And for £15 from John de Birne[39] and Richard Taverner in payment of £20 for the tithe of corn sheaves and hay for part of Snaith sold to them from the produce of the previous year, in addition to 100s. paid the year before.

And for £6 13s.4d. from William Broun[40] in payment of 24 marks for the tithe of corn sheaves and hay belonging to the grange of Heck from the produce of the previous year, in addition to 14 marks paid the year before, and in addition to 40s. pardoned him by the lord abbot.[41]

And for £8 0s.6d. from the same person as part (payment) of 31 marks for the tithe of corn sheaves etc. belonging to the said grange sold to him from the produce of the present year.

And for 40s. from the same person as part (payment) of 6 marks for the tithe of Whitley sold to him from the produce of the present year.

And for £8 6s.8d. from Thomas Dilcok[42] for the tithe of corn sheaves etc. of Balne and of the orchards (gardinorum) of Pollington sold to him from the produce of the present year.

And for £25 from John de Birne as part (payment) of 45 marks for the tithe of the corn sheaves and hay from two thirds of the parish of

---

[38] The division of the tithes of Brayton into fractions was an ancient one. In 1218 Archbishop Gray included a third of the church of Brayton among the endowments of the prebend of Wistow in York Minster. *York Minster Fasti*, ed. C. T. Clay, II, YAS, Record Series 124, 1958, p. 87.

[39] An important servant of the abbey (see below, p. 56 n. 86).

[40] The bursars purchased 10 quarters of wheat from him at Gowdall for the use of the granger (see *Purchase of grain*, p. 71).

[41] As the mark was worth 13s.4d., 24 marks equals £16 and 14 marks £9 6s.8d. The two payments equal the full sum of the debt, so that one must assume that the pardoned 40s. is to be understood as additional to the 24 marks.

[42] The bursars purchased 30 quarters of oats from him this year (see *Purchase of grain*, p. 72). Thomas Dilcok senior and junior were farmers of the tithes of Balne for the next 30 years, at least until 1432 (see HUL, DDLO 20/54d and 20/1; WDA, Se/Ac/10).

Brayton sold to him from the produce of the previous year, in addition to 100s. which John Lascy and Thomas Danyel[43] claim from the lord abbot.

From the farm of the land and marsh belonging to the grange of *Loune* they answer for nothing this year, because Roger Pog[44] who holds them cannot pay on account of his great loss.

And for £4 from Richard de Drax from the farm of the holdings in Selby acquired by Walter, lord bishop of Durham, as part (payment) of £8 spent for alienation in mortmain of the same, paid by (*per manus*) John de Brun.[45]

And for 20s. received from Master John de Petreburgh at Collingham for the benefit of the cloister.[46]

And for £80 received from John Tuch for the pension of 10 marks sold to him and to his present wife Margaret for the term of their lives.[47]

And for £18 from Katherine Dreng for one corrody sold to her,[48] in addition to certain acres of land granted to the monastery, and in addition to 40s. credited to her for the same amount of money borrowed from her by Brother Thomas de Houeden 4 years before by order of the lord abbot.

---

[43] In 1343 one John de Lascy was steward of the abbot of Selby (*The Coucher Book of Selby*, II, p. 323). This may be the same family as the Lascys of Gateforth, near Selby, described as merchants in the Poll Tax returns of 1379 (*YAJ*, 61, 1881, p. 130), who had lands and tenements in Selby by the 15th century (*Testamenta Eboracensia*, II, pp. 1–2). Thomas Danyel, or Daynell, of Selby dealt in cloth (*The Early Yorkshire Woollen Trade. Extracts from the Hull Customs' Rolls, and Complete Transcripts of the Ulnagers' Rolls*, ed. J. Lister, YAS, Record Series 64, 1924, p. 95).

[44] Roger Pogge of Swinefleet was a juror in an inquisition *post mortem* of 1401 (*Inquisitions post mortem relating to Yorkshire of the reigns of Henry IV and Henry V*, p. 13).

[45] This entry may refer to the costs incurred in relation to a grant of property in Selby to the abbey by Walter Skirlaw, bishop of Durham, which was to provide revenues for the chantry of one priest-monk he established there. John de Brun, described as steward of Selby in 1404, was one of his agents in this transaction. (See *CPR, 1396–99*, p. 219; British Library, Cotton Vit. E.XVI, fos 135v–136v for the chantry, and f.116 for the reference to Brun as steward). Richard de Drax was bailiff of Selby in 1404, and received a fee from the house of 40s. in this account. See *Yorkshire Deeds*, VII, ed. C.T. Clay, YAS, Record Series 83, 1932, p. 121; and *Pensions and fees*, p. 56).

[46] See *Restoration of the monastery*, pp. 74–76. Master John de Petreburgh was involved in other grants to the abbey (see *Expenditure of the lord abbot*, p. 65; and *CPR, 1374–77*, p. 476). He had been admitted as rector of Lambourne, Essex, in 1395. His biography appears in A. B. Emden, *A Biographical Register of the University of Oxford to 1500*, Oxford, 1957–59.

[47] The grant of the pension is recorded in the abbey's register (British Library, Cotton Vit. E.XVI, fos 142v–143), the entries being dated 10–11 February 1399. John Tuch was a mercer of York (see *York Memorandum Book*, ed. M. Sellers, I, Surtees Society 120, 1912, p. 251).

[48] The grant is recorded in the abbey's register (British Library, Cotton Vit. E.XVI, f.143v). She is described there as 'of Wrelton' (North Yorkshire).

And for £26 13s.4d. received from Peter Talbot and Beatrice his wife for the office of porter and the corrody belonging to the same, sold to them for the term of their lives.[49]

And for £20 received from Peter de la Haye as a loan under bond.[50]

And for £20 received from William de Asthill as a loan without bond.

And for £25 from William de Wath as a loan for the allowance of clothing (*ex mutuo in liberationem pannorum*).[51]

And for £60 received from Alan de Hamerton as a loan.[52]

Total £351 9s.10d.

Sum total of receipts £774 7s.8d.

Excess
(*Excessus*)

From which the same persons account for the excess of expenditure (over income) of their previous final account, as it appears at the foot of the said account £75 11s.7½d.

Total £75 11s.7½d.

Pensions and fees
(*Pensiones et feoda*)

Likewise the same persons account for the payment made to the abbot of the blessed (St) Mary's York for his annual pension 50s.

And to the choristers of Lincoln yearly 40s.[53]

And to the prior of St Andrew's York yearly for the houses in Skeldergate in York 8s.[54]

And to the lord duke of Lancaster for Eastoft in county York yearly 4s.

---

[49] The grant is recorded in the abbey's register (British Library, Cotton Vit. E.XVI, fos 144v–145).

[50] Peter de la Haye was an East Riding landowner and local official (see C.D.Ross, *The Yorkshire Baronage 1399–1435*, D.Phil. thesis, Oxford, p.382).

[51] The abbey made various purchases of cloth from William de Wath both this year (see pp.65, 73, and 74), and later.

[52] He was a mercer of York (R.B.Dobson, 'The Foundation of Perpetual Chantries by the Citizens of Medieval York', in *Studies in Church History*, ed. G.J.Cuming, IV, 1967, p.29). The bursars purchased sturgeon, eels, and wine from him this year (see pp.67 and 73).

[53] The pension was paid from the revenues of Selby's appropriated churches in Lincolnshire, Crowle, Luddington, Redbourne, and Stallingborough (see *The Registrum Antiquissimum of the Cathedral Church of Lincoln*, II, ed. C.W.Fowler, Lincoln Record Society 28, 1933, pp.140 and 164).

[54] For the grant to Selby Abbey of a messuage in Skeldergate and the rent of 8s. due from it to St Andrew's Priory, see *The Coucher Book of Selby*, I, pp.330–332 and 334. It was a small Gilbertine house with three canons and a prior in 1380–81 (D.Knowles and R.N.Hadcock, *Medieval Religious Houses: England and Wales*, pp.197 and 199).

And to the abbot of Thornton for the site of the grange at *Loune* 33s.

And to the collector of the lord pope yearly 7s.2d.[55]

And to the boy-bishop of York yearly 6s.8d.[56]

And to John Tuch for his pension yearly £10.[57]

And to the same and Margaret his wife for their pension at the due date (*pro termino*) of the Nativity of St John the Baptist (24 June) 66s.8d.

And to Katherine Dreeng for her[58] pension yearly 106s.8d.

And to John Chaumbrelayn, corrodarian of the lord king,[59] with half a mark given to him by the lord abbot 66s.8d.

And to Joan, who was the wife of Nicholas Rose, for her pension yearly 40s.[60]

And to Brother William Pygot[61] at Oxford yearly £10.

And to Robert Potman for his provisions yearly 40s.[62]

And to Alice Spicer for her clothing yearly 5s.[63]

---

[55] This sum represented a pension of 7s. p.a. for procurations, plus 2d. for acquittance (see W. E. Lunt, *Financial Relations of the Papacy with England 1327–1534*, Cambridge, Mass., 1962, ch. XIV).

[56] A reference to the celebrations of the festival of Holy Innocents (28 December), which included the election by the cathedral choristers of one of their number as boy-bishop. The boy-bishop made a 'visitation' of his diocese and was entertained by various of the nobility and ecclesiastical institutions along the way, receiving gifts from each. See *The Camden Miscellany* VII, Camden Society NS 14, 1875, pp. v–xxxii and 31–33, for a discussion of the festival and an account roll of the 'visitation' of the York boy-bishop in 1396.

[57] See above p. 51.

[58] *sua* repeated in the MS. For Katherine Dreeng, see above p. 51.

[59] It was common practice for the crown to demand for its servants corrodies and pensions in monastic houses in the royal patronage. See J. H. Tillotson, 'Pensions, Corrodies, and Religious Houses: An Aspect of the Relations of Crown and Church in Early 14th-Century England', *Journal of Religious History*, 8 (1974), pp. 127–143. Chaumbrelayn had been granted the corrody by the crown in 1394 (*CCR*, 1392–96, p. 262).

[60] Nicholas Rose, one of the abbey cooks, had been granted the pension in 1386 (British Library, Cotton Vit. E.XVI, f.144).

[61] Pygot, elected abbot of Selby in 1408, was maintained at Oxford University by the house in accordance with the Benedictine statute that each house of the order maintain one student at the university for every 20 monks in the community. His inception as bachelor of canon law is recorded later in the account (see *Foreign expenses*, p. 81)

[62] Potman was clearly a corrodarian of the house, receiving turves for his fuel later in the account (see *Costs of fuel*, p. 81). He was the father of Master Ralph de Selby, Baron of the Exchequer (see *Payment of debts*, p. 84); and he was possibly the Robert Potteman, merchant of Selby, who paid 3s.4d. to the Poll Tax of 1379 (see *YAJ*, 6, 1881, p. 146).

[63] Another corrodarian of the house, receiving turves for her fuel later in the account (see *Costs of fuel*, p. 81). Under a mortmain licence of 1377 a messuage in Selby was to revert to the abbey on her death (*CPR*, 1374–77, p. 476).

And to Deonise Loef for her clothing and her fuel yearly, in addition to 3,600[64] turves 9s.8d.[65]

And to the lord prior for his fee yearly 10s.

And to the sub-prior yearly 6s.8d.

And to the third prior yearly 5s.

And to the treasurers yearly 6s.8d.

And to the pittancer for Eastoft in County York yearly 6s.8d.

And to the keeper of the altar of the blessed Mary for *CourtNayland* annexed to the vicarage of Brayton yearly 12d.

And to the chaplain of the lord abbot for his fee yearly 13s.4d.

And to Brother John de Cave, scribe in the storehouse,[66] yearly 6s.8d.

And to Master Alan de Newerk[67] for his fee in respect of the terms of Pentecost (26 May) and St Martin (11 November) *anno domini* etc. (13)98 and of Pentecost (18 May) *anno* etc. (13)99 60s.

And to John de Catisby,[68] steward of Stanford, yearly 20s.

And to Thomas de Frisby,[69] steward of Queniborough, yearly 20s.

And to Thomas de Brunhom,[70] steward of Crowle, yearly 40s.

And to the same for his fee previously granted 20s.

And to Thomas de Egmanton,[71] steward of Stallingborough and Rawcliffe, yearly 20s.

[64] The long hundred of six score (where 'C' = 120, 'D' = 600, and 'M' = 1200) is in use in this account for items other than money amounts; and all such hundreds have been converted to normal hundreds. Hence here *iii M*[1] becomes 3,600.

[65] Deonise Loef was another corrodarian of the house, receiving turves for her fuel later in the account (see *Costs of fuel*, p. 81).

[66] The word 'keeper' (*custos*) was used instead of 'scribe' (*scribenti in celario*) in the bursar's roll of 1431–32, and his fee was for recording the daily expenses in food of the monastery (HUL, DDLO 20/1, s.v. *Feoda*).

[67] Master Alan de Newerk begins the list of counsellors and officials of the abbey in receipt of fees. King's clerk and advocate in the Consistory Court of York, he became archdeacon of Durham 1408–09 (see *Testamenta Eboracensia*, I, Surtees Society 4, 1836, pp. 51–54; *CPR*, 1388–92, p. 276; *John Le Neve: Fasti Ecclesiae Anglicanae 1300–1541*, compiled by Joyce M. Horn, B. Jones and H. P. F. King, 12 vols, London, 1962–67, VI, p. 112).

[68] A landowner in Northamptonshire and Warwickshire, appointed to the commission of the peace in both counties (see *Inquisitions and assessments relating to feudal aids*, ed. H.C. Maxwell-Lyte, HMSO, 1920, VI, p. 492; and *CPR*, 1396–1399, pp. 98, 232, 435–437. Also *The 'Status Maneriorum' of John Catesby 1385 and 1386*, ed. J. Birrell, Dugdale Society, Miscellany I, 31, 1977, pp. 15–28).

[69] A justice of the peace in counties Leicester, Rutland, and Nottingham (see *CPR*, 1396–99, pp. 235, 238, and 436; 1399–1401, pp. 560 and 563).

[70] Thomas de Brunhom or Burnham was a Lincolnshire landowner (*Feudal Aids*, VI, p. 483).

[71] Thomas de Egmanton of Fockerby, escheator for Yorkshire in 1403 (*CCR*, 1402–05, p. 66).

And to William de Gascoigne[72] yearly 26s.8d.

And to Robert Tirwhyt[73] yearly 26s.8d.

And to Thomas de Gaytford[74] yearly 20s.

And to Alexander de Stayndrop, attorney of the lord abbot in the Court of Common Pleas, yearly 20s.

And to William de Waldby,[75] attorney of the lord abbot in the Court of King's Bench, yearly 20s.

And to William Passelewe, auditor of the serjeants' accounts, yearly 20s.

And to William de Ludyngton[76] yearly 20s.

And to Nicholas Rocelyn[77] yearly 20s.

And to John Amyas[78] for the previous and present years 40s.

---

[72] Most probably the king's serjeant (1397) and later chief justice of King's Bench (1400) of that name, who had strong connexions with the Duchy of Lancaster administration. He was retained as counsel with Henry, earl of Derby, 1392–93; was made chief steward in Lancashire c.1395–96, and chief justice at Lancaster in 1397; and died in 1419. Of Gawthorpe, co. York. (See R. Somerville, *History of the Duchy of Lancaster*, I 1265–1603, London, 1953, pp. 363, 386, and 468). On the retaining of lawyers, see N. Ramsay, 'Retained Legal Counsel, c.1275–c.1475', *Royal Historical Society, London, Transactions*, 5th Series 35, 1985, pp. 95–112.

[73] A lawyer and landowner in Lincolnshire and Yorkshire, retained also by the abbey of Meaux, Ramsey Abbey and the Duchy of Lancaster, he served as justice of the peace for all three Ridings of Yorkshire and the liberty of Beverley between 1396 and 1429. He was appointed king's serjeant in 1399 and judge of King's Bench 1409 (see *Feudal Aids*, VI, pp. 483 and 545; C. Ross, *The Yorkshire Baronage 1399–1435*, p. 121; R. Somerville, *History of the Duchy of Lancaster*, I, p. 450; and J. R. Maddicott, *Law and Lordship: Royal Justices as Retainers in thirteenth- and fourteenth-century England, Past and Present* Supplement 4, 1978, pp. 75–76).

[74] This may be the Thomas de Gaytford, attorney, of Gateforth near Selby who paid 6s.8d. to the Poll Tax of 1379 (see *YAJ*, 6, 1881, p. 130).

[75] Perhaps the William Waldeby, attorney in the court of King's Bench of the Duchy of Lancaster, who served as justice of the peace for the East and West Ridings and the liberty of Beverley between 1399 and 1422 (see R. Somerville, *History of the Duchy of Lancaster*, I, pp. 457, 486, 488).

[76] Possibly the William Lodington constituted the king's attorney in Common Pleas and elsewhere by Henry IV in 1399 (*CPR*, 1399–1401, p. 9). The family were Lincolnshire landowners, and William Lodington is found in several of the commissions of the peace for the county under Henry IV (*Feudal Aids*, VI, p. 483; R. Somerville, *History of the Duchy of Lancaster*, I, pp. 450, 453, 575).

[77] Appointed to the commission of the peace in the East Riding of Yorkshire in 1397, 1399, and 1400 (*CPR*, 1396–99, p. 235; 1399–1402, p. 566). In 1399 he was nominated one of the attorneys of Thomas Percy, earl of Worcester, on Percy's departure for Ireland with Richard II (*CPR*, 1396–99, p. 531).

[78] Probably John Amyas of Sitlington in the West Riding of Yorkshire, where the abbey had a mill. In 1379 John Amyas senior of Sitlington, franklin, paid 3s.4d. in Poll Tax; and John Amyas junior, merchant, paid 2s. (*YAJ*, 6, 1881, p. 159). A John Amyas was appointed king's alnager in the West Riding of Yorkshire in 1397 (*CFR*, 1391–99, p. 231). In 1408 John Amyas of Sitlington was associated, among others, with William Gascoigne and Robert Mauleverer in a grant to the priory of Nostell (*CPR*, 1408–13, p. 4).

And to Robert Mauleverer[79] yearly 20s.

And to William Barker of Tadcaster[80] yearly 20s.

And to John Marshall[81] yearly 20s.

And to Richard de Drax[82] yearly 40s.

And to Robert Broune[83] yearly 26s.8d.

And to William de Wessyngton[84] yearly 26s.8d.

And to John Martyn[85] for his fee and robe yearly 32s.

And to John de Birne[86] yearly 66s.8d.

Total £79 4s.10d.[87]

Salaries of staff
(*Stipendia famu-
lorum*)

Likewise the same persons account for the salary of John de Selby, chamberlain of the lord abbot, for the year 13s.4d.

And for the salary of Henry Droury, cook of the same lord, during (*pro*) the term of St Martin[88] 10s.

And for the salary of Thomas Warde, servant in the storehouse, for the year 13s.4d.

---

[79] In 1407 and 1410 he was described as the abbot's steward, and he was steward of Monk Fryston 1416–17 (British Library, Cotton Vit. E.XVI, f.132v; HUL, DDLO 18/1; WDA, Se/Ac/9, s.v. *Feoda*). This may be the Robert Mauleverer, under-sheriff of co. York, appointed sheriff in September 1406 (*CFR*, 1405–1413, p.44). He was remembered in the will of another Selby counsellor, William Barker of Tadcaster (*Testamenta Eboracensia*, I, pp.327–328).

[80] Appointed king's alnager in the West Riding of Yorkshire 1395 and 1399, and collector of a tenth and fifteenth there in 1398 (*CFR*, 1391–99, pp.165 and 264; 1399–1405, p.45; *The Early Yorkshire Woollen Trade*, ed. J. Lister, p.95). He left 6s.8d. to the fabric of Selby Abbey in his will, dated 1403 (*Testamenta Eboracensia*, I, pp.327–328).

[81] A Selby man, associated with other officers of the abbey in the business of monastery and town (see *CPR*, 1391–96, p.219, and 1405–8, p.17).

[82] He was described as an esquire of the abbot in 1384, when he was granted a corrody and pension of 40s. p.a. for life in return for his services in suitable offices (British Library, Cotton Vit. E.XVI, f.143v). In 1400 and 1404 he was serving as bailiff of Selby (*Yorkshire Deeds*, ed. C.T. Clay, VII, p.121; British Library, Cotton Vit. E.XVI, f.116).

[83] A serjeant's account roll of 1423–24 describes him as the abbot's butler (HUL, DDLO 20/66, s.v. *Compotus bladorum et stauri*).

[84] He received a legacy in the will of William, son of John de Escryk, priest of Selby, along with other servants of the abbey both feed and salaried (*North Country Wills*, ed. J.W. Clay, pp.2–5).

[85] He was described as the abbot's clerk in 1396, when he was present at the performance of homage by tenants of Stallingborough at Selby (British Library, Cotton Cleo. D.III, f.197).

[86] He was described as the clerk of the extern cellarer and bursar in a document of 1402 (British Library, Cotton Vit. E.XVI, f.140).

[87] See also *Restoration of the Monastery*, p.75, where a fee of 40s. is paid to the abbey's master mason, and *Allowances* under Queniborough, p.86, where a fee of 6s.8d. annually granted to John Folvil of Rearsby for life is mentioned.

[88] i.e. 11 November 1398, since he died during the period of the account and John Hasand took over as cook (see below and *Expenditure of the lord abbot*).

And for the salary of Henry Sampson, servant in the guest house, for the year 13s.4d.

And for the salary of John Marshall, palfreyman of the lord abbot, for the year 13s.4d.

And for the salary of John Hasand, cook of the lord abbot, this year 11s.8d.[89]

And for the salary of John Sperwe junior, usher of the lord abbot, during the term of St Martin[90] 5s.

And to the same for taking care of the hunting dogs, during the same term 3s.4d.

And for the salary of John de Hamelton, usher of the said lord, for the year 10s.

And for the salary of John Droury, groom[91] of the chaplain of the said lord, for the year 10s.

And for the salary of John Sperwe senior, groom in the stable of the said lord, for the year 10s.

And for the salary of Robert de Crofton, groom in the same, for the year 10s.

And for the salary of Alice Trim, laundress of the lord abbot, for the year 10s.

And for the salary of John de Cadnay, groom of the bursar, for the year 10s.

And for the salary of William de Duffeld, page in the kitchen of the said lord, for the year 6s.8d.

And for the salary of John Bewe, page in the same, during the Pentecost term[92] 3s.4d.

And for the grant to Simon the stableman for footwear for the same year 3s.4d.

And for the salary of Richard Smyth, workman in the pool, for the year in addition to grain and clothing 16s.

Total £8 12s.8d.

---

[89] The full year's salary was apparently 20s., and Hasand was paid this amount in the bursar's account for 1416–17 (WDA, Se/Ac/9, s.v. *Stipendia famulorum*). He took over from Henry Droury during 1399 on the latter's death.

[90] i.e. for half the year, starting 11 November 1398.

[91] The account roll uses three general terms for servant, depending on salary. *Servientes* were paid 13s.4d. a year; *garciones* 10s.; and *paietti* 6s.8d. They have been translated respectively 'servant', 'groom', and 'page'.

[92] i.e. for half the year, starting about 18 May 1399.

Gifts
(*Dona*)

Likewise the same persons account for the gift to Brother John de Cawod, Dominican of York, at his inception in theology,[93] by command of the lord abbot 20s.

And to Master John de Lepyngton, clerk of the archdeacon of York, making a visitation of the church of Brayton on behalf of the said archdeacon about the festival of St Andrew (30 November, 1398) 3s.4d.

And to the clerks of Selby singing (*psallentibus*) on St Nicholas eve (5 December, 1398) 12d.

And to a certain servant of the rector of the church of Hemingbrough[94] about the said time 18d., paid by (*per manus*) Brother Adam de Crosseby at the lord abbot's command.

And to Nicholas de Oklay on Christmas Eve 3s.4d.

And to 4 boys of York performing (*ludentibus*) before the lord abbot on Christmas Day 12d., paid by Robert Broun.[95]

And to John de Brikhill, forester of Crowle, at the festival of St John the Apostle (27 December, 1398) 3s.4d.[96]

And to John Warst, lowest grade minstrel (*ministrallo pessimo*) of the lord duke of Lancaster,[97] at the same time 18d.

And to Hugh the waferer of the lord archbishop of York at the said (time)[98] 18d.

And to 3 minstrels of Sir (*domini*) Henry de Percy[99] at the same time 3s.4d.

---

[93] i.e. on his admission to a degree in theology, which involved an elaborate and expensive ceremony (see C. E. Mallet, *A History of the University of Oxford*, I, London, 1924, pp. 189 and 196–198).

[94] The rector was Thomas de Walworth, made vicar-general for the diocese of York in 1389, and a man high in the favour of Archbishop Scrope (see T. Burton (ed. and enlarged J. Raine), *The History and Antiquities of the Parish of Hemingbrough in the County of York*, YAS, Extra Series 1, 1888, pp. 56–58).

[95] For Robert Broun, see above p. 56 n. 83.

[96] Brikhill's appointment as forester was made at the request of Thomas de Mowbray, earl of Nottingham, of whose chase at Crowle he was warden (see Lincolnshire Archives Office, CM 1/44).

[97] John of Gaunt, duke of Lancaster and Richard II's uncle, who died 3–4 February 1399. His death precipitated the crisis which led to the usurpation of his son, Henry Bolingbroke, earl of Derby and duke of Hereford, at the end of September 1399.

[98] The word *tempus* has apparently been omitted in error.

[99] This is presumably Henry 'Hotspur' Percy, son and heir of the first earl of Northumberland. The Percies ranked second only to the duke of Lancaster as Yorkshire landowners, with castles at Spofforth, Topcliffe, and Wressle (see C. D. Ross, *The Yorkshire Baronage*, ch. III).

And to 3 minstrels of Sir Philip Darcy[100] at the said time 3s.4d.

And to 2 minstrels of Selby at the same time 2s.

And to John Careaway of York and his companions performing before the lord abbot and the convent at the festival of St Silvester (31 December, 1398) 3s.4d.

And to Richard de Riplay, brother of Robert de Waterton,[101] at the same time by command of the lord abbot 6s.8d.

And to 6 minstrels of the lord earl of Northumberland[102] about the said time 6s.8d.

And to the messenger of the lord archbishop of York inviting the lord abbot to lunch with the said lord archbishop at the festival of Epiphany (6 January, 1399) 3s.4d.

And to 3 clerks of William Gascoigne[103] at the same time 5s.

And to 2 servants (*valettis*) of the same 2s.

And to a certain minstrel of the lord de Roos[104] at the said time 20d.

And to a certain servant of William Barker[105] bringing to the lord abbot 12 partridges about the festival of St Hillary (13 January, 1399) 6d.

And to Roger Payn, lessee (*Firmario*) of Queniborough, and Nicholas de Holt, servant (*valetto*) of the duke of Aumale,[106] about the festival of St Vincent (22 January, 1399) 3s.4d.

---

[100] Philip, lord Darcy, who died in April 1399, a minor baron distinguished from the knights and gentry only by his rank and not by wealth. His most important lands were in North-East Yorkshire, but he also had estates in Lincolnshire, Derbyshire, Northumberland, and Nottinghamshire (see C. D. Ross, *The Yorkshire Baronage*, ch.IX).

[101] The Waterton family, all of whom were to show themselves devoted followers of Henry IV, took their name from the manor of Waterton in the Hundred of Crowle, co. Lincoln. Robert was the third son of William Waterton of Waterton, and an esquire of Henry Bolingbroke as duke of Hereford. He was one of the earliest supporters of Bolingbroke after his landing in the north of England in 1399. Under the Lancastrian kings he was prominent both at court and in Yorkshire, and he was in receipt of the large annual fee of 100s. from Selby Abbey by 1413 (see J. W. Walker, 'The Burghs of Cambridgeshire and Yorkshire and the Watertons of Lincolnshire and Yorkshire', *YAJ*, 30, 1930–31, pp. 349–419; and HUL, DDLO 20/54b, List of fees 1413–14).

[102] Henry Percy, first earl of Northumberland, who was to join Henry Bolingbroke with his son at Doncaster on or about 13 July 1399 in an alliance that led directly to Richard II's deposition. For the Percies, see above p. 58 n. 99.

[103] For Gascoigne see above, p. 55 n. 72.

[104] William, lord Roos of Hamelake, another early supporter of Henry IV and leading personality at his court in the first years of the reign. He was Treasurer 1403–04 and died in 1414. The family had an important seat at Helmsley in Yorkshire; but William's favourite residence was Belvoir, astride the Lincolnshire and Leicestershire border (see C. D. Ross, *The Yorkshire Baronage*, ch.IV).

[105] For Barker see above, p. 56 n. 80.

[106] Edward of York, son of Edmund duke of York and cousin of Richard II. He was created Duke of Aumale in 1397, but degraded from the rank to earl (of Rutland) after the revolution of 1399.

And to Reginald de Gaytford and 2 esquires of Master Ralph de Selby[107] at the same time 10s.

And to 3 servants of the same 3s.8d.

And to John Daunay[108] on the morrow (of the festival) of the Purification of the blessed Mary (3 February, 1399) 13s.4d.

And to William, the son of John Scot, on the same day 3s.4d.

And to John de Beltoft, courier of Oxford, about the festival of St Valentine (14 February, 1399) 12d., paid by Brother J(ohn) de Cave.

And to a certain young man, the son of one of the esquires of the lord earl of Arundel,[109] a beggar, by command of the lord abbot about the same time 20d.

And to John de Sutton, *adulator*,[110] 6d.

And to a certain minstrel of Sir Ralph de Lumlay[111] about the said time 12d., paid by J(ohn) de Birne.[112]

And to one waferer at Stainer about the same time 12d., (paid) by the same John 12d.

And to Thomas Harpour of Tadcaster, a blind man, at the same time 2s.

And to John Mauleverer, esquire of Sir Stephen le Scrope,[113] about the said time by command of the lord abbot 6s.8d.

---

[107] A creditor of the abbey, whose father was one of its corrodarians (see pp. 84 and 53 n. 62).

[108] Possibly John Dawnay of Escrick, co. York, with property also in Cowick and Snaith (*VCH*, Yorkshire East Riding 3, OUP, 1976, p. 21; *CCR*, 1392–96, p. 90), who is recorded as refusing to pay a rent of 12d. for a holding in Cowick in this account (see *Allowances*, p. 89). He later became the recipient of an annual fee from the abbey as one of its counsellors, though the rent of 12d. could still not be collected (1413–14: HUL, DDLO 20/54b, s.v. *Pensiones et feoda*; 1416–17: WDA, Se/Ac/9, s.v. *Feoda and Allocationes*).

[109] Richard fitz Alan, earl of Arundel, was one of the Appellants of the Merciless Parliament and he was executed in 1397. His only surviving son and heir was restored to the title in 1400 after the Lancastrian usurpation.

[110] The literal meaning 'flatterer' seems inappropriate. Possibly *cauillator* or 'jester' was intended? The word occurs in the *Gift* section of other account rolls of the abbey, including one reference to the *adulator* of the archbishop of York (WDA, Se/Ac/9, 1415–16).

[111] Ralph, lord Lumley (1384–1400), associated with the Percy family in the defence of the north of England against the Scots, and a commissioner of the peace in Yorkshire NR 1394–1397. He joined an unsuccessful conspiracy against Henry IV at Christmas 1399 and was beheaded at Cirencester the following January (G. E. Cokayne, *The Complete Peerage of England, Scotland, Great Britain, and the United Kingdom, Extant, Extinct, or Dormant*, revised edition, ed. V. Gibbs, H. A. Doubleday, G. H. White, and R. S. Lea, 12 vols, London, 1910–1959, VIII, pp. 269–70).

[112] For John de Birne, see above p. 56 n. 86.

[113] Stephen, lord Scrope of Masham 1392–1406, a Yorkshire baron with estates in Wensleydale, the Vale of York, and the East Riding, and a favourite residence at Faxfleet near York (see C. Ross, *The Yorkshire Baronage*, ch. V).

And to a certain servant of the same Sir S(tephen) who brought porpoise (*porpays*) to the lord abbot at the said time 12d.

And to a certain servant of lord de Roos who brought one letter to the lord abbot about the middle of Lent 12d.[114]

And to 2 nuns of Nunburnholme[115] begging at the festival of the Annunciation of the blessed Mary (25 March, 1399), by command of the said lord 2s.

And to John de Lincoln, esquire of Sir Stephen le Scrope, who invited the lord abbot to lunch with the same Sir Stephen in Easter Week 3s.4d.

And to one servant of the same Sir S(tephen) at the same time 20d.

And to Nicholas de Oklay at the same time 12d.

And to 2 minstrels of the duke of Norfolk[116] at the said time 3s.4d.

And to Thomas del Kirk, servant of dominus[117] Thomas de Haxay[118] who brought one letter to the lord abbot about the said time 12d.

And to Richard de Gascoigne[119] about the festival of St George (23 April, 1399) by command of the lord abbot 13s.4d.

And to 2 minstrels of Baron de Greystoke[120] and to a certain lowest grade fiddler (*Phialatori pessimo*) 2s.

And to a certain servant of the abbot of Whitby, who brought to the lord abbot a letter about visitation of the monastery[121] around the said time 18d.

---

[114] *xiid.* interlined. Easter day in 1399 was on 30 March. Lent was the 40 week-days preceding Easter.

[115] A small priory for Benedictine nuns in the East Riding of Yorkshire, with 6 inmates and an income of about £8 a year in the early 16th century (see D. Knowles and R. N. Hadcock, *Medieval Religious Houses, England and Wales*, pp. 262 and 254).

[116] Thomas de Mowbray, earl of Nottingham and duke of Norfolk, one of the Appellants of the Merciless Parliament but a supporter of the king in the Westminster Parliament of 1397 that destroyed his former allies. He was exiled for life in 1398 as a consequence of allegations of treasonable words spoken to the duke of Hereford (Henry Bolingbroke), and he died at Venice 22 September 1399 a few days before Bolingbroke became king (see *Complete Peerage*, IX, pp. 601–04).

[117] The title *dominus* was commonly given to the clergy.

[118] A king's clerk and a pluralist, who had acted as proctor of the abbot of Selby in the parliament of 1 January 1397. At that parliament he introduced a bill for reform of the royal household, and was adjudged a traitor for it, though pardoned soon afterwards. See M. McKisack, *The Fourteenth Century*, p. 477.

[119] Possibly Richard de Gascoigne of Hunslet, younger brother of William Gascoigne the lord chief justice (see *Testamenta Eboracensia*, I, p. 403).

[120] Ralph, lord Greystoke (1359–1418), a border magnate but whose family held Fangfoss in the East Riding of Yorkshire (see *Complete Peerage*, VI, pp. 195–196; and *Victoria History of the Counties of England*, Yorkshire East Riding 3, p. 165).

[121] The abbot of Whitby was presumably the visitor appointed in the northern province by the general chapter of the English Benedictines, which met every three years at Northampton

And to a certain chaplain 2s., paid by Brother Richard de Harewod.

And to John Dowcel, minstrel, on Ascension Day (8 May, 1399) 3s.4d., (paid) by Brother John de Cave.

And to a certain knight named Adam, a beggar, who brought as evidence of his condition a charter of the lord king, about the said time by command of the lord abbot 6s.8d.

And to the servant of Edward de Clynton, who brought to the lord abbot one letter (*unam l'ram*) for one ambling horse in Pentecost week[122] 18d.

And to William Haliday, kinsman of Brother Thomas de Wakefeld, on his departure (*in recessu suo*) from the lord prior by command of the lord abbot 2s.

And to Brother John de Parys, Dominican of York, about the said time 6s.8d.

And to a certain blind chaplain, kinsman of John Barbour,[123] at the same time 12d.

And to a certain chaplain of the court of the lord archbishop at the said time 3s.4d.

And to William Belassys, *adulatori*, 6d.

And to a certain foreign minstrel 12d., paid by J(ohn) de Birne.

And to 2 Austin friars mendicant taking Brother Thomas de Craven away from the monastery to York to remain in the said order,[124] by command of the lord abbot 10s.

And to 2 women beggars from London 12d.

And to Huburdouncy, lowest grade minstrel (*ministrallo pessimo*) 6d.

And to Roger Wayt, who brought wafers to the lord abbot about the festival of St Barnabas (11 June, 1399) 20d.

---

under the statutes of Benedict XII and appointed visitors for its houses in each province (see D. Knowles, *The Religious Orders in England*, II, pp. 3–7; and W. A. Pantin (ed.), *Documents Illustrating the Activities of the General and Provincial Chapters of the English Black Monks, 1215–1540*, I, Camden Society, third series 45, 1931, pp. 86–88).

[122] Whit sunday 1399 was 18 May. Edward de Clynton was master forester and chief keeper of the chase in the Isle of Axholme, co. Lincoln, to Thomas Mowbray duke of Norfolk, with a fee of £20 p.a. (see *CPR*, 1399–1401, p. 90).

[123] Presumably the John Barbour of Selby earlier involved in business transactions with the abbey (see British Library, Cotton Vit. E.XVI, fos 126 and 150).

[124] No other reference to Brother Thomas de Craven has been found in the Selby Abbey records. It would appear from this entry that he was transferring from Benedictines to Austin Friars, a change possible because the latter would be regarded as a stricter Order.

And to John, chamberlain of lord de Roos, about the said time by command of the lord abbot 10s.

And to a bishop of Ulster (*Huluest'*) in Ireland, begging, on the 2nd day of the month of July by command of the lord abbot 6s.8d.

And to a certain courier of Oxford about the said time 12d., (paid) by Brother John de Cave.

And to William de Duffeld on his departure from the kitchen of the lord abbot to his brother 12d.

And to Dan Richard de Brunby, monk of York, by command of the lord abbot 3s.4d.

And to a servant of William Passelewe[125] on the eve of (the festival) of St James the Apostle (24 July, 1399) 18d.

And to Master Thomas Wright of Rothwell, who brought to the lord abbot a letter of the lord Henry, duke of Lancaster, to borrow money (*pro pecunia mutuanda*)[126] about the said time 6s.8d.

And to a servant of William Ketring,[127] who brought to the lord abbot 2 herons about the said time 6d.

And to John de Moslay, cook of the lord bishop of Durham,[128] bringing news to the lord abbot about the lord H(enry), duke of Lancaster, on the 2nd day of the month of August 2s.[129]

And to Richard Emson of Crowle, who brought to the lord abbot one deer sent by Thomas de Brunhom[130] about the said time 12d.

And to a certain waferer at the festival of St Bartholomew (24 August, 1399) 12d.

---

[125] Auditor of the serjeants' accounts (see above, *Pensions and fees*, p. 55).

[126] Henry Bolingbroke had landed in Yorkshire at Ravenspur on the lower Humber early in July, on the invasion which replaced Richard II by his cousin on the throne of England. A servant of his father Gaunt, named Thomas Wright of Rothwell, had received a grant of a house in Cowick near Snaith, county Yorkshire, for his services (*John of Gaunt's Register, 1379–1383*, ed. E. C. Lodge and R. Somerville, Camden Society third series 56 and 57, 1937, II, p. 311).

[127] John of Gaunt, duke of Lancaster, had an esquire of this name who was granted the manor of Kirkby near Ouseburn, co. Yorkshire, by the duke for life in 1380. He may also have held the manor of Osgodby, where Selby Abbey had a small estate (see *John of Gaunt's Register*, ed. E. C. Lodge and R. Somerville, I, pp. 10 and 146; II, pp. 303–304; and *VCH*, Yorkshire East Riding 3, p. 65).

[128] Walter Skirlaw, bishop of Durham 1388–1406, a former Keeper of the Privy Seal (1382–1386), since 1386 mainly occupied in his northern diocese and after 1397 released by Richard II from attendance at parliaments and councils by reason of his services and advanced age (see T. F. Tout, *Chapters in the Administrative History of Medieval England*, 6 vols, Manchester, 1928–37, III, p. 436, n. 1). For his chantry at Selby see above, p. 51 n. 45.

[129] Bolingbroke was now in the south–west of England. At Bristol on 29 July Richard II's councillors Bussy and Green had been executed, two days after the king had left Ireland. See M. McKisack, *The Fourteenth Century*, p. 492.

[130] Steward of Crowle (see above, *Pensions and fees*, p. 54).

And to the messenger of the lord king, who brought to the lord abbot a writ of summons to parliament (*brevem de parliamento*) about the festival of St Giles (1 September, 1399)[131] 2s.

And to the crier of the court of York about the said time 3s.4d.

And to Alexander de Stayndrop, who went as proctor of the lord abbot to parliament at London about the festival of St Matthew (21 September),[132] by command of the lord abbot 6s.8d.

And to Thomas de Hoghlay, brother of Agnes the wife of Master William Coke, by command of the lord abbot 3s.4d.

And to Adam, minstrel of the lord duke of York,[133] 20d. paid by J(ohn) de Hamlton.[134]

And to the servant of William de Waldby,[135] who brought to the lord abbot a writ of the lord king directed to the sheriff of York touching a false presentment made against the lord abbot for obstruction of Foulness (*Fulnay*) water at Holme upon Spaldingmoor, by command of the said lord 12d.

And to a certain waferer at the festival of the burial of St German (1 October, 1399) 20d.

And to William Swalwe,[136] who brought to the lord abbot large eels from Crowle 12d.

And for 2 pairs of knives bought and given by the lord abbot to two clerks of the court of the lord archbishop of York 3s.2d.

And to a certain servant of the lord bishop of Durham, (paid) by J(ohn) de Birne 20d.

---

[131] Writs for a parliament to meet at Westminster on the last day of September were issued from Chester in Richard II's name on 19 August. The king was by now Bolingbroke's prisoner, and his act of abdication was read to this assembly when it met. See M. McKisack, *The Fourteenth Century*, pp. 493–494.

[132] Alexander de Stayndrop was the abbot of Selby's attorney in the court of Common Pleas (see above, *Pensions and fees*, p. 55). For Abbot John de Shirburn's record of attendance at parliament, see Appendix p. 255.

[133] Edmund of Langley, duke of York (d.1402), uncle of both Richard II and Henry Bolingbroke, and regent during the king's Irish expedition of 1399. He held the Yorkshire castle and lordship of Conisborough, and the lordship of Thorne near Snaith (see *Complete Peerage*, XII, pp. 895–905; *Inquisitions post mortem*, ed. W. P. Baildon and J. W. Clay, pp. 24–25).

[134] Hamlton (or Hamelton) received a salary of 10s. in this account roll as the abbot's usher (see above, *Salaries of staff*, p. 57).

[135] Attorney of the abbot in the court of King's Bench (see above, *Pensions and fees*, p. 55).

[136] Perhaps the same person who was later serjeant of Crowle (see HUL, DDLO 20/54c, 1413–1414).

And to a servant of William Pund of Hull,[137] (paid) by the said J(ohn) 8d.

Total £12 15s.

Expenditure of the lord abbot (*Expense domini Abbatis*)	Likewise the same persons account for the expenditure of the lord abbot at York for the convocation of the clergy there in the 4th week of Lent.[138] Nothing (is accounted for) here because (met) from the sum of 100s. given to the monastery by Master John de Petreburgh.[139]

And for the expenditure of the same lord at York for the convocation of the clergy there after the festival of the Ascension (8 May, 1399), (certified) by bill 35s.10½d.

And they have paid[140] to the chaplain of the lord abbot for presents to be given to various persons against Christmas 52s.

And to the same chaplain for this sort of thing on Maundy Thursday (27 March, 1399) 2s.

And for spices bought from William Martyn for the use of the lord abbot this year, (certified) by 3 bills £9 1s.1d.

And for 6 cushions (*in vi peciis de Cosyne*) bought at London by John de Birne for the use of the lord abbot 10s.6d.

And for green ginger and other things bought at Hull by John, chamberlain of the lord abbot, for the use of the said lord, together with the expenditure of the same John going to Hull to buy wine, and with transport of the said wine, (certified) by bill 15s.2½d.

And for green ginger bought by John de Birne for the use of the same lord about the feast of St Valentine (14 February, 1399) 3s.4d.

And for 8 ells of black cloth bought from William de Thorp for the use of the said lord 14s.

And for one ell of black cloth bought for the cowl of the same lord 3s.

And for 3 ells of cloth of burnet bought from William de Wath for the use of the said lord 9s.

And for 6 ells of blanket cloth bought by Walter del Sartry for the said lord 3s.

---

[137] A wine merchant (see *Purchase of wine*, p.73).
[138] Convocation met on 11 March 1399. See F. M. Powicke and E. B. Fryde, *Handbook of British Chronology*, 2nd edition London, 1961, p.559.
[139] See also above, *Foreign receipts*, p.51.
[140] *liberavit* written in the manuscript for *liberaverunt*.

And for 10 ells of blanket cloth bought for the same lord by the said Walter 5s.

And for 8 ells of stamyn cloth bought for the same person by the same Walter 2s.8d.

And for one ounce of silk bought for stitching the clothes of the said lord by the said Walter 14d.

And for the payment to John Shether, skinner, for mending the furs and lining the clothes of the lord abbot with fur in the past and present years before the festival of Christmas (certified) by bill 6s.8d.

And for 20 ells of linen cloth bought from Alice Banes for the chamber of the lord abbot by John, his chamberlain, 7s.11d.

And for 36 ells of canvas bought for table-cloths for the said lord's chamber 15s.

And for 8 ells of canvas bought for the kitchen of the same lord 3s.4d.

And for the service of Ellen de Helagh in mending and stitching the napery of the said lord this year and last year 20d.

And for soap bought for the laundress of the lord abbot for washing table-cloths and other cloths of the same this year 8½d.

And for payment for various necessities appurtenant to the chamber of the said lord by J(ohn) de Hamlton this year 2s.

And for payment to John de Brighton for boots and other things received from him for the use of the said lord this year and last year before the festival of Christmas (certified) by bill 42s.

And for 20 stones of Paris candles purchased both for the chamber of the lord abbot and for the corrodarians this year 26s.8d.

And for[141] 16 dozen goblets, 8 candlesticks, 4 bowls, purchased from Robert Turnour for the chamber of the said lord this year and last year before the festival of Christmas 14s.1d.

And for half a dozen decorated pewter pots purchased for the lord abbot by Brother A(dam) de Crosseby 8s.4d.

And they have paid to Henry Droury, the lord abbot's cook, for victuals purchased for the use of the same lord this year on 8 occasions 47s.7d.

And for payment to various persons after the same Henry's death for various victuals received from them for the use of the said lord whilst he (Henry) was alive, as the bills show £7 11s.

---

[141] *in* interlined.

And to John Hasand, the lord abbot's cook after the death of the same Henry, for various victuals purchased by the same John for the use of the same lord this year on 22 occasions £10 5s.

And for one measure (*una copula*)[142] of figs and raisins purchased for the use of the said lord 8s.

And for 55 capons purchased this year for the use of the said lord at a price of 4d. each 18s.4d.

And for one barrel of olive oil purchased for the kitchen of the said lord 8s.

And for half a barrel of sturgeon (*Sturgeon*) purchased from William Spenser for the same lord 16s.

And for a quarter of a barrel of sturgeon (*Sturgen*) and one barrel of salted eels purchased from Alan de Hamerton for the use of the said lord 13s.4d.

And for 6 barrels of salted eels purchased from William Spenser for the use of the said lord 30s.

And for payment to Thomas Deken of York for various copper vessels purchased from the same and repaired by him for the kitchen of the same lord 17s.5d.

And for 2 saddles, with 2 bridles and 3 *poles*, bought for the said lord's stable 13s.10d.

And for one fishing-net called a *Dikenet* and 3 kiddle-nets (*kidellis*)[143] purchased at Crowle for the fishery in the dam (*stagno*) 17s.8d.

And for the service of various men transporting the lord abbot by water to Wheel Hall (*le Welehall*)[144] on various occasions this year 2s.10d.

Total £50 15s.2½d.

| Expenditure on visitors (*Expense super-venientium*) | Likewise the same persons account for 8 gallons of wine purchased for the guest house on account of the visits of William de Skipwith, John de Amyas, Robert Mauleverer,[145] and others whilst the lord abbot was absent this year 6s.8d. |

---

[142] The cope (*copula*) is a measure of capacity of uncertain size (see R. E. Zupko, *Dictionary of English Weights and Measures from Anglo-Saxon times to the Nineteenth Century*, University of Wisconsin Press, 1968).

[143] A kiddle was a 'dam, weir, or barrier in a river, having an opening in it fitted with nets, etc. for catching fish.' (*OED*)

[144] A residence of the bishops of Durham on the River Ouse close to Riccall (see W. W. Morrell, *The History and Antiquities of Selby*, p. 106).

[145] Amyas and Mauleverer were both paid fees in this account (see above, *Pensions and fees*,

And for meats and fishes purchased for the same reason 3s.4d.

And for horse-bread purchased for visitors' horses at the guests' stable by Simon the stableman this year 10s.

And for 6 pounds of paris candle purchased by the same for lighting in the said stable this year 9d.

Total 20s.9d.

Small expenses (*Minute*)	Likewise the same persons account for the expenses of John Hasand and John Droury (going) to Crowle for the purpose of taking rabbits there about the festival of St Katherine (25 November, 1398) 16d.

And for payment to William Farrier for shoeing the horses hired at Oxford by Brother William Pygot[146] to bring him thence to Selby 6d.

And for the expenses of the same Brother William, John de Birne, and others with them, going with 8 horses from Selby to Stanford on Avon; together with the expenses of the same Brother William thence to Oxford, and with the expenses of John Palfryman returning from that place with the aforesaid horses to Selby; and also with the expenses of the aforesaid John de Birne in going from Stanford on Avon to London, in order to speak with Master Ralph de Selby[147] and on other business of the monastery, and in returning from that place by way of Stanford on Avon and Queniborough to Selby; with the money given to the servants for boots in the accustomed fashion about the festival of St Andrew (30 November, 1398) 68s.4d.

And for the service of 2 men with the fisherman from Crowle transporting by water from Crowle to Selby one boar, swans, rabbits, capons, and fishes for the lord abbot's consumption, together with victuals bought for the consumption of the same men and with money given to the said fisherman 2s.8d.

And for 1 quarter of oats purchased by the said fisherman for feeding the rabbits and swans at Crowle 20d.

And for the expenses of Robert Broun going to York in order to speak with John Tuch,[148] and in the second place to Stilling-fleet in order to speak with the steward there, about the said time 10d.

---

pp. 55–56. William de Skipwith is possibly the lord of Skipwith, a few kilometres north-east of Selby, of that name (*VCH*, Yorkshire East Riding 3, p. 63).

[146] Supported by Selby Abbey as a student at Oxford (see above, *Pensions and fees*, p. 53).

[147] A creditor of the abbey, whose father was one of its corrodarians (see p. 84). Selby was a doctor of canon and civil law, Baron of the Exchequer, and archdeacon of Buckingham (see *John Le Neve: Fasti*, I, p. 15; and T. F. Tout, *Chapters*, IV, p. 45 n. 2).

[148] His purchase of a pension is recorded above, *Foreign receipts*, p. 51. Broun received a fee of 26s.8d in this account (see above, *Pensions and fees*, p. 56).

And for the expenses of Brother Richard de Secroft going to York on 2 occasions in order to speak with Masters Ralph de Selby and Alan de Newerk[149] there 6s.

And for the expenses of Brother Peter de Rouclif and others with him going to York in order to speak with John Tuch, and on other business of the monastery, about the festival of the Conversion of St Paul (25 January, 1399) 4s.6d.

And for the payment to the lord prior as fee for the common seal with which the deed of the said John Tuch concerning his corrody is sealed, beyond the 40d. which John himself has paid 3s.4d.

And for 6 deed-boxes purchased to put deeds in and carry them 9d.

And for the expenses of the same Brother Peter and Brother Robert de Selby and others with them going to York in order to speak with John Tuch (and) William de Muston,[150] and on other business of the monastery about the festival of St Valentine (14 February, 1399) 6s.8d.

And for the expenses of John de Birne going to York in order to speak with the sheriff there, with Sir Gerald Salvayn,[151] and others on various occasions in the past and present year before the festival of St Vincent (22 January, 1399) 8s.9d.

And for the expenses of the same John and others with him going to Stanford on Avon and Queniborough to collect the farms, and with the expenses of John Palfrayman going from Stanford on Avon to Oxford in order to bring Brother William Pygot his pension; going and returning about the festival of the Annunciation of the blessed Mary (25 March, 1399). With the money given to the servants in the accustomed manner 18s.7d.

And for the expenses of the same John going with 2 horses to Stanford on Avon and Queniborough for repairing the houses of the tenants there about the festival of the Discovery of the Holy Cross (3 May, 1399) 13s.4d.

And for the expenses of Brother Richard de Secroft going to York for the synod after Easter (30 March, 1399), going and returning in the course of 3 days 8s.

[149] For Master Ralph de Selby see above, n.147. Master Alan de Newerk was paid a fee of 60s. in this account (see above *Pensions and fees*, p.54).

[150] Muston was a creditor of the abbey (British Library, Cotton Vit. E.XVI, f.124v), who purchased a corrody and pension from it in 1402 (*Ibid.*, f.137v).

[151] Sir Gerald Salvayn of North Duffield, co. Yorkshire, where Selby Abbey also had property (see *Feudal Aids*, VI, pp.172, 224, and 271). The sheriff of county Yorkshire was Sir James Pykeryng (Public Record Office, *Lists and Indexes*, 9, 1898, List of Sheriffs for England and Wales from the earliest times to A.D. 1831, p.162).

And for the expenses of the aforesaid Brother Peter going with 4 horses to Lincoln and Collingham[152] on various business of the monastery, going and returning in the course of 8 days about the festival of the Discovery of the Holy Cross (3 May, 1399). With victuals purchased on account of the wife of Gerard de Suthill[153] 16s.

And for the expenses of the same person going to York in order to speak with Master Alan de Newerk[154] and on other business of the monastery, going and returning in the course of 3 days after the festival of the Lord's Ascension (8 May, 1399) 5s.

And for the expenses of John de Birne and others with him going with 6 horses to Queniborough and Stanford on Avon to collect the farms; together with the expenses of the same persons going to Oxford, and with the expenses of Brother William Pygot, John de Birne, and others going with the same number of horses thence to Northampton to the general chapter;[155] and also with the expenses of the same persons returning to Selby about the festival of the Translation of St Thomas Martyr (7 July, 1399) 51s.2d.

And for the gift to the aforesaid Brother William for boots 3s.4d.

And for the expenses of the aforesaid Brother Peter going to York in order to pay John Tuch his pension and on other business of the monastery; going, staying, and returning about the festival of St Laurence (10 August, 1399) 5s.

And for the expenses of Peter Talbot[156] going to Rampton in order to speak with *dominus* Thomas de Haxay[157] concerning business of the lord abbot about the festival of the Nativity of the blessed Mary (8 September, 1399) 3s.4d.

And for the expenses of Brother William Pygot and others with him going with 4 horses to Oxford about the festival of St Matthew (21 September, 1399), together with the expenses of the men bringing back the said horses to Selby, and with the expenses arising from medical attention for the said horses whilst sick 28s.

---

[152] The gift of 20s. by Master John de Petreburgh at Collingham 'for the benefit of the cloister' is recorded above under *Foreign receipts*, p.51.

[153] Sir Gerard de Suthill, knight, is described under *Allowances*, p.87, as holding Stainton Waddingham, co. Lincoln, from the abbey for the term of his life.

[154] He received a fee of 60s. in this account (see above, *Pensions and fees*, p.54).

[155] The general chapter of the Benedictine Order in England met every three years at Northampton under the statutes of Benedict XII. See D. Knowles, *The Religious Orders in England*, II, p.4, and W.A.Pantin (ed.), *Documents Illustrating the Activities of the General and Provincial Chapters of the English Black Monks, 1215–1540*, Camden Society 3rd Series, vols 45, 47, and 54, 1931–37.

[156] His purchase of the office and corrody of porter is recorded in this account under *Foreign recipts*, above p.52.

[157] For Haxay see above, p.61 n.118.

And for the expenses of Brother Richard de Secroft going to York for the synod after the festival of St Michael (29 September, 1399) 3s.4d.

And for the expenses of John Palfrayman going to Blyth on business of the lord abbot 10d.

And for the expenses of the aforesaid Brother Peter, Thomas de Egmanton,[158] John de Birne, and others with them going with 8 horses to the soke of Crowle, Redbourne, and Stallingborough on various occasions this year, together with the money given to various servants and workmen in various places 30s.

And for the expenses of John de Birne going to the soke of Crowle, Redbourne, and Stallingborough to collect the farms on various occasions this year, with the money given to servants and workmen in various places 33s.

And for 15 skins of parchment purchased for court rolls (and) accounts of the bursars and serjeants this year 3s.9d.

And for 24 skins of parchment purchased for the same things 4s.

And for the purchase of 6 quires of paper 2s.6d.

And for shoeing the horses of Brother Peter in the past and present year before the festival of St Valentine (14 February) 15s.

And for shoeing the horses of John de Birne during the aforesaid time 6s.

And for 2 andirons bought for the lord abbot's hall in addition to the old andirons 8s.

Total £18 3s.6d.

Purchase of grain, with transport of the same (*Emptio bladorum cum cariagio eius-dem*)

Likewise the same persons account for 10 quarters of wheat purchased from William Broun at Gowdall for the use of the granger, with transport of the same from the Carlton crossing[159] to the abbey 51s.8d.

And for 40 quarters of wheat purchased at *Stretton in the Clay*, with the transport of the same by water thence to Selby, and with the expenses of those engaged in purchasing the same £10 10s.

And for 34 quarters of wheat purchased at Stallingborough at (*prout dat'*) 4s.4d. a quarter £7 7s.4d.

And for 3 quarters of beans purchased for pottage in the kitchen 9s.

---

[158] Steward of Stallingborough and Rawcliffe (see above, *Pensions and fees*, p. 54).
[159] i.e. over the River Aire.

And for 3 quarters 4 bushels of green peas purchased at York for the same 19s.3d.

And for 1 quarter 4 bushels of oats purchased from John Sperwe for horse fodder 2s.1d.

And for 20 quarters of oats purchased at Wistow for the fodder of the horses of the lord abbot and visitors, with the transport of the same thence to the abbey 38s.4d.

And for 28 quarters of oats purchased by the serjeant of Monk Fryston for horse fodder within the abbey, with the transport of the same to the abbey 51s.4d.

And for 61 quarters of oats purchased at Rawcliffe, with the transport of the same to the abbey 106s.2d.

And for 30 quarters of oats purchased from Thomas Dilcok for fodder, with the transport of the same to Carlton 60s.

And for the service of John Adcok in transporting 40 quarters of wheat from Stallingborough to Selby by water for the use of the granger 6s.8d.

And for the service of the same person in transporting 120 quarters of wheat by water from Garthorpe to Selby on 3 occasions for the use of the granger 12s.

And for the service of 2 men of Thorne with their ship in transporting 60 quarters of barley and dredge by water from Eastoft to Selby on 2 occasions 9s.

And for the service of men with their 12 wagons in carrying 110 quarters of oats from Carlton to Selby 10s.

And for the payment to Robert Brid and his fellows on the lord's ship for collecting grain (*querentium bladum*) at *le Gullath* this year 4s.

Total £36 16s.10d.

Purchase of wine, with transport of the same
(*Emptio vini cum cariagio eiusdem*)

Likewise the same persons account for one and a half[160] gallons of wine purchased for the lord abbot by Brother Adam de Crosseby 18d.

And for 6 gallons of wine purchased by Brother Thomas de Wakefeld for the said lord 3s.

---

160 *dimidio* interlined.

And for 6 gallons of red wine purchased in the town for the same lord's consumption 4s.

And for 2 pipes of red wine purchased at Hull by John, the lord abbot's chamberlain, for the use of the same lord £7 13s.4d.

No entry here (*nichil hic*) for transport of the same (pipes) and of one tun of wine sent to the lord abbot by William Pund, but (it is included) in other bills of the said chamberlain.

And for the expenses of the aforesaid chamberlain going to York and to Hull for the purchase of 6 pipes of wine at the aforesaid places, with the transport of the same by water from the said places to Selby, (certified) by 2 bills 14s.5d.

And for 2 pipes of wine purchased from Alan de Hamerton for the lord abbot's use, with transport of these from York to Selby £6 16s.1d.

And for 4 pipes of wine purchased from William Palmer for the said lord's use £14 13s.4d.

And for the payment to William Pund, as part of 21 marks for 1 tun of red wine and 2 pipes of white wine purchased from the same person for the use of the said lord £6 13s.4d.

Total £36 19s.

Purchase of cloths (*Emptio pannorum*)   Likewise the same persons account for the payment to Robert Broune[161] for one gown purchased for him in the previous year 5s.

And for cloth purchased from William de Wath for one gown with a hood for John de Selby, chamberlain of the lord abbot, about the festival of St Lucy the Virgin (13 December, 1398) by order of the same lord 5s.

And for cloth purchased for one gown with a hood for William de Brayton, clerk of John de Birne, 5s.

And for cloth purchased for one gown with a hood for William de Duffeld, page in the lord abbot's kitchen, by order of the said lord 2s.4d.

And for cloth purchased for the livery (*pro vestura*) of William de Mundevill by order of the lord abbot 6s.5d.

And for cloth purchased for the livery of Thomas, groom in the tailor's shop, because he did not have cloth of the lord abbot's livery 4s.6d.

---

[161] He received a fee of 26s.8d. in this account (see above, *Pensions and fees*, p. 56).

And for 2 ells of cloth of ray purchased for the livery of Richard Smyth, workman in the pond, 2s.6d.

And for cloth purchased from Adam Banes for 3 summer gowns for Richard de Drax, Robert Broun, and William de Wessyngton[162] 9s.3d.

And for various cloths purchased from William de Wath for the livery of the esquires and others of the household of the monastery this year, as the indenture shows £24 18s.7d.

And for 10 lambs' skins purchased for the esquires' livery 15s.

Total £27 13s.7d.

Restoration of the monastery, with the costs of the quarry and renovation of the cloister (*Resumptio monasterii cum custibus quarere et Renovationis claustri*)	Likewise the same persons account for various things purchased by Brother Thomas de Wakefeld for furnishing the better parlour of the lord abbot, (certified) by bill 10s.

And for the services of John Broune senior clearing the quarry at Monk Fryston and quarrying stones in the same for the renovation of the cloister for 57 days between the festival of St Barnabas the Apostle (11 June, 1398) in the preceding year and the festival of St Martin (11 November) A.D. 1399, at a wage of 5d. a day without food[163] 23s.9d.

And for the services of the men similarly employed (*ad idem*) between the aforesaid festivals, (calculated) as if (there were) 130 and a half for one day each receiving 4d. a day without food 43s.6d.

And for gifts to the same persons for drink at times within the said period 2s.6d.

And for the services of the aforesaid John Broune with his cart getting the quarried stones out of the quarry for 8 days, at a wage of 10d. a day 6s.8d.

And for carrying 2 cart-loads of the aforesaid stones from the quarry to the abbey in winter time 2s.

And for carrying 108 cart-loads of the aforesaid stones from the same quarry to the abbey in summer time, at a cost of 10d. for each £4 10s.

---

[162] All received fees in this account. See above, *Pensions and fees*, p. 56.

[163] Daily wages to workmen vary in amount in the account depending on whether they received food from the abbey as part of their terms of employment.

And for payment to the aforesaid John Broune for various iron tools purchased and repaired for use at the quarry 2s.3d.

And for payment to William de Suthwell, master mason, as his annual fee by agreement 40s.

And for the services of the same person working on the building of the new cloister for 2 weeks 6s.8d.

And for the services of John del Wod, mason, working both in the quarry and elsewhere on the aforesaid building for 46 weeks (and) 4 days in the present year, at 3s. a week without food £7.

And for the service of John de Hilton, mason, working on the same building for[164] 50 weeks (and) 4 days, at the above wage £7 12s.

And for the services of Robert de Drax, mason, working on the said building for 27 weeks (and) 4 days, at the above wage £4 3s.

And for the services of John Smyth fashioning and sharpening various tools of the masons in the past and present year 11s.

And for the services of the men helping the masons and others to dismantle the old cloisters, and dig and prepare the soil in front of the masons, and to fix stakes in that place (*ad pilas inibi figendas*), and helping the masons to erect the new cloister building, (calculated) as if (there were) 228 for 1 day each receiving 4d. without food 76s.

And for the services of one man felling alder trees in order to make stakes from them for the aforesaid work 6d.

And for 6 cart-loads of lime purchased for the aforesaid work at a price of 2s.8d. for each 16s.

And for sand purchased for the same work 4s.

And for wax and resin purchased for repairing the stones (*pro lapidibus consolidandis*) 10d.

And for 780 pounds, 3 stones, of Spanish iron purchased for fashioning bars and other ironwork from it 30s.9d.

And for fashioning the said iron, at an agreed price of 3s. for each hundredweight 20s.6d.[165]

And for 2 barrels purchased for making tubs from them for the masons 11d.

And for 2 bowls purchased for the aforesaid work 6d.

And for 360 boards of wainscot (*Waynshot*) purchased at York for the roof of the said cloister 102s.9d.

---

[164] *per* interlined.
[165] It appears that a hundredweight of 120 pounds was used here. For variations in the weight of the hundredweight, see R. E. Zupko, *Dictionary of English Weights and Measures*.

And for carrying the said boards from the water into the abbey 8d.

And for sawing 26 rods of timber and boards for the aforesaid work, at a price of 40d. for each rod £4 6s.8d.

And for the services of John Rothing, master carpenter, working on the roof of the said cloister for 12 weeks at 4s. a week without food 48s.

And for the services of John Brennand, carpenter, carving the bosses for the joints of the ceiling (*sculpantis nodos pro iuncturis celature*) of the aforesaid building for 11 weeks at 40d. a week 36s.8d.[166]

And for the services of 6 carpenters working on the said building for 12 weeks, each receiving 3s. a week without food £10 16s.

And for the services of one carpenter working on the said [167] building for 8 weeks (and) 4½ days at the above wage 26s.3d.

And for victuals purchased for the aforesaid carpenters and others helping them whilst they were working in the woodland at the beginning of their work, by courtesy[168] 8s.7d.

And for payments to the same persons for gloves 5s.

And for 5640 spike-nails (*spikyng*) purchased for the aforesaid work 11s.5d.

And for 240 large spike-nails, 240 brad-nails (*broddis*), purchased for the same work 13d.

And for iron bands, with hooks, hasps, and bars, purchased for the south door of the cloister 12d.

And for the services of John Hare, plumber, taking down the lead roof of the old cloister and casting lead sheets and roofing the new cloister with them for 9 weeks at 40d. a week without food 30s.

And for 2400 lead-nails (*leednayl*) purchased for the aforesaid work 5s.

And for various tools and nails purchased for preparing one bowl with them (*pro una patella inde paranda*) for casting the lead sheets 12d.

And for ropes purchased for hauling the sheets on to the roof of the said cloister 2s.6d.

And for the services of one glazier repairing the defects of one window on the north side of the choir, and mending the great

---

[166] *d.* interlined.

[167] The words 'more on the dorse' (*Plus in tergo*) follow on the next line, and the account continues on the other side of the parchment.

[168] *ex curialitate*, i.e. not part of the contract between workmen and abbey.

window in the chamber of the lord abbot, and restoring a coat of arms of Richard, the lord archbishop of York, in the chapel of the lord abbot 3s.4d.

And for the services of William de Bardenay, glazier, and his servant mending defects in the windows in the nave of the church and in the great window in the dormitory, for 4 days with food 2s.8d.

And for the services of the same person replacing (*facientis de novo*) one glazed window measuring (*continentem*) 16 feet at the end of the lord abbot's hall 13s.4d.

And for the services of the smith fashioning iron bars from 3 stones of his own iron 2s.6d.

And for the services of the same person, and for the services of the same glazier and his servant, repairing defects in the great window in the refectory, and defects in the windows in the sacrist's chamber, for 5 days with food 3s.4d.

And for glass, lead, and tin purchased for soldering the aforesaid windows by the said glazier himself (*per manus dicti vitriarii*) 3s.2d.

And for one lock with a key purchased for the door of the lead-house to keep safe the lead 8d.

Total £68 14s.11d.

Repair of buildings inside and outside the abbey (*Emendatio domorum infra Abbatiam et extra*)

Likewise the same persons account for the services of 2 carpenters dismantling 4 rods of old roofing of boards in one portion of the refectory on the south side, and splitting long laths for roofing the same with stones, and repairing defects in the timber work of the same for 1 week without food 5s.

And for 240 large spike-nails, 1800 brad-nails purchased for the same work 3s.

And for expenses incurred in respect to roofing the same portion with stones from Pudsey (*de Pudsay*), namely for purchasing the stones with carting of them thence to the abbey, and with the services of the slaters fitting the same together into a roof (*aptantium et tegentium eosdem*) without food £4.

And for the services of John Hare, plumber, roofing 8 corners of the higher lantern (*coni superioris*) of the great kitchen with lead from the old roof of the cloister for 18 days, at a wage of 8d. a day without food 12s.

And for the payment to William Muto, assisting him in the same work 12d.

And for the services of the smith repairing the iron spindle and weathercock placed on top of the said kitchen 6d.

And for nails purchased for the aforesaid work 12d.

Likewise for the services of Roger preparing the ground in front of the masons repairing the walls of the oriel (*del Oriell*) and serving them whilst they were making the said walls in the past and present year for 40 days, with food 6s.8d.

And for 6 cart-loads of lime purchased for the aforesaid work and for other buildings inside the abbey 16s.

And for sand purchased for the same 16s.

And for the payment to Adam Smyth for locks, keys, and other items of iron made by him for various doors within the hall and chamber of the lord abbot and at Stainer,[169] (certified) by bill 2s.10d.

And for expenses incurred in respect to repair of the house of the master of the forge and the plumbery, and of the stable of the lord prior, the chamber of John de Birne, and the stable of the extern cellarer, all of which were threatened with ruin, namely for the wages of the carpenters, sawyers, (and) wall-plasterers, for tiles purchased both for roof and for walls, (and) for iron bands and nails, in addition to the stones from the quarry, the lime and the sand £6.

Likewise for repairing various defects of the houses in Skeldergate in York this year, (certified) by Hugh de Cotum 4s.

And for repairing various defects in two houses of tenants in Snaith, paid by (*per manus*) John de Birne 15s.9d.

And for timber purchased for repairing one house there formerly (in the possession) of John de Thornhill 6s.

And for the services of the carpenter repairing the same (house) for a fixed price (*ad tascam*) 6s.

Total £14 15s.9d.

Costs of ditches and enclosure (*Custus Fossatorum et Inclusionis*)	Likewise the same persons account for making 80 rods of ditch around Warde Shawe (*Wardshagh*),[170] with as many rods of hedge made on the same, at a price of 2d. a rod 13s.4d.

---

[169] The abbot of Selby acquired Stainer Grange in the mid-thirteenth century, and it probably served as a place to which the monks could go for short periods of relaxation. It was about 1 kilometre from the abbey. See R. B. Dobson, *Selby Abbey and Town*, p. 24.

[170] A survey of 1543 states that the wood was 7 miles (11 km) from Pontefract and contained 4 acres (see *The Coucher Book of Selby*, II, p. 371).

And for the services of 4 men for 1 day repairing the fences of the meadows at Roscarrs (*Roukerres*), paid by R(obert) de Gretham[171] 16d.

And for the services of 10 men for 1 day repairing defects in the portions of the new sewer within the soke of Crowle that concern the monastery 3s.4d.

And for the services of one man cleaning out reeds and grass in the portions of the Mere Dyke (*le Mardyk*)[172] that concern the monastery for 12 days, without food 4s.

Total 22s.

Costs of hay and straw (*Custus feni et litere*) Likewise the same persons account for mowing of the meadows at Roscarrs (*Roukerres*) this year, for an agreed salary (*in conventione*) 15s.10d.

And they have paid to Brother Richard de Secroft for the wages of the workmen making and stacking hay therefrom 15s.

And for victuals purchased for those carrying the said hay, paid by (*per manus*) Simon the stableman 2s.

And for mowing 5½ acres of meadow in *Haysted*[173] for a fixed price (*ad tascam*) 4s.2d.

And for making hay therefrom and stacking it, paid by Robert de Croftun[174] and John de Raghton 9s.10d. So much on account of the rainy weather.

And for carrying 9 cart-loads of the said hay from that place to the abbey, at a cost of 5d. for each 3s.9d.

And for 10 acres of meadow grass purchased in Wistow meadows, with the tithe of the same 40s.

And for mowing the said grass and spreading it for a fixed price 8s.9d. All of which was flooded and carried off by suddenly rising flood-waters.

They account for no tithe hay at Carlton this year, because it was flooded and destroyed by the flood-waters as above.

---

[171] He was the lessee of the abbey at Roscarrs, which was part of the manor of Stainer (see HUL, DDLO 21/15 and 16).

[172] Mr G.S. Haslop informs me that it seems to have been an important sewer running from the Hatfield area through Eastoft and Crowle to the River Trent, co. Lincoln. The point of entry to the Trent was between Amcotts and Waterton (see *CCR*, 1385–89, p.73).

[173] Five acres of meadow in Wistow Ings, customarily reserved for the mill horses of the abbey, according to a Valor of 1540 (see *The Coucher Book of Selby*, II, pp.350 and 356). Wistow is about 5 kilometres north-west of Selby.

[174] Croftun was a groom in the abbot's stable (see above, *Salaries of staff*, p.57).

And for 25 cart-loads of hay purchased at Hemingbrough from *dominus* John de Ellerton, in gross £4 3s.4d.

And for 60 thraves of straw purchased for the horses' bedding 5s.

Total £9 7s.8d.

Costs of fuel in addition to Rawcliffe[175] (*Custus Focalis preter Rouclif*)

Likewise the same persons account for 12 chaldrons of sea-coal purchased for fuel in various buildings inside the abbey, at a price of 4s.4d. a chaldron 52s.

And for 10¼ chaldrons of this kind of coal purchased for the same, at a price of 4s. for each (chaldron) 41s.

And for the salaries of 3 men on the bigger ship with Robert Brid getting one ship-load of furlong-turves (*furlangorum*)[176] at Rawcliffe for the lord abbot's fuel about the feast of Sts. Peter and Paul (29 June, 1399), with 6d. given to the said Robert 6s.

And[177] for the services of the men and women carrying the said turves from the ship into *le Oldhall* 5s.

And for food purchased for consumption by these same persons by John Hasand[178] 2s.8d.

And for the salaries and provisions (*companagio*) of the men taking one half boat-load of furlong-turves (*furlangorum*) from Rawcliffe to Selby for the lord abbot's chamber 3s.

And for the services of the men and women carrying the said turves from the ship to *le Oldhall*, paid by (*per manus*) John de Hamlton[179] 20d.

And for victuals purchased for consumption by these same persons, paid by John Hasand 2s.

And for 240 pieces of split wood (*astelwod*) purchased for the fuel of visitors of standing (*proborum supervenientium*) in the guest house 3s.

---

[175] The abbots of Selby took recreation at their manor house of Rawcliffe in the late 14th century. See G.S. Haslop, 'The Abbot of Selby's Financial Statement for the year ending Michaelmas 1338', p. 161.

[176] The subsequent entries make the nature of the cargo clear, turves for fuel. But the proper translation of the word is doubtful.

[177] *Et* interlined.

[178] The abbot's cook (see above, *Salaries of staff*, p. 57).

[179] Hamlton was the abbot's usher (see above, *Salaries of staff*, p. 57).

And for the payments to Alice Spycer, Deonise Loef, Robert Wright, William Porter,[180] and the two laundresses of the lord abbot and the convent, for 20,400 mixed turves owed to them this year 11s.10d.

And for 6,000 turves of this kind for the fuel of Robert Potman[181] they do not account here, because he had the turves from the lord's fuel.

Total £6 8s.2d.

| Foreign expenses (*Forinsece expense*) | Likewise the same persons account for 4 writs sued out at London by John de Birne directed to the sheriffs of York, Lincoln, Leicester, and Northampton, that they should not trouble (*de non molestando*) the lord abbot and his tenants in the aforesaid counties 6s.8d. |

And for the expenses of William de Ludyngton and John de Birne[182] at Lincoln for the assizes on account of a certain plea initiated between the township of Amcotts and the township of Keadby concerning common of pasture about the festival of St Nicholas (6 December, 1398) 4s.6d.

And for gifts to various jurors impanelled on the jury 20s.

And for the expenses of Richard de Drax[183] at York on the lord abbot's business on 2 occasions 19d.

And for gifts to the clerks of the sheriff of York for writing copies of various statutes, letters of the lord king, and presentments against the lord abbot of various matters in the tourns of Sir John de Depeden, sheriff of York[184] 14d.

And for the payment to Brother William Pygot[185] for expenses incurred at his inception to the degree of bachelor of canon law, by command of the lord abbot £6 13s.4d.

---

[180] The grant of a corrody to Wright, dated 1397, is recorded in the abbey register (British Library, Cotton Vit. E.XVI, fos 143v–144). Spicer and Loef appear above (pp. 53–54) in receipt of a clothing allowance. William Porter may be the William del West of Bolton granted a corrody as porter's groom (*Garcionis janitoris*) in the 1390s (British Library, Cotton Vit. E.XVI, fos 144–144v), since Peter Talbot who purchased the porter's corrody in 1399 (see above, *Foreign Receipts*, p. 52) is thereafter sometimes called Peter Porter in the abbey records.
[181] Potman was clearly receiving a corrody from the abbey. See above, *Pensions and fees*, p. 53.
[182] Ludyington was recorded as receiving a fee of 20s. in the *Pensions and fees* section of the account, whilst Birne received one of 66s.8d. See above, pp. 55–56.
[183] On Drax see above, p. 51 n. 45.
[184] Depeden was sheriff of Yorkshire 18 October 1392–7 November 1393, and again 30 September 1399–3 November 1399 when he was succeeded by Sir John Constable (PRO, *Lists and Indexes*, 9, 1898, p. 162).
[185] For Pygot see above, p. 53 n. 61. The rules for the degree of bachelor in canon law

And for 6 pheasants purchased and sent to Richard, lord archbishop of York,[186] with 6 swans and 12 rabbits, on behalf of the lord abbot 12s.6d.

And for the services of the sailors transporting all the aforesaid items to Cawood[187] by water 2s.

And for payment to Robert Broune for his expenses and those of John Bernard and John Bewe going to London with the lord archbishop of York for parliament[188] 20s.

And to Master John de Banbiry, proctor of the monastery in county Lincoln, and other clerks of the bishop of Lincoln and archdeacon of Stow, appearing at convocations and sessions on behalf of the lord abbot 20s.

And for 30 pairs of ash trees purchased and given to Thomas Broket[189] by the lord abbot, with transport of the same del pilehag to Cawood 10s.6d.

And for 30 pairs of ash trees purchased at Habholme[190] and given to the prior of St Andrew's York to renovate one house as a dwelling for one canon recluse, by command of the lord abbot 8s.9d.

And for one grey ambling horse purchased and given to Robert de Waterton[191] by the lord abbot £4 10s.

Total £16 11s.

Payments (*Solutiones*)	Likewise the same persons account for payment to the abbot of Sulby, collector of one tenth granted to the lord king, for the temporalities of the monastery in county Northampton 71s.

---

stipulated 5 years study; and as with the other higher degrees, the ceremony of admission or inception was an expensive one (see C. E. Mallet, *A History of the University of Oxford*, I, pp. 189, 194–198; and W. A. Pantin, *General and Provincial Chapters*, II, pp. 56–57).

[186] Third son of Henry, lord Scrope of Masham, consecrated as Archbishop of York in 1398. There is no strong evidence that Archbishop Scrope was particularly involved in forwarding the revolution of 1399, but he certainly assisted in the formalities of establishing Henry IV's title. In 1405, however, he rebelled against Henry IV and was executed. For details of his career, see P. McNiven, 'The Betrayal of Archbishop Scrope', *Bulletin of the John Rylands Library Manchester*, 54, 1971–72, pp. 173–213.

[187] Where the archbishop of York had a residence, near York.

[188] See above p. 64 n. 131. Broune received a fee of 26s.8d. in this account (*Pensions and fees*, p. 56), and was described as the abbot's butler during the next abbacy (HUL, DDLO 20/66). Bewe was a lesser servant of the abbot (*Salaries of staff*, p. 57).

[189] One of the abbot's attorneys in a plea in the court of Exchequer c.1401 (British Library, Cotton Vit. E.XVI, f.116v).

[190] Near Hambleton, co. Yorkshire.

[191] See above, p. 59 n. 101.

And for 2 acquittances 4d.

And for the expenses of one man paying the said money 8d.

And to the same abbot for this sort of tenth for the temporalities of the monastery in county Leicester 76s.4d.

And for 2 acquittances 4d.

And for the expenses of one man paying the said money 16d.

And to the abbot of Swineshead, collector of this sort of tenth, for the spiritualities and temporalities of the monastery in the arch-deaconries of Lincoln and Stow, in respect of the first payment £11 12s.7d.

And for an acquittance 2d.

And for the expenses of John de Birne paying the said money at Lincoln 3s.4d.

And to the prior of Monk Bretton, collector of this sort of tenth, for a quarter of one tenth[192] for the spiritualities and temporalities of the monastery in the diocese of York £12 16s.2¼d.

And for an acquittance 2d.

And to Henry, lord bishop of Lincoln,[193] for the half of one tenth granted to him in respect of the spiritualities and temporalities of the monastery in the archdeaconries of Lincoln and Stow £11 12s.7d.

And for an acquittance 2d.

And for the expenses of Brother Peter going from Crowle to Stow Park to pay the same money 3s.8d.

And to Sir Richard de Redemane, knight, master of the horse of the lord King Richard, bringing to the lord abbot a writ under the privy seal of the said lord king for sending horses to the said lord king, to buy horses[194] £6 13s.4d. in addition to one colt given to him by the lord abbot.

---

[192] The abbey of Selby was receiving relief from taxation at this time for lands adversely affected by flooding, specifically by the Humber (see Borthwick Institute of Historical Research, Archbishop's Register 16, Richard le Scrope, f.213; and *CFR*, 1399–1405, pp. 160–161).

[193] Henry Beaufort, son of John of Gaunt, duke of Lancaster, by Katherine Swynford, was consecrated bishop of Lincoln on 14 July 1398. See F. M. Powicke and E. B. Fryde, *Handbook of British Chronology*, p. 236.

[194] Presumably for Richard II's second Irish expedition in 1399. Sir Richard de Redemane of Harewood (co. Yorkshire) and Levens Castle (co. Westmoreland) was one of the wealthiest Yorkshire parliamentary representatives, and the recipient of valuable grants from Richard II (see C. Ross, *The Yorkshire Baronage*, p. 413).

And for[195] one bridle (and) one saddle-cloth (*houce*) purchased for the said colt 3s.4d.

And for gifts to the servants of the same Sir Richard 10s.

Total £51 5s.6¼d.

Payment of debts (*Acquietantia debitorum*)   Likewise the same persons account for payment to Master Thomas de Dalby, archdeacon of Richmond,[196] for money borrowed from the same person under bond in the preceding year £40.

And to John Tuch[197] for money borrowed from the same person in the preceding year under bond £26 13s.4d.

And to Master Ralph de Selby in part (payment) of two hundred marks borrowed from the same person in preceding years, by means (*per manus*) of Robert Potman his father[198] £13 6s.8d.

And to William Punde of Hull in payment of sixteen pounds for wine purchased from the same person in the preceding year £15 3s.4d.

And to William de Helmeslay[199] of York for money owed to him by Brother Thomas de Warnefeld, by order of the lord abbot 40s.

And to the executors of Robert Wrench for money owed to him by the said Brother Thomas 71s.

And to *dominus* John Porter, chaplain, for money owed to him by the same Brother Thomas, by order of the lord abbot 30s.

And to Adam Olyf[200] for money owed to him by the said Brother Thomas 13s.4d.

Total £102 17s.8d.

Payments of cash (*Liberatio denariorum*)   Likewise the same persons account for paying over to Brother Robert de Selby, kitchener, at intervals (*per vices*) this year £108 10s.6d.[201]

---

[195] *in* interlined.

[196] He was archdeacon of Richmond from 1388 to his death in May 1400. See *John le Neve: Fasti*, VI, p. 26.

[197] For the purchase of a pension by Tuch, see above p. 51.

[198] See above pp. 53 n. 62 and 68 n. 147.

[199] Citizen and merchant of York. See *York Memorandum Book*, II, Surtees Society 125, 1915, p. 37.

[200] Farmer of the demesnes and tithes of Rawcliffe. See below, p. 85.

[201] The Selby kitchener's income of under £100 was insufficient for the expenses of the office, and he was subsidised this year by cash payments from the bursars' revenues. See G. S. Haslop, 'A Selby Kitchener's Roll of the Early Fifteenth Century', *YAJ*, 48, 1976, pp. 119–133.

And to Adam Olyf, farmer of the demesnes and tithe of Rawcliffe, for various reprises (*reprisas*) there and for storage (*ad hospitationem*) of the tithe of Hook £16 9s.6d.

Total £125.

Allowances (*Allocationes*) Stanford on Avon	Likewise the same persons ask that they be allowed £6 10s.8d. from the revenues of Stanford on Avon this year, namely 2s. from the rent of William Purfray in Misterton [202] because he will not pay and it is not known where he may be duly distrained for the same;

12d. from the close of the chapel in le Doune,[203] in the hands of the farmer of the manor;

1d. from the toft formerly (in the possession) of Stephen Waleys, because Thomas Doyl who occupies it unjustly refuses to pay;

12d. from the rent of Roger Gilbert yearly, because he used to pay five shillings yearly, (but) now he shows a deed under the common seal of the monastery that he is bound to pay only four shillings;

2s. pardoned to John Coke, pauper;

12d. pardoned to John Sharp, tenant of the common oven there this year;

12d. from 2 acres of the new foreland (*forland*) which John de Norton and William Gilleson held, in the lord's hand for want of tenants;

3s. for the decrease in rent (*in decasu redditus*) of one virgate of land formerly Roger Gibbe's of *la Doune*, which Roger de Gunthorp, tailor (*Tailliour*), now holds for twelve shillings a year where formerly he paid fifteen shillings;

20s. lost by negligence among the reeves there and (the negligence) of John de Cadnay in checking the totals (*in talliando summas*) of rent paid whilst John de Birne was sick;

13s.4d. debited (to them) in error (*nimis oneratis*) from 2 years past (because) paid to the pittancer;

---

[202] A lost village in Leicestershire. See M. Beresford, *The Lost Villages of England*, London, 1954, p. 317.

[203] Another lost village, this time in Northants. See J. E. B. Gorer, A. Mawer, and F. M. Stenton, *The Place-Names of Northamptonshire*, English Place-Name Society Publications 10, CUP, 1933, p. 74.

41s.8d. for various expenses incurred by John del Grene, farmer of the manor there, about the repair of tenants' houses in *Stormworth*[204] and about the cultivation of the former land of Geoffrey Smyth in the lord's hand for lack of tenants;

7s.6d. from arrears of Peter Sandre, former reeve of Stanford on Avon in A.D. (13)94, which cannot be collected because of the plea pending between John de Catesby[205] and Robert de Waner concerning certain tenements from which the aforesaid (sum) is owed;

9s. from arrears of Roger Waryn, reeve there in A.D. (13)95, the reason as above;

15s. from arrears of William Gilleson, reeve there in A.D. (13)96, which cannot be collected both for the aforesaid reason and on account of the poverty of the said reeve;

4s.9d. from arrears of Richard Norrays, reeve of *Stormworth* A.D. (13)96, which cannot be collected on account of his poverty;

8s.4d. from arrears of John Reve junior, reeve *del Doune* in the aforesaid year, which cannot be collected for the aforesaid reason.

Queniborough	And £6 17s.8d. from the revenues of Queniborough this year, namely 10d. from the rent of John Folvill of Rearsby[206] yearly, which cannot be collected;

2½d. from the rent of the abbot of Leicester, because he refuses to pay;

2s. from head-silver (*del hedesilver*) there, which cannot be collected;

6s.8d. given to John Folvill for his fee yearly, granted to him for the term of his life so that he pay his rent more willingly;

18s. from 1 toft, 1 virgate of land which John Warde held, in the lord's hand this year for lack of tenant;

10s. from 1 toft, 1 bovate of land which John Carter held, in the lord's hand this year for lack of tenant;

8s. for the decrease in rent of one toft and 1 virgate of land which John Arketill held, because it used to pay eighteen shillings yearly, (but) now it pays only ten shillings;

[204] Now a lost village, co. Leicestershire. See M. Beresford, *The Lost Villages of England*, p. 207.
[205] Steward of Stanford-on-Avon. See above, p. 54.
[206] A Leicestershire landowner, coroner of the county in 1396. See *CPR*, 1391–96, p. 716 and *Feudal Aids*, III, p. 119.

6s. for the decrease in rent yearly of one toft and one virgate of land which John Slek held, because it used to pay eighteen shillings, (but) now it pays only twelve shillings;

8s.6d. from the rent of Thomas Bernard this year, which cannot be collected on account of his poverty;

20d. from 1 toft which William Slek held, in the lord's hand for the term of Candlemas (2 February);

12d. from the rent of Ralph de Segrave this year, which cannot be collected on account of his poverty;

12s. given to William Tailliour to buy timber for renovating his barn (*grangia*);

56s.1½d. from arrears of Richard Bikyn, reeve there, in respect of various years in which he was in the said office, which for the most part cannot be collected and the rest (was) pardoned him at the festival of St Martin (11 November) A.D. (13)96 because of his work;

6s.8d. from the yearly farm of Roger Payn, farmer there, for 8½ acres of meadow called *Milneholm* which the heir of Sir Ralph Basset of Drayton,[207] lord of Ratcliffe on the Wreake, occupies unjustly.

Stainton Waddingham	And 9s. from Stainton Waddingham yearly, in the hands of Sir Gerard de Suthill knight[208] for the term of his life.
Redbourne	And 3s.4d. from Redbourne yearly, because the serjeant there is debited with it (*inde oneratur*) in his account.[209]
Stallingborough	And 24s.8d. from Stallingborough this year, namely 2s. from the rent of Thomas de Missenden of Healing,[210] because he refuses to pay;

---

[207] Ralph, lord Basset of Drayton, died without heirs of his body on 10 May 1390. The heirship of his estates was somewhat doubtful, with one inquisition naming Thomas earl of Stafford alone, and another the said earl and Alice wife of William Chaworth. Ralph himself devised all his estates to his nephew, Hugh Shirley; and the Shirley family certainly inherited considerable estates in counties Nottingham, Leicester, and Warwick. See *The Complete Peerage*, II, pp. 3–4.

[208] This considerable Lincolnshire family held, among other possessions, half a knight's fee in Redbourne, whose church was appropriated to Selby Abbey (see *Feudal Aids*, III, p. 247).

[209] That is, the serjeant of Redbourne accounted to the abbey separately for this rent.

[210] Healing is near Stallingborough, co. Lincoln. The will of Thomas Mussenden esquire, dated 20 July 1402, is printed in N. H. Nicolas, *Testamenta Vetusta*, London, 1826, p. 161, where he is described as the second son of Sir Thomas Mussenden of co. Buckingham and husband of Johanna, daughter of Sir John Hawley.

10½d. from the rent of William del Hagh for the aforesaid reason;

3d. from the rent of Sir William de Belesby knight[211] for the aforesaid reason;

1½d. from the rent of the heir of Sir William de Haulay[212] for the aforesaid reason;

5s.9d. from the fishermen's stalls near the Humber there carried out to sea (*eiectis ad mare*);

15s.8d. allowed to the miller there for the time which the said mill stood empty.[213]

Crowle   And 21s. from Crowle this year, namely 8s. allowed to the miller for renovating one iron mill-spindle (*fusilli ferrei*) and one mill-rind (*Ryne*)[214] for the said mill;

8s. allowed to the reeves from the rents of Ealand in the past and present years, which cannot be collected because of the poverty of the tenants;

5s. pardoned to John de Brikhill,[215] Beatrice Kemme, and others, which cannot be collected.

Elvesthwait   And 10s.6d. from *Elvesthwayt* this year, namely 7s.2d. from arrears of Robert Johnson, reeve there this year, who is dead and has nothing from which they can be collected;

3s.4d. from the rent of Richard atte Brigg, deceased, for the aforesaid reason.

Eastoft   And 9s.11½d. from the revenues of Eastoft this year, namely 2s.7½d. from arrears of Robert Watson, late reeve there, which cannot be collected because of his poverty;

16d. for the decrease in rent yearly of the holding which Ralph Bust (? held);[216]

---

[211] He held property in Stickford and Horsington, co. Lincoln, in 1401–02 (see *Feudal Aids*, VI, p. 610).
[212] Lincolnshire Hawleys mentioned by E. G. Kimball (*Some Sessions of the Peace in Lincolnshire 1381–1396*, The Lincoln Record Society 49, 1955, p. xxiv) include Sir Robert Haule (d. by 1390) of Riby and Stallingborough, and Sir William Haule (d. 1387) of Utterby, co. Lincoln, a relative of Sir Robert.
[213] *stetit vac'* interlined.
[214] The rind was 'an iron fitting serving to support an upper millstone on the spindle.' (*OED*)
[215] Forester of Crowle (see above, *Gifts*, p. 58).
[216] No verb in the manuscript.

6s. from the farm of one intake (*Intak*) near the Mere Dyke (*le Muredyk*) in respect of the 3 preceding years, which cannot be collected.

Amcotts	And 24s. from the rents of Amcotts this year, namely 2s. from the rent of Richard de Amcotes yearly, because he refuses to pay;

22s. from the fishery of *Crasegarth*, in the lord's hand for lack of a tenant.

Garthorpe	And 13s.8½d. from the rents of Garthorpe this year, namely 6d. from the marshland which John Nom held, in the lord's hand;

3s.6d. allowed to the miller for various reprises made in respect of the mill there;

9s.8½d. from arrears of Robert de Messingham, late reeve there, which cannot be collected.

Reedness	And 16d. from one acre of land in Reedness, because the proctor (*procurator*) there accounts for it.

Hook	And 6s.8d. from tithe of the mill and fishery of Hook yearly; the reason appears in the preceding account.

Rawcliffe	And 4s.0¾d. from Rawcliffe this year, namely 14¼d. which cannot be collected;

18d. pardoned to John Cok on account of his poverty;

4½d. pardoned to Richard Bagier, for the aforesaid reason;

12d. pardoned to William Urry, because of the burning of his buildings.

Snaith	And 7s.6d.[217] from Snaith etc. yearly, namely 3s.2d. from the old rent of the holding lately acquired by Brother John de Balne;

12d. from the holding of John Daunay[218] in Cowick, because he refuses to pay;

16d. for depreciation of the holdings in Cowick which Henry de Horden holds;

[217] The sums below in fact add up to 8s.0d.
[218] See above p. 60 n. 108.

6d. from the holdings which John Garnet held;

19d. from the holdings of Sir Thomas de Meteham[219], because he refuses to pay;

5d. from the holdings of William atte Freres and John Edmund, because they lie empty.

Hillam	And 11s.1½d. from Hillam this year, namely 6s.8d. given to John de Marrays on account of his diligence towards the monastery and the tenants there;

4s.5½d. given to the former wife of Robert Tombarum, a poor old woman.

Monk Fryston	And £10 9s.1d. from Monk Fryston this year, namely 10s. from the holding which William Base held, in the lord's hand for Pentecost term;[220]

5s. this year from the holding which John Benneson held;

10d. pardoned to William atte Kirk because of his poverty;

£9 13s.3d. for expenses incurred about the repair and renovation of various houses in the aforesaid township which William Base, William de Snaythe, John Benneson, and John de Goldesburgh held, all of which were almost ruined; as appears by the schedule of costs of the same.

Thorpe Willoughby	And 12d. pardoned to John Hudson of Thorpe Willoughby, a poor and blind man.

Brayton	And 9½d.[221] from Brayton which cannot be collected from Thomas de Berlay and others this year.

Acaster Selby	And 42s.8d. from Acaster Selby this year, namely 18d. from the fishery in *le Flete*, in the lord's hand;

20s.8d. from the holdings[222] which John de Glasedale, a thief (who was) hanged, held,[223] in the lord's hand;

3s.2d. for decrease in rent of the cottages which are called *Romayntoft*, *Helwistoft*, and *Raghtontoft*;

---

[219] Of Metham in Howdenshire, co. York. The tenement in question was in Pollington, where the family held a moiety of the manor (see *Inquisitions post mortem*, ed. W. P. Baildon and J. W. Clay, pp. 121–123).

[220] Whit Sunday was on 18 May in 1399.

[221] *d'* interlined.

[222] *de ten'* interlined.

[223] *tenuit* interlined.

5s. given to Nicholas Jakson for repair of his buildings;

9s.4d. pardoned to William de Tankirlay of York from the farm of the pasture called *les leeghes*, because of his great loss;

12d. for the cleaning out of 15 rods of ditch around the site of the manor-house there;

2s. given to John Fenton, reeve there, for his work.

Stillingfleet And 7s. from the revenues of Stillingfleet this year, namely 3s. in respect of the amercement imposed on the lord abbot in the court of the heir of lord de Gray[224] there;

2s. in respect of the fine of the lord abbot for obtaining a postponement of performing his fealty to the same heir;

2s. given to the forester of the said heir and to Richard de Gaby, a tenant there.

Breighton And 6s. from the rents of Breighton this year, namely 5s. from the rent of John de Ask for the former holding of Richard de Lunde, because he refuses to pay;

12d. for decrease of rent of the holding which Thomas Alkes holds.

And 40s. to these same accountants for their work.

Total £36 1s.8¾d.

Total of all expenses, payments, and allowances £779 17s.5d. And thus the accountants are owed 109s.9d., in addition to reprises made in respect of the manors of Crowle, Redbourne, and Monk Fryston, in the four years past and present by Brother Peter de R(ouclif), extern cellarer, which are accounted for in the accounts of the serjeants and not in the accounts of the bursars for the aforesaid time.

---

[224] See above p. 47 n. 32.

II

THE COMMUNITY AND ITS NEEDS

(a) The offices of Pittancer and Chamberlain

Until the early decades of the fifteenth century these were separate offices with their own officials, providing in origin quite different services for the community. The pittancer's task was to pay the abbot, prior, monks, and novices, the sum of money that was allowed to them annually in cash for their personal expenditure, the 'pittance'.[1] The responsibility of the chamberlain was the clothing of the monks.[2] No separate chamberlain's account has survived to provide the necessary evidence, but it is assumed that at Selby as elsewhere this official had originally fulfilled his responsibilities by providing cloth and finished garments for the community. At some stage, however, an annual money payment was substituted for goods,[3] and the two offices of pittancer and chamberlain were united as the responsibility of a single official paying to each member of the house one money payment for both pittance and clothing. In 1415–16 this union had not yet taken place; by 1431–32 the change had happened, and was never it seems reversed during the rest of the abbey's history.[4] Even the scale of payments[5] remained the same, at least until 1516–17, the date of the last

[1] In 1362, the earliest surviving pittancer's roll, the amounts paid to the community were: 20s. to the abbot; 15s.4d. to the prior; 13s.6d. to priest-monks; and either 5s.2d. or 6s. to novices (WDA, Se/Ac/2). For a discussion of pittances, see D. Knowles, *The Religious Orders in England*, II, ch. XVIII. Such payments were a subject of concern to the reformers of 1421 (see W. A. Pantin, *General and Provincial Chapters*, II, p. 113).
[2] As at Durham Priory (see R. B. Dobson, *Durham Priory 1400–50*, p. 255).
[3] This was also the cause of disquiet to the reformers of 1421 (see W. A. Pantin, *General and Provincial Chapters*, II, p. 113).
[4] See HUL, DDLO 20/15 and 16. The survey made in 1535 of the revenues of the various Selby offices mentions only the pittancer; and it seems likely that even in the account rolls of the office the use of the name 'chamberlain' was dropped in the second half of the 15th century.
[5] 66s.8d. for the abbot; 53s.4d. for the prior; 40s. for priest-monks and 20s. for novices. See HUL, DDLO 20/16 and below, pp. 111–112.

surviving pittancer's account. More account rolls have survived for the pittancer's office at Selby than for any other obedientiary of the house, some 37 in all though a few are not complete. Their main value to the student of the house lies in the lists which they provide of the members of the community, since all from abbot to novice received a pittance each year. What they indicate is considerable stability of numbers. In 1362 the pittancer's roll for that year lists 27 monks and novices, including the abbot and prior;[6] and a community of approximately that size was maintained throughout the fifteenth century, as the figures below show:[7]

1412–13, 30	1452–53, 26	1469–70, 25
1415–16, 35	1453–54, 26	1470–71, 25
1431–32, 36	1454–55, 26	1472–73, 28
1432–33, 36	1455–56, 31	1474–75, 25
1437–38, 30	1456–57, 29	1475–76, 26
1438–39, 29	1457–58, 27	1479–80, 30
1446–47, 23	1458–59, 27	1496–97, 29
1447–48, 26	1467–68, 26	1497–98, 27
1450–51, 27	1468–69, 25	1516–17, 25

As Professor Dobson has remarked: 'Throughout the fifteenth century there was apparently no shortage of aspirants to the life of a cloistered monk at Selby.'[8]

In its ability to maintain its membership at a stable level Selby Abbey follows the general pattern for houses of its type. Durham Priory, for example, provides similar evidence, with about 70 monks maintained at the mother house and its cells throughout the fifteenth century.[9] Whatever its effects on other aspects of religious life, the dramatic fall in population that followed the arrival of the bubonic plague in England in 1348 did not occasion a continuing decline in monastic numbers after the initial catastrophic losses. Rather recruitment was able to make up a considerable proportion of the losses in a population that may well have continued to decline for much of the fifteenth century.[10] Whilst we may speculate that the living-standards of fifteenth century monastic houses may have had something to do with their ability to attract recruits, we cannot altogether deny their vitality in their society.

---

[6] WDA, Se/Ac/2.

[7] The figures are taken from all complete surviving pittancers' rolls other than those translated below. HUL, DDLO 20/15, 16, 17, 19, 20, 22, 23, 25, 27, 28, 29, 30, 32, 33, 34 and 36. WDA, Se/Ac/7, 16, 18 and 21. York Minster Library, HH 21.3a and 3b.

[8] R.B. Dobson, 'The Election of John Ousthorp as Abbot of Selby in 1436', *Yorkshire Archaeological Journal*, 42, 1967, p. 40.

[9] R.B. Dobson, *Durham Priory 1400–50*, pp. 52–54.

[10] On population decline see J. Hatcher, *Plague, Population and the English Economy 1348–1530*, London, 1977. Knowles estimated that the total number of religious in all orders in c.1500 was 50% higher than the low-point reached in the later fourteenth century (D. Knowles, *The Religious Orders in England*, II, p. 257).

Two pittancer's rolls have been selected for inclusion in this section, in order to illustrate the original form of the office and its union with the chamberlain's office discussed above. These are for the years 1403–1404 and 1441–1442.[11] The earlier account has suffered substantial damage from a tear at the bottom left of the single piece of parchment, resulting in the loss of portions of the entries in the final, 'Allowances', section. But it has been included here because it comes nearest of surviving accounts to providing a profile of the Selby community at the time of the bursars' account of 1398–99. The later of the two accounts, the pittancer and chamberlain's roll for 1441–42, has been selected for inclusion over five earlier and similar rolls as a result of its superior condition of preservation.[12] It has suffered slight damage from damp, but virtually nothing has been rendered illegible.

Neither of the monk-accountants in these rolls appears to have had a particularly distinguished or in any way unusual career at Selby. Brother John de Milyngton, pittancer 1403–04, had become a full member of the community in 1388, but his earliest known employment as an obedientiary was as pittancer 1402–03. He was chamberlain 1413–14 and kitchener 1415–16; and he appears as representative of the abbot in the court of Selby in 1403 and 1411. Payment of his pittance shows him to have been still a member of the community in 1415–16; but he does not appear in the pittancer's account for 1431–32 or subsequently.[13]

The accountant of 1441–42, Brother William Snayth, entered the house about 1422 and was ordained a priest in 1427. He served as pittancer with some frequency: 1435–36, 1440–42, and 1452–59. And he was also bursar 1459–60, and possibly 1451–52. He died either late in 1470 or early in 1471, his pittance being paid to him only for the earlier half of the year.[14]

[11] HUL, DDLO 20/14 and 21.
[12] The earlier pittancer and chamberlain's rolls are 1431–32, 1432–33, 1433–34, 1437–38, 1438–39 (HUL, DDLO 20/16, 17, 18, 19, 20).
[13] See Borthwick Institute of Historical Research, Archbishop's Register 14, Thomas Arundel, f. 11b; HUL, DDLO 20/14, 15, 16 and 54c, DDLO 21/91, and DDX 145/1; and WDA, Se/Ac/10 and Se/CR/4.
[14] See Borthwick Institute of Historical Research, Archbishop's Register 18, Henry Bowet, f. 412r, and Register 19, John Kempe, f. 231; HUL, DDLO 20/20, 21, 25, 26a and 30, DDLO 2/2; WDA, Se/Ac/18; and R. B. Dobson, 'The Election of John Ousthorp', p. 38.

Pittancer's account of 1403–04

Table of Contents

The account of Brother John de Milyngton, pittancer of the abbey of Selby, from the festival of Pentecost (3 June) A.D. 1403 to the same festival (18 May) A.D. 1404

Arrears (*Arreragia*)	No arrears (from the previous account) are held because (the expenditure and allowances of) this same accountant in his last account exceeded income.
Rents and farms (*Redditus et firme*)	The same person answers for £33 0s.4d. from all rents and farms belonging to the office yearly according to the new rental, in addition to the profit of the Selby dam (*stagni*).
Total £33 0s.4d.	
Other receipts (*Aliud Receptum*)	The same person answers for 55s. from 220 thraves[15] of grass and rushes coming from produce of the Selby dam this year, at a price of 3d. a thrave, and

---

[15] The form of the number (*CVxx*) indicates that the long hundred of six score is in use in this account, and *CVxx* has been translated as 220 (i.e. C = 120; *Vxx* = 100).

not more because of the flooding (*superundationis aquarum*) at the time of mowing.

Total 55s.

Sum total of receipts £35 15s.4d.

Excess (*Excessus*)	From which the same person accounts for the excess of expenditure (over income) in his preceding account, as it appears at the foot of the said account £13 13s.3d.

Total £13 13s.3d.

Transfer of a farm, with small expenses (*Resolutio firme cum Minutis*)	Likewise he accounts for the money transferred to the keeper of the altar of the blessed Mary for the farm due to him from the toft in Gowthorpe which Thomas Rosell[16] holds, and from the toft in Church Lane (*le Kirklane*) which John de Babthorp holds, yearly 5s.3d.

And for gifts to the various persons collecting the rents of the office this year 5s.

And for mowing and binding 220 thraves of grass and rushes in the dam, at (*prout data*[17]) ¾d. a thrave 13s.9d.

And for the service of Walter Coke of Thorpe Willoughby transporting[18] the said thraves by water from the aforesaid dam to the houses of the various persons in the town in which they were sold (*in quibus vendebantur*) 5s.

Total 29s.

Repair of houses (*Emendatio dom-orum*)	Likewise he accounts for 6 thraves of thatch (*Dam-thak*) purchased for repair of one gutter (*gutter'*) for the house (*in domum*) of Thomas Mound and the house of the office in Gowthorpe 18d.

And for the service of the man thatching over the said gutter for one day 4d.

And to the same person's mate 2d.

And for 11 thraves of thatch (*Damthak*) purchased for the roof[19] of the house there which Beatrice Frere holds on the northern side 2s.9d.

---

[16] One Thomas Rosell received a wage as a brewer in the granger's account of 1404–05 (see below, p. 134).

[17] *a* has been added to *falcand'*, *ligand'*, and *dat'*, in dark ink by a different hand.

[18] *is* added to *navigant'* as above.

[19] *a* added to *tectur'* as above.

And for the service of the man thatching on the same for 2 days without food (being provided) 8d.

And for the service of his mate for the said time 6d.

And for stowers (*stoures*) purchased for repair of the malt-kiln house (*domus thoralis*) in the garden of the toft there which John Mody holds 11d.

And for 21 thraves of thatch (*Damthak*) purchased for the said house 5s.3d.

And for the payment to John Mody for repair and roofing of the said house by contract 5s.

And for payment to John Jeb for one screen (*spera*) made in the house which he holds there 12d.

And for the payment to John Hamund for one door made in the house which he holds there, with the braces (*ligamentis*) and hooks purchased for the same[20] 15d.

And for outlays and expenses incurred (*factis*) by Thomas Rosell about the renovation of one house built in the garden of the toft which he holds there 16s.

And for 48 thraves of thatch (*Damthak*) purchased and delivered[21] to the same person for thatching the said house 12s.

And for 70 thraves of thatch (*Damthak*) purchased for the roof of the malt-kiln house in the garden of the toft in Micklegate which William Belnays holds 17s.6d.

And for the service of one man roofing on the same for 7 days 2s.4d.

And for the service of his mate for the said time 21d.

And for 15 thraves of thatch (*Damthak*) purchased for the roof of the malt-kiln house in the garden of the toft there which Robert Eleson holds 3s.9d.

And for the service of the man thatching on the same for 2 days 8d.

And for the service of his mate for the said time 6d.

And for 16 thraves of thatch (*Damthak*) purchased for the roofs of 4 cottages near the water-mills 4s.

And for the service of the man thatching on the same and ridging the same for 6 days 2s.

And for the service of the woman assisting him 12d.

---

[20] *e* added to *eod'* by a different hand.
[21] *s* interlined after *liberat'* as above.

And for 8 oak saplings purchased for making[22] into beams for one of the aforesaid cottages 16d.

And for the service of Simon Wright and his mate working as carpenters and[23] putting 4 tie-beams (*copulas*) into the aforesaid cottages for 2 days 2s.

And for one oaken timber purchased for repair of one house in the garden of the toft there which William Kay holds 5d.

And for the service of Simon Wright and his mate repairing the said house by contract 2s.8d.

And for 12 thraves of thatch (*Damthak*) purchased for the roof of the same 3s.3d.

And for the service of the man thatching on the same for 2 days 8d.

And for the service of his mate for the said time 6d.

And for 12 thraves of thatch (*Damthak*) purchased for the roof of the house in Wren Lane which John Smyth holds 3s.

And for the service of the man thatching and ridging the same for 2 days 8d.

And for the service of his mate 6d.

And for expenses incurred by *dominus* John de Blakewell[24] on a certain stable in the garden of one cottage in Wren Lane 2s.8d.

And for the wattling and daubing (*periettatione et dealbatione*) of the houses which Margery de Bylton holds, paid by (*per manus*) Brother William Pygot[25] 2s.

And for daubing various defects in the walls of the houses in Ousegate which Richard Beawe held, by contract 3s.

And for 200 tiles purchased for the roof 2s.4d.

And for the service of William Geve roofing on the said house for 2 days and a half 14d.

And for the service of his mate for the said time 10d.

---

[22] *i*ˢ added to *fac'* by a different hand.

[23] *s et* interlined after *carpentant'* as above.

[24] The title *dominus* was commonly given to the clergy, as here. Blakewell was the parish chaplain of Selby (see British Library, Cotton Vit. E.XVI, f. 145v).

[25] Brother William Pygot was elected abbot of Selby in 1408, having graduated from Oxford University in 1399 as bachelor of canon law (see above, p. 81). For a discussion of the use of wattle and daub in building, see L. F. Salzman, *Building in England down to 1540. A Documentary History*, Oxford, 1967, ch. XII.

And for the repairs done on the house in the garden of the toft there which John Inglot holds, paid by the said John 7s.

Total 114s.9d.[26]

Payments of cash (*Liberationes denarii*) Likewise he accounts for the payment to the lord abbot[27] for his pittance yearly 33s.4d.

And to the lord prior yearly 26s.8d.

And to Brothers Thomas Wakefeld, Robert de Cayton, Adam de Crosby, (and) Stephen de Duffeld yearly £4.

And to Brothers William de Lathum, Thomas de Warnefeld, William de Snayth, and William de Saltmarssh yearly £4.

And to Brother Peter de Roucliff, Thomas de Houeden, Robert de Selby, and Richard de Secroft £4.

And to Brothers Thomas de Allerton, John de Anlaby, Richard de Harewod, and John Milyngton £4.

And to Brothers John de Coventr', John Paselew, William Pygot, and Robert de Schyrburn £4.

And to Brothers John de Cave, John de CrosthWayt, Thomas de Drax, John Lincoln, and Peter de Sutton 100s.

And to Brothers John de Gaynesburgh, John de Ousthorp, John de Grayngham, John Hales, and Thomas de Bolton 10s.

Total £28 10s.

Allowances (*Allocationes*) Likewise he asks that he be allowed 2s.6d. from the farm of John de Duffeld, shoemaker, this year because he has nothing.

And 5s. from the farm of John Blakst' ...[28] for the aforesaid reason.

And 16d. from the farm of Robert Broune this year because he refuses to pay.

And 5s. from the farm of John Gayt this year because he has nothing.

... from the farm of Roger de Kyrkeby this year because he says that £4 and more are owed to him for repairs done on the houses which he held in ... of Brother Richard Harewod.[29]

---

[26] The total should be 114s.10d.

[27] John de Shirburn, abbot of Selby 1369–1408.

[28] The manuscript has a tear down the last 8 cm of the left side and a number of words have been lost.

[29] Brother Richard was already a full member of the community by 1395 when he was representing the abbot in the court of Selby; and he appears in the pittance list of 1415–16, but not that for 1431–32 (see HUL, DDLO 20/15 and 16).

And 6d. from the rent of Robert de Bolland this year because he refuses to pay.

And 6d. from the rent ... for the aforesaid reason.

And 4d. from the site of the hermitage (*herimitagi*) at the end of New Lane, in the lord's hand this year for want of tenant.[30]

... Brayton which John de Lyndsay held, in the lord's hand for want of repair.

And 5s. from the tenement in Snaith ... he has nothing.

And 2s.6d. from one marsh (*mora*) there, in the lord's hand for want of tenant.

And 4s. from one .....

And 9d. from the rent of John Burdeux this year, because he says that he will not pay for the tenements in .....

... de Vaslay for the tenements in Brayton, for the aforesaid reason.

And 18d. from one bovate of land in Burton .....

... rent of Sir Thomas de Metham[31] and William de Wintworth for the tenements in Pollington .....

... to this (accountant)[32] himself for his labour.

Total 69s.3d.

(Sum total of all)[33] expenses, payments, and allowances £52 6s.3d.[34]
(And thus he exceeds income by) £16 10s.11d.

---

[30] Recluses were common figures in late medieval England (see R. M. Clay, *The Hermits and Anchorites of England*, London, 1914; and F. D. S. Darwin, *The English Mediaeval Recluse*, SPCK, 1944), where 'there was a strong contemporary current setting towards the solitary life' (D. Knowles, *The Religious Orders in England*, II, p. 222). The Selby hermitage, however, seems to have been unoccupied, and perhaps had been so for some time, since the site was rented to a tenant when one was available.

[31] Of Metham in Howdenshire, co. York. The family held a moiety of the manor of Pollington (see *Inquisitions post mortem*, ed. W. P. Baildon and J. W. Clay, pp. 121–123).

[32] In 1415–16 the pittancer's fee was 6s.8d. (HUL, DDLO 20/15, s.v. *Allocationes*).

[33] Words in brackets are surmised from other accounts, as several words have been lost at this point through the tear mentioned earlier.

[34] This figure should be £52 16s.3d.

The Pittancer and Chamberlain's account of 1441–42

Table of Contents

The account of Brother William Snayth, pittancer and chamberlain of the monastery of Selby, from the festival of St Martin in winter (11 November) A.D. 1441 to the same festival A.D. 1442 for one whole year

Arrears
(*Arreragia*)

No arrears (from the previous account) are held, because (the expenditure and allowances of) this same accountant in his last account of the preceding year exceeded income.

Total nothing.

Rents and farms
(*Redditus et firme*)

Firstly the same person answers for £37 15s.3d. from rents and farms belonging to the pittancer's office yearly according to the rental.

And for £33 10s.5d. from rents and farms both of the freehold tenants and of the tenants at will, together with the pensions and farms of the mills of Monk Fryston, belonging to the chamberlain's office yearly according to the new rental.

And for 2s. from the profit of the dove-cot over the chapter-house this year.

And for 3s.4d. from the rent of one moor (*unius more*) in Rawcliffe formerly in the tenure of John Marshall.

And for 3s.9d. from the increase in the rent of one toft formerly (in the possession) of Walter de Sartryne, which used to return 15d. and now (is) in the tenure of John Dobbe for 5s. yearly.

And for 6s. yearly from the rent of the tenement in New Lane formerly (in the possession) of John Marshall of Brayton.

And for 10s. yearly for the toft near the gates of the abbey.

And for 18d. from the rent of one acre and a half of land across the Ouse, formerly in the tenure of William Saxton freeholder[1] and now in the tenure of William Fraunceys.

And for 12d. this year from the rent of one selion of land formerly in the tenure of Margery Warde.

And for 46s. received from rushes, reeds, and hay (*herbagio*) growing in the Selby dam (*stagno*) this year.

And for 16d. from John de Lunde for one bovate of land this year.

And for 4d. received from Roger Burwod for one carr (*Karr'*)[2] in the dam this year.

---

[1] *libere tenentis* interlined.
[2] A 'Carr' is a 'pond or pool; bog or fen'. (*OED*)

And for 10s. this year received from Lawrence Wylson and William Dust[3] from branches of oaks cut down in various assarts of the office (and) sold to them for this (*sic eis venditis*).

Total of receipts £75 10s.11d.[4]

Excess (*Excessus*)	From which he accounts for the excess of expenditure (over income) of his last account of the year next preceding, as it appears at the foot of the account of that year, 78s.3¾d. and half a farthing.

Total 78s.3¾d. and half a farthing.

Transfers of rent[5] (*Resolutiones redditus*)	And he accounts for the money transferred to the keeper of the altar of the blessed Mary from the rents of the pittancer for the toft formerly in the tenure of John Chapman in Gowthorpe, and the two tofts (in?)[6] Church Lane (*le Kirklane*) yearly 5s.3d.

And to the same kitchener for the tenement formerly (in the possession) of *dominus* Peter Hugate, chaplain, in respect of (*pro*) the lands formerly (in the possession) of Katherine Dreng[8] belonging to the chamberlain's office, yearly 17d.

And to the same kitchener for the tenement formerly (in the possession) of *dominus* Peter Hugate, chaplain, by virtue of (*pro*) the lands formerly (in the possession) of Katherine Dreng[8] belonging to the chamberlain's office, yearly 17d.

And to the keeper of the altar of the blessed Mary for the aforesaid tenements yearly 18d.

And to the kitchener for one and a half acres of land across the Ouse formerly (in the possession) of William Saxton yearly 3d.

And to the same kitchener for the toft formerly (in the possession) of Margery Warde 3d.

And to the keeper of the altar of the blessed Mary for the same toft yearly 9d.

---

[3] *et Willelmo Dust* interlined.

[4] There are dots in the margin used by the accountant in calculating this total. For an explanation of the system see C. T. Martin, *The Record Interpreter*, 2nd edn, London, 1910, pp. xii–xiii.

[5] i.e. payment to other monk-officials of the house of rents belonging to their offices collected (presumably for convenience) by the officers of the pittancer and chamberlain.

[6] The manuscript is damaged at this point and the word surmised.

[7] Formerly a corrodarian of the abbey (see above, Bursars' Account, p.53 n.62). There is a record of property formerly belonging to him passing to the abbey in 1404 in the abbey register (see British Library, Cot. Vit. E.XVI, f.116).

[8] Also a former corrodarian of the abbey (see above, Bursars' Account, pp.53 and 51 n.48).

And to the keeper of the fabric for the houses in the cemetery and the land in *Marchalridding* formerly (in the possession) of Robert Potman yearly 8d.

And to the pittancer for the tenement built in Church Lane formerly (in the possession) of Katherine Dreng yearly 2s.

And to the kitchener for the tenement in le .. *Welane*[9] formerly (in the possession) of John Marschall of Brayton yearly 4d.

And to the keeper of the altar of the blessed Mary[10] for *le Dawepighell* yearly 1d.

Total 15s.7¾d.

Repairs of houses[11] (*Reperationes Domorum*)	(And for?)[12] the service of Reginald Wright and his companion for 3 days working and repairing the fence of the tenement in Gowthorpe formerly in the tenure of Geoffrey Dynelabe, each receiving 4d. (a day?)[12] 2s.

And for 200 large spike-nails (*spykyng*) purchased for the same work 8d.

And for 100 medium spike-nails (*Middelspykyng*) purchased for the same work 3d.

And for the service of Peter Bynglay (and?)[12] Reginald Wright for 4 days this year repairing various faults in the houses there in the tenure of John Branes and John Muston 3s.8d.

And for the service of Thomas Pachet working on the same job for 1 day and a half 9d.

And for 400 laths purchased for the same work 22d.

And for 800 brad-nails (*broddis*) purchased for the same work 12d.

And for the service of John Pulter stripping the houses there for one day 4d.

And for the service of two sawyers sawing stooths (*stothes*)[13] for the said houses 12d.

(And?)[14] for 4 waggon-loads of mud purchased for the said houses 8d.

---

[9] Possibly New Lane. The manuscript is damaged at this point.
[10] *Marie* interlined.
[11] A sub-heading further down this side of the manuscript has been lost. It was almost certainly *Gouthorp*.
[12] The manuscript is damaged by damp and some words made illegible.
[13] 'A post, an upright lath'. (*OED*)
[14] The manuscript is damaged by damp and a word illegible.

And for the service of John Hoggeson and his companion for 2 days mixing the mud and daubing the walls of the said houses 16d.

And for two bands (*ligaminibus*) with iron hooks purchased for the door of John Branes' house 5d.

And for one lock with key purchased for the door of the store-room (*celarii*) (of the said?)[14] John 4d.

And for one lock with key purchased for the door of John Muston's house 4d.

And for one lock with key purchased for the door of the store-room of …[14] Hamonde 4d.

And for the service of James Couper for one day repairing one louver (*lover*) of the house formerly in the tenure of Robert Rolle 4d.

And for 100 large spike-nails purchased for the same work 4d.

And for 60 medium spike-nails purchased for the same work 1½d.

And for 15 boards of 5 feet purchased for the said louver …[15]

And for the service of Thomas Wylde roofing for 11 days and a half on six houses there on the northern side in the tenure of the said John Branes and others, receiving 5d. a day 4s.9½d.

And for the service of his mate for the same time, receiving 3d. a day 2s.10½d.

And for the service of Thomas Wate and Richard Bordclever (for?)[16] one day and a half working and repairing faults in the building (*domus*) there in the garden of the house in the tenure of Thomas Thryston 18d.

And for 8 spars (*sparres*) purchased for the same work 8d.

And for 100 laths purchased for the same work 6d.

And for 260 brad-nails purchased 5d.

And for 2 waggon-loads of mud[17] purchased for the said building 4d.

And for the service of William Butler for one day mixing the mud and daubing the walls of the said house 4d.

And for the service of Thomas Wylde for 2 days roofing on the said building 10d.

And for the service of his mate for the same time 6d.

[15] The sum is possibly 7½d.
[16] The manuscript is damaged by damp and a word illegible.
[17] *luti* interlined.

And for 11 thraves of thatch (*Damthak*) purchased for the said work 22d.

Total 30s.11d.

Micklegate (*Mikelgate*)	And for the service of Thomas Whitehede and three carpenters working on and renewing one building (*domum*) for the malt-kiln[18] within the garden of the house in Micklegate in the tenure of Lawrence Wylson, by contract (*in conventione*) 22d.

And for the service of Thomas Belyce and his companion for one day making the stone foundations of the said building 10d.

And for 200 wall-tiles (*Walteghell'*) purchased for the said malt-kiln 12d.

And for spars (*sparres*) purchased for the said building 16d.

And for 24 stowers (*stoures*) purchased for the said building 5d.

And for the service of James Couper for one day and a half working on the said malt-kiln 6d.

And for large spike-nails (*Spykyng*) purchased for the same work 4d.

And for 100 medium spike-nails (*Middelspykyng*) purchased for the same work 3d.

And for brags (*bragg'*) purchased 1d.

And for 200 sap-laths (*Sappelatt'*)[19] purchased 12d.

And for 500 brad-nails (*broddis*) purchased 10d.

And for the service of Robert Bouland carting 8 waggon-loads of mud to the said building 16d.

And for the service of Thomas Schawe carting 2 waggon-loads of sand to the same work 4d.

And for the service of John Whallay and his two companions mixing the said mud and daubing the walls of the said house, and making one malt-floor (*Maltflore*) in the said building, by contract 2s.

And for the service of Thomas Wylde for 11 days roofing on the house there at *Milnebrig*, receiving 5d. a day, 4s.7d.

And for the service of his mate for 4 days, receiving 3d. a day, 12d.

And for the service of the two women helping the same Thomas for 7 days, each receiving 3d. a day, 3s.6d.

---

[18] *pro thorali* interlined.
[19] i.e. laths made of sap-wood. (*OED*).

And for 400 wall-tiles (Walteghell') purchased at Cawood, with the transport of the same thence to Selby, for repair of the house[20] there in the tenure of Peter Bynglay 2s.6d.

And for the service of William Greve and his mate for two days repairing one *Kilnehorne* and 2 ovens (*fornacia*) in the said house 18d.

And for the service of Thomas Resyte and his mate roofing and pointing for 2 days on the said house 18d.

And for the service of William Butler and his companion for one day cutting down underwood in the dam and making a hedge of it in the garden of the said house 8d.

And for the service of John Thorp carting 6 waggon-loads of mud to the said *Kilnehorne* 9d.

And for paris candles purchased for the same work 1d.

And for the service of 2 men daubing the walls of the said house for 1 day 8d.

And for 4 locks with 4 keys purchased for the doors of the said house 12d.

And for one key purchased 2d.

And for the service of Thomas Wylde for 3 days and a half[21] roofing on the house in the garden of Peter Bynglay this year, receiving 4d. a day, 14d.

And for the service of his mate for the same time, (receiving) 3d. a day, 10½d.

And for 15 thraves of thatch (*Thak*) purchased for the roof of the said house 2s.6d.

Total 34s.6½d.

Wren Lane
(*Wrenlane*)
And for the service of Thomas Wylde roofing for 3 days on the house in Wren Lane formerly in the tenure of Katherine Hugate 15d.

And for the service of the 2 women helping him for the same time, each receiving 3d. a day, 18d.

And for the service of John Webster and James Couper for 1 day and a half repairing various defects in the said house 15d.

And for 160 sap-laths (*saplatt'*) purchased for the same work 9d.

And for 300 brad-nails purchased for[22] the same work 4½d.

[20] *domus* interlined.
[21] *et dimidium* interlined.
[22] *ad* repeated in the manuscript.

And for large spike-nails (*spykyng'*) purchased 4d.

And for 2 bands (*ligaminibus*) with 2 iron hooks purchased for the said house 3d.

And for the service of Robert Boulande carting 4 waggon-loads of mud to the said house 6d.

And for the service of John Weston and his companion mixing the mud and daubing the walls of the said house for 2 days 16d.

And for 16 thraves of thatch (*Damthak*) purchased for the roof of the said house 2s.8d.

And for the service of William Brigham and his companion for 1 day and a half repairing the kitchen of the house there in the tenure of John Uscher 16½d.

And for the service of Geoffrey Dynlabe carting 1 waggon-load of timber from *le Trenche* to the said house 6d.

And for 60 large spike-nails (*spykyng*) purchased for the same work 2d.

And for 80 sap-laths (*sappelatt'*) purchased for the said house 4d.

And for 200 brad-nails purchased 3d.

And for the service of Robert Boweland carting 3 waggon-loads of mud to the said house 4½d.

And for the service of John Weston and his companion[23] mixing the said mud and daubing the walls of the said house for 1 day and a half 12d.

And for the service of William Brigham for 2 days roofing and pointing on the house in the tenure of the said John this year 10d.

And for the service of his mate for the same time 6d.

And for the service of William Brigham for 2 days roofing and pointing on the house there in the tenure of Agnes Wright this year 10d.

And for the service of his mate for the same time 6d.

Total 16s.10½d.

Ousegate	And for the service of William Brigham for 3 days and a half roofing and pointing on the house in Ousegate in the tenure of John Maltake this year 17½d.

And for the service of his mate for the same time 10½d.

Total 2s.4d.

---

[23] *et socii sui* interlined.

Church Lane
(*Kirkelane*)
And for the service of Edmund Brighton and his brother George for 4 days roofing and pointing on the house in Church Lane in the tenure of Cecily Bawetre this year 16d.

And for[24] 60 laths of heartwood (*hertlattis*)[25] purchased for the said house 5d.

And for 100 nails purchased for the said house 2d.

And for the service of Edmund Brighton and his brother George for 2 days roofing and pointing on the house in the cemetery this year, the lord providing food (*ad cibum domini*) 8d.

And for the service of William Butler cutting down underwood in the dam for 4 days to make a hedge with it in various tenements of the office 16d.

And for 500 tiles purchased this year from Brother Robert Skipwyth[26] for various repairs 5s.7d.

And for 5 quarters of sand purchased this year 15d.

And for 2 waggon-loads of lime purchased this year 4s.

Total 14s.9d.

And for 2 stones and a half[27] of Spanish iron purchased for the windmill at Monk Fryston this year 20d.

And for one hurter (*hurtour*)[28] purchased 2d.

And for the service of William Synderby of Milforth working the said iron into bands and[29] hoops (*hopes*) for the axle-tree (*le Axeltree*) and the trundle wheels (*lez trendells*)[30] of the said mill 14d.

Total 3s.

---

[24] *in* interlined.
[25] Heartwood is a 'name for the central part of the timber of exogenous trees, hardened and matured by age'. (*OED*)
[26] Brother Robert entered the monastery c.1429 and was ordained a priest in March 1430. His activities as a monk-official included terms as bursar 1431–32 and 1435–36, and extern cellarer 1435–36. He is known to have been a member of the guild of Corpus Christi at York with other Selby monks, and was still alive in 1475 (see Borthwick Institute of Historical Research, Archbishop's Register 19, John Kempe, fos ccxxxv and ccxxxvib; HUL, DDLO 20/1 and 33; B. Dobson, 'The Election of John Ousthorp', p. 38; *The Register of the Guild of Corpus Christi in the City of York*, ed. R. H. Scaife, Surtees Society 57, 1872, p. 87).
[27] *et dimidio* interlined.
[28] 'The shoulder of an axle, against which the nave of the wheel strikes; also a strengthening piece on the shoulder of an axle.' (*OED*)
[29] *et* interlined.
[30] An axle-tree is a 'fixed bar or beam of wood, etc., on the rounded ends of which the opposite wheels of a carriage revolve'. (*OED*) Trendle-wheels or lantern wheels are a form of conversion gear on the actual mill-stone spindle.

Cost of ditches
(*Custus fossatorum*) And for the service of John Barker (cleaning out?)[31] 24 rods and a half of ditch of the assart called *Dawpighell* 2s.0½d.

And for the service of the said John cleaning out 41 rods of ditch of the assart called *Palycokridding*, and making a hedge thereon (*desuper*), receiving 1d. a rod, 3s.5d.

And given to John Dobbe for enclosing of 2 acres of land in Snaith Ings (*Snathyng*) 8d.

And for the service of one man (cleaning out)[32] 3 rods of ditch at the end of the garden formerly in the tenure of Geoffrey Dynelabe ...d.[33]

Total 6s.4½d.

Costs of the ferry
(*Custus passagii*) And for one ferry-boat (*batella passagii*) purchased from Brother Thomas Crull,[34] bursar of the monastery this year, 66s.8d.

And for the service of two men sawing 1 rod of timber into planks (*plauncheours*) for the said boat 3s.

And for the service of William Cauthorne working on and repairing (*facientis*) the said boat by contract 6s.8d.

And for iron brags (*bragg'*) purchased for the same work 4d.

And for 100 large spike-nails (*spyking*) purchased 4d.

And for the service of Richard Goldale shaping the said timber into posts (*postantis dictum meremium*) for 1 day 6d.

And for the service of 2 men sawing 1 sapling (*sappelyng*) into ledges (*leggas*) for the said boat 4d.

And for trenails (*clavis ligneis*)[35] purchased for the same work 2d.

And for ale purchased and given to the men dragging the said boat from the dam to the waters of the Ouse 7½d.

Total 78s.7½d.

---

[31] The word is partly illegible.

[32] The sentence lacks a verb and was apparently a late addition to the account.

[33] The sum is illegible, but should be 3d.

[34] First mentioned as a novice of the abbey in 1408 (Borthwick Institute of Historical Research, Archbishop's Register 18, Bowet I, f.39), Brother Thomas Crull served in a variety of offices: kitchener 1413–14 and 1436; bursar 1416–17 and 1441–42; granger 1421–22 and 1423–25; almoner 1431–32 as well as 1433–34 (HUL, DDLO 20/1, 21, 54d, 66, and 4/3; WDA, Se/Ac/8a and 8b, 9, and 12; R. B. Dobson, 'The Election of John Ousthorp', p. 38). He received a legacy of a gold ring and a pair of ivory tablets under the will of a Selby corrodarian, Isabella Hamerton, in 1433 (*Testamenta Eboracensia II*, pp. 22–23); and he was still alive in 1453 (HUL, DDLO 20/25).

[35] 'A cylindrical pin of hard wood used in fastening timbers together, especially in ship building and other work where the materials are exposed to the action of water.' (*OED*)

Wages with small expenses
(*Stipendia cum Minutis*)

And for the wage of Lawrence Wylson, tailor of the convent this year, 13s.4d.

And for the wage of Thomas, groom in the tailor's shop this year, 10s.

And for the wage of the laundress of the convent this year 5s.

And for blanket cloth purchased for the slippers (*ad pedul'*) given to the rector of Averham[36] this year 4d.

And for thread purchased for sewing the habits (*indumentorum*) of the convent this year 9s.8d.

And given to John Grewe, keeper of the Selby ferry, for his clothing this year 6s.8d.

And for 4 lbs of paris candle purchased for lighting in the said office this year, at 1¼d. a lb., 5d.

And for 9 rods of linen cloth purchased for towels to be hung in the cloister,[37] at 5d. a rod, 3s.9d.

Total 49s.2d.

Payments of cash
(*Liberationes denariorum*)

And for the payment to the lord abbot for his pittance and clothing this year 66s.8d.

And to the lord prior for the same reason yearly 53s.4d.

And to Brothers Robert Shirburne, John Acastre, Thomas Crull, and Richard Athelyngflete this year, each receiving 40s., £8.

And to Brothers William Bridlyngton and Stephen Farnehill this year, receiving as above, £4.

And to Brother Thomas Savage this year for the terms of Martinmas (11 November) and Pentecost (20 May) 33s.4d.[38]

And to Brothers John Farneworth, William Snayth, Robert Skipwith, Thomas Normanton, and John Farnehill this year, each receiving as above, £10.

And to Brothers John Hull and Robert Bank, each receiving as above, £4.

---

[36] Co. Nottingham. The abbey received an annual pension of £2 from the rector, representing commuted tithes. See G.S. Haslop, 'The Abbot of Selby's Financial Statement for the Year ending Michaelmas 1338', p. 161 and n. 7.

[37] Presumably near the lavatorium, where the monks washed their hands before entering the refectory.

[38] *iiiid* interlined.

And to Brother Thomas Duffeld this year for the term of Martinmas (11 November) 20s.[39]

And to Brothers Thomas Estoft, Richard Cave, Robert Whitwode, and James Mershden this year, each receiving as above, £8.

And to Brothers John Barlay, William Wencelowe, William Batlay, John Alkbarowe, and Robert Thorp this year, each receiving as above, £10.

And to Brothers John Scharowe, William Skipwith, John Rither, John Northerby, and Walter Cotyngwith, novices this year, each receiving 20s., 100s.

Total £57 13s.4d.

Payment (*Solutio*)	And for money paid to Brother William Bridlyngton, former pittancer and chamberlain[40] of the monastery, as part of the 57s.4d. from the excess (of expenditure over receipts) of his[41] last account, as it appears at the foot of the account of that year 20s.
Total 20s.	

Allowances (*Allocationes*)	Likewise the same accountant is allowed 6s.8d. for the decline in the rent of one house in Gowthorpe formerly in the tenure of Geoffrey Dynelabe, because (it was) in the lord's hand this year for want of a tenant.

And for 12d. for loss of rent of one house there formerly in the tenure of John Hamonde, which used to return 6s. and now returns only 5s. a year.

And 4s. for loss of rent of one house there in the tenure of Thomas Thriston, which used to return 12s. and now returns only 8s. a year because of repair (*causa reperationis*).

And 6s.8d. for loss of rent of one house there in the tenure of Thomas Thorp, cook, which used to return 20s. and now returns

---

[39] In April 1442 Brother Thomas Duffeld obtained a papal dispensation to receive and hold a benefice with cure of souls for life, including a parish church or perpetual vicarage (*CPL*, IX, 1431–1447, p. 261). See above, pp. 26–27.

[40] The account referred to here survives and was for the years 1432–33. The original excess was £12 2s.10½d., of which the accountant pardoned to the convent £6 2s.10½d., received 20s. from the pittancer in his account of 1440–41, and was paid a further £2 2s.8d. by the abbot from the sacristan's 'Arrears', leaving the £2 17s.4d. mentioned above (HUL, DDLO 20/17).

[41] *sui* interlined.

only 13s.4d. a year, leased for this to the same Thomas by indenture for a term of years.

And 3s. for loss of rent of the tenement in New Lane, formerly (in the possession) of John Marschall of Brayton, because (it was) in the lord's hand for Martinmas term for want of a tenant.

And 3s. for loss of rent of one barn in Micklegate formerly in the tenure of Richard Gleson, because it is filled with thatch (*Damthak*) for the office's use.

And 3s. for loss of rent of one barn there formerly in the tenure of William Glover, because it is filled with thatch (*Damthak*) for the office's use.

And 2s.6d. for loss of rent of one house there formerly in the tenure of Lettice Bedale this year for the term of Pentecost, for want of a tenant.

And 6s. for loss of rent of one house in *Middilthorp*[42] formerly in the tenure of John Dent, because (it was) in the lord's hand this year for want of a tenant.

And 4s. for loss of rent of one house in Wren Lane formerly in the tenure of Richard Dent, because it is filled with lime, sand, and tiles, for the use of the office this year.

And 5s. for loss of rent of one house there formerly in the tenure of Katherine Hugate, because (it was) in the lord's hand this year for the sake of repair.

And 8d. for loss of rent of one house in Church Lane in the tenure of Henry Littester, which used to return 14s. and now returns only 13s.4d. a year.

[43] And 9s. for loss of rent of one house in Ousegate formerly in the tenure of Henry Sutton, because (it was) in the lord's hand this year for the sake of repair.

[44] And 6s. for loss of rent of one house there formerly in the tenure of Thomas Difford, because (it was) in the lord's hand this year for Pentecost term for want of a tenant.

[44] And 2s.8d. for loss of rent of one house there in the tenure of John Grewe, which used to return 16s. and now returns only 13s.4d. a year, leased for this to the same person for a term of 60 years by indenture, this year being the seventh.

---

[42] This appears to have been originally a hamlet between Selby and Over or Upper Selby (see G. S. Haslop, 'A Selby Kitchener's Roll', p. 123).

[43] *b* written above the line at this point. The reason is unclear.

[44] *a* written above the line, as above.

And 6s. for loss of rent of one assart called *Whetecroft*, which used to return 16s. and now returns only 10s. a year.

And 12d. for loss of rent of one assart called *Aviceridding*, which used to return 16s. and now returns only 15s. a year, leased for this to Richard Freman by indenture for a term of 15 years, this year being the fourth.

And 12d. for loss of rent of one house in Brayton in the tenure of Thomas Thomasson, which used to return 4s. and now returns only 3s. a year, leased for this to the same Thomas by (entry on) the court rolls.

And 10d. for loss of rent of one acre of land in *Claypitridding* formerly in the tenure of Richard Clook, because (it was) in the lord's hand for want of a farmer (*conduct'*).

And 1½d. from the rent of one selion and one rood of land called *AshWelrode* at Lund, because distraint could not be found therefrom.

And 2d. from the rent of half an acre of land in the open field (*campo*) of Gateforth formerly in the tenure of James Whitlay, for the same reason.

And 2d. for the decrease in rent of one bovate of land in the open field of Burton in the tenure of William Burdeux, because it used to return 12d. and now it returns only 10d.

And 2d. for the decrease in rent of one bovate of land in the said open field in the tenure of the said William, because it used to return 10d. and now it returns only 8d. a year.

And 1d. for the decrease in rent of one garden in Brayton called *Lyndesay garth*, of one selion and one butt[45] there in the tenure of Thomas Smyth, because it used to return 14d. and now it returns only 13d. a year.

And 4d. for the decrease in rent of one acre of land in *Marschall ridding* near the gates of Stainer in the tenure of Thomas Esyngwalde, which (used?)[46] to return 18d. and now returns only 14d. a year.

And 13d. for the decrease in rent of 5 acres of meadow in the parks of Barlow this year.

And 2s.6d. for loss of rent of one marsh in the marshes of Snaith formerly in the tenure of Alexander Hayne, because (it was) in the lord's hand for want of a farmer.

And 13s.4d. for the small tithes (*minutis decimis*) at Adlingfleet this year.

---

[45] ''Butt' and 'selion' are used interchangeably, and the former also has the meaning of 'a small piece of ground disjointed in whatever manner from the adjacent lands.' (*OED*)

And 2s. for the decrease in rent of one house in Micklegate in the tenure of Peter Bynglay, because it used to return 16s. and now it returns only 14s. a year.

And 23s.6d. for loss of rent of the mills at Monk Fryston for the terms (ending at the festivals) of the Purification (2 February), the Finding of the Holy Cross (3 May), St Peter Advincula (1 August), and the feast of All Saints (1 November), within the period of the account.

And to this accountant himself for his diligence in the said office this year by courtesy 13s.4d.

And for paper and parchment purchased for the writing of the items of this account 4d.

Total £6 9s.1½d.

Total of all payments, liveries, and allowances £81 13s.0d. (and) half a farthing.

And thus the accountant exceeds (income by) £6 2s.1d. (and) half a farthing.

(Whereof there is due from?)[47]

Thomas Metham for the free rent of his tenements in Pollington this year 5s.[48]

Thomas Wentworth for the free rent of his tenements in Pollington this year 5s.[49]

From the rent of the tenement of Tristan Stalworth in Selby this year 3s.6d.

Robert Dilcok for the rent of one bovate of land in the open field of Snaith near *Bowerflatt* this year 6d.

Total 14s.

These (sums) being due and not yet levied, the accountant exceeds (receipts by) £6 16s.1d. (and) half a farthing.

---

[47] Some words are illegible at this point, but the phrase is surmised to be *Unde pendent super*.
[48] In the account of the pittancer for 1403–04 Sir Thomas de Metham also appears to have owed rent for these tenements (see above, p. 100).
[49] In the account of the pittancer for 1403–04 one William de Wintworth appears to have owed rent for these tenements (see above, p. 100).
[46] There is a small hole in the manuscript at this point, and a word lost.

(b) The office of Extern Cellarer

The function of the extern cellarer was to purchase livestock to supply the community's needs for meat, principally through the kitchener. That at least is clear from the few surviving documents of this office. However, only five extern cellarer's accounts have certainly survived, and of these three have come down to us complete, separated in time by more than seventy years.[1] There is no certain evidence from these that the office was ever assigned a fixed income from the abbey's resources. Like the chamberlain's the office seems to have ultimately disappeared after frequently being held in conjunction with another obedience, most often the bursar's, but also at times the chamberlain's, abbot's chaplain's, and even the abbacy itself.[2] When a list of Selby monk-officials and their revenues was compiled shortly before the Dissolution, no mention of the extern cellarer was made.[3]

The account translated here has been included because, being compiled in the abbacy of William Pygot (1408–29), it falls within the period of time on which this study of Selby Abbey seeks to concentrate. It is also virtually undamaged, and illustrates well enough the particular form of such accounts, with their division into two sections recording respectively receipts and expenditures of money, and the movement of stock in and out of the office. Compared with other cellarer's records, however, it has some peculiar features that need discussion.

In the first place the account has survived as part of a composite bundle of obedientiary rolls for the year 1413–14, sewn together at the head,[4] which as a whole suggests that the house had embarked on short-term or experimental measures of financial reorganization, presumably in response to the financial difficulties that caused the abbey to seek royal aid in 1410.[5]

---

[1] The five accounts are dated 1411–12 (printed in YAS, Miscellanea VI, RS 118, 1953, pp. 38–41), 1413–14 (HUL, DDLO 20/54c), 1479–80 (HUL, DDLO 20/56), 1489–90 (HUL, DDLO 20/49), and 1492–93 (WDA, Se/Ac/20). The three complete rolls are those for 1413–14, 1479–80 and 1489–90.

[2] Chamberlain and cellarer 1355 (British Library, Cotton Vit. E.XVI, f.147v); bursar and cellarer 1386–87, 1396–97, 1398–99, 1436, 1478– 79, and 1479–80 (Lincolnshire Archives, Crowle Manor 1/39 and 47; WDA, Se/Ac/5; HUL, DDLO 20/56; R.B.Dobson, 'The Election of John Ousthorp', p.38); abbot's chaplain and extern cellarer 1413–14 (HUL, DDLO 20/54c and g); abbot and extern cellarer 1489–90 and 1491–92 (HUL, DDLO 20/49; WDA, Se/Ac/20).

[3] HUL, DDLO 20/60 and *Valor Ecclesiasticus*, V, 1825, pp. 12–14.

[4] The account owes its good preservation to its inside position in the bundle, which also contains the accounts of the fabric keeper, the receiver of certain revenues belonging to the bursary assigned to pensions and fees, the kitchener, the granger, the bailiffs of Stanford on Avon, *Stormesworth*, *Doune*, and Queniborough, and the chaplain and procurator of the abbot's household. Each of the accounts is written on a separate membrane of parchment, the whole being tied together at the head.

[5] The abbot and convent complained of corrodies and yearly payments of £200 p.a. and debts

These measures involved diversion of the revenues and alteration of the responsibilities of various obedientiaries, possibly including the cellarer. Thus the receipts recorded in this account are half those recorded in a similar account for 1411–12, and less than half those in later fifteenth century rolls.[6] Similarly, stock purchased and delivered to the kitchener by the accountant of 1413–14 is tiny in number by comparison with other complete accounts, those of 1479–80 and 1489–90, and restricted in type to bullocks and sheep where the later accounts include pigs.[7]

The kitchener's account of 1416–17 suggests that the restricted responsibilities of the extern cellarer in 1413–14 persisted for at least a few years. The number of cattle listed as received from the extern cellarer in this account is a minute proportion of the total consumption of the community that year and easily exceeded by the number purchased or received directly from the serjeants of the Selby manors.[8] The conclusion seems to follow that in these years of Pygot's abbacy the cellarer had only a limited roll in supplying beasts to the kitchen, though at other times his responsibilities could be expanded to cover virtually the whole of the abbey's needs for victuals of this kind.

The monk responsible for compiling the account which follows was Brother John Crossethwayt, whose career at Selby Abbey seems to have been relatively short but notably active in administration. He entered the house about 1399 and became a priest in the next year.[9] As well as being extern cellarer in 1413–14 he was also abbot's chaplain, an office that he had also held in 1412–13.[10] He was kitchener 1411–12 and 1414–15, and extern cellarer again 1416–17.[11] Whilst his duties as extern cellarer may not themselves have been extensive, he is found in his account for 1413–14 actively involved with the abbey estates, holding views and making new rentals for several manors, a task that may also have been part of the

---

of £1040, and secured royal protection and a licence for the abbot to stay and teach within the university of Oxford or Cambridge for 3–4 years in order to reduce costs. *CPR, 1408–13*, p. 244.

[6] Total receipts were £64 7s.5d. in 1411–12 (YAS, RS 118, 1953, p. 40); £79 9s.9d. in 1479–80 (HUL, DDLO 20/56); £89 2s.11d. in 1489–90 (HUL, DDLO 20/49); and £98 13s.1d. in 1492–93 (WDA, Se/Ac/20).

[7] In 1413–14 he delivered to the kitchener 20 bullocks and 69 sheep. This compares with 23 oxen, 106 bullocks, bulls, and cows, 500 sheep, and 38¼ pigs, delivered to the kitchener by the cellarer of 1479–80 (HUL, DDLO 20/56); and 24 oxen, 85 bullocks etc., 765 sheep, and 59½ pigs delivered by the cellarer of 1489–90 (HUL, DDLO 20/49).

[8] The kitchener's roll for 1416–17 (WDA, Se/Ac/10) is translated in full below. He appears to have received only 10 bulls and oxen and 13 cows from the extern cellarer in a year when he accounted for 21 oxen, 51 cows, 25 bullocks and heifers, 21 calves, 86 pigs, 37 piglets, 396 sheep, and 66 lambs.

[9] Borthwick Institute of Historical Research, Archbishop's Register 16, Richard le Scrope, fos 283 and 285v.

[10] HUL, DDLO 20/54g.

[11] HUL, DDX 145/1 and DDLO 20/54c; WDA, Se/Ac/10.

abbey's efforts to restore its financial position in the years after its 1410 petition to the crown. Similarly, a bursar's account for 1416–17 shows Brother John Crossethwayt involved in repairs to buildings on the abbey estates and in discussions about disputed rents at Carlton near Lincoln; whilst the kitchener's account for the same year indicates his involvement with the Selby court.[12] So far as we can tell, however, his career at Selby must have come to an end about this time, for his name has not been found in the records of the abbey after 1417.

[12] WDA, Se/Ac/9 and 10. See below, p. 183.

The Extern Cellarer's account of 1413–1414
Table of Contents

The account of Brother John Crossethwayt, extern cellarer of the monastery of Selby, from the morrow (of the festival) of St Michael the Archangel (30 September) A.D. 1413 to the same festival of Michael (29 September) A.D. 1414 for one whole year.

Arrears
(*Arreragia*)

No arrears (from the previous account) are held because (this is) his first year as accountant.

Total nothing.

Receipts (*Receptum*)

Redbourne

Firstly the same person answers for £4 received from 20 quarters of barley from Redbourne, sold for this (*sic venditis*) to John Haynson and Emma Turnour this year, at (*prout dat'*) 4s. a quarter.

Total £4.

Crowle

And for £6 13s.4d.[13] received from 42 quarters of dredge from Crowle, sold for this to John Byrne this year, at 3s.4d. a quarter.

And for 40s.[14] from customary services remitted to the tenants there this year, paid by (*per manus*) William Swalowe.[15]

Total £8 13s.4d.

Whitgift

And for £7 received from Robert West, farmer of the tithes there leased to him at farm by indenture, for the terms of Candlemas (2 February) and St Peter Advincula (1 August).

And for £4 received from 26 stones of tithe wool there this year, sold for this to Robert Courtenay.[16]

And for 53s.4d. for the tithes of *Estmorefeld* in the tenure of William Stansfeld this year he does not answer, because Brother John Milyngton,[17] chamberlain of the monastery, will be answerable for it.

Total £11.

---

[13] The price received should be £7 and not £6 13s.4d.
[14] *xxx* crossed out and *xl* written above.
[15] Serjeant of Crowle. See p. 127.
[16] One Robert Courtenay was paid a wage of 16s. p.a. as baker and brewster of the abbey in a granger's account of this year. See HUL, DDLO 20/54e, *Stipendia Famulorum*.
[17] For Brother John Milyngton see above p. 94.

Reedness
: And for 24s. received from 8 quarters of dredge-malt (*brasii drageti*) by the razed measure, sold for this to *dominus* John Oliff[18] this year, at 3s. a quarter.

Total 24s.

Hook
: And for 44s. received from tithe beans and peas of Hook, sold for this collectively to John Sparke this year.

Total 44s.

Lowne
: And for £6 6s.8d. received from John Arnald, farmer [19] this year of the tithes of *Riddyngate*, for the terms of the Purification (2 February) and St Peter Advincula (1 August).

Total £6 6s.8d.

Foreign receipts (*Forinsecum Receptum*)
: And for 12d. received from the profit of pasture within the abbey belonging to the office of Brother Thomas Bolton,[20] kitchener of the monastery this year.

Total 12d.

Sum total of receipts £33 9s.

Purchase of stock (*Emptio Instauri*)
: From which the same person accounts for 70 sheep purchased by *dominus* John Oliff, chaplain, at 18d. a head 105s.

And for 3 bullocks purchased from Richard Marshall for fattening towards the festival of Easter (8 April) 36s.

And for 12 bullocks purchased at Pontefract by *dominus* John Oliff, at a price of 12s.8d. a head £7 13s.[21]

---

[18] A chaplain (hence the title *dominus*) who was serving the abbey this year and in previous years as serjeant at Reedness and Rawcliffe. He was later rector of Stanford-on-Avon, a living in the abbey's patronage. See HUL, DDLO 20/54e; WDA, Se/Ac/9 and 10; and YAS, Record Series 118, 1953, p. 39.

[19] *grangie ibidem* crossed out. A John Arnald appears as the purchaser of tithes at Whitgift in 1397–98 (HUL, DDLO 20/65, Proctor's Account).

[20] A novice in the house in 1404, Brother Thomas Bolton was ordained priest in 1406. He was serving as keeper of the guest house as well as kitchener this year, and was abbot's chaplain 1416–17. There are several references in the kitchener's account for 1416–17 that suggest Brother Thomas' involvement in hunting. See Borthwick Institute of Historical Research, Archbishop's Register 16, Richard le Scrope, f.310, and 5A, *Sede Vacante* 1405–07, f.100v; WDA, Se/Ac/8 and 9; and below, p. 183.

[21] The total should be £7 12s. and not £7 13s.

And for 24 bullocks purchased by the same person at Doncaster, at a price of 11s.1d. a head £13 6s.

And for 12 bullocks purchased there by the same person, at a price of 12s.9¼d. a head £7 7s.8d.[22]

Total £35 7s.8d.

Cost of ditches (*Custus fossatorum*)	And for the service of 4 men working and cleaning out (the channel) in *le Gote*[23] at Roscarrs and from there to *le Thistelcroft*, and for sinking a ditch from the arable land of Roscarrs through the middle of the meadows to *Roukerbuskes* for 20 days, each receiving 4d. a day without food (being provided) 26s.8d.

Total 26s.8d.

Tithe-barn of Snaith (*Snayth Grangia decimalis*)	And for repairs done at the tithe-barn of Snaith by the labour (*per manus*) of William Pulterer and his companions this year 2s.6d.

Total 2s.6d.

Tithe-barn of Heck (*Hek grangia decimalis*)	And for repairs done around the tithe-barn of Heck by the labour of John Went this year 5s.

Total 5s.

Manors of Rawcliffe and Adlingfleet (*Rouclif et Athelingflet maneria*)	And for 12 hurdles (*flectis*) purchased for the manor of Rawcliffe this year 4s.

And for 6 hurdles purchased for the manor of Adlingfleet this year 3s.

Total 7s.

Small expenses (*Minute*)	And for 5 gallons of red wine purchased for the sake of William Ludyngton, Thomas Egmanton, Thomas Sheffeld, Robert Sheffeld, Robert Lyolf and others at Crowle for a certain session concerning the Mere Dyke (*le Maredyke*)[24] 4s.2d.

---

[22] The total should be £7 13s.3d. and not £7 7s.8d.
[23] A Northern dialect word meaning a watercourse or sluice. (*OED*)
[24] William Lodyngton, Thomas Egmanton, and Thomas Sheffeld were appointed to a royal commission for walls and dykes (*de walliis et fossatis*) in Crowle and elsewhere in June 1413

And for salted fish, salmon, and other payments made at Crowle for the sake of Thomas Burnham, William Waldby,[25] and others in the second week of Lent[26] 3s.4d.

And for 2 gallons of red wine purchased for the sake of the same persons 16d.

And for 4 gallons of wine purchased for the sake of Thomas Burnham, Thomas Egmanton, William Waldby, and others at Garthorpe for holding a session of this kind there concerning the Mere Dyke at the same time 3s.4d.

And for gloves, knives, and other things purchased and given to various persons 13s.4d.

And for the expenses of Brother John Crossethwayt,[27] *dominus* John Olif, and others with them for holding a view in the manors within Marshland (*Mershland*) and the soke of Crowle on 7 occasions this year, with the money given to various workmen there 20s.

And for 8 ells of cloth of lake (*de lake*) purchased for one tablecloth, 2 long towels and 2 short towels for the manor-house of Crowle, at 8d. an ell, with the stitching together of the same 5s.7d.

And for the expenses of William Pekton[28] (going) to the soke of Crowle and other places on business of the monastery this year 8s.

And for the expenses of William Carter[29] (going) to the soke of Crowle and Stallingborough on various occasions on business of the monastery this year 3s.

And for 12 skins of parchment purchased for writing the account rolls of the serjeants (*servientium*) and other records (*munimentis*) with this year 4s.

(*CPR*, 1413–16, p.37). William Ludyngton and Thomas Egmanton, the latter steward of Rawcliffe and Stallingborough, both received fees from Selby Abbey in this year; whilst Robert Sheffeld was later the recipient of a Selby fee (1431–32). See HUL, DDLO 20/1 and 20/54b, *Pensiones et Feoda*. For commissions of this kind and their work in inquiring about defects in river embankments, dykes, gutters and sewers, and fixing responsibility for repair, see *Public Works in Mediaeval Law*, ed. C.T.Flower, 2 vols, Selden Society, vols 32 and 40, 1915 and 1923. There are pleas involving the abbot of Selby to be found in II, vol.40, 1923, pp.239 (1348), 252 (c.1348), 255 (1375 and 1392) and 295 (1362).
[25] Thomas Burnham was appointed to the same commission in 1413 (*CPR*, 1413–16, p.37). He was steward of Crowle, whilst William de Waldby was attorney of the abbey in King's Bench, both receiving fees. See HUL, DDLO 20/54b, *Pensiones et Feoda*.
[26] Lent in 1414 began on 21 February.
[27] i.e. the accountant himself.
[28] William Pekton's wife received a pension of 40s. p.a. from the abbey this year. He is described in later accounts as the servant in the guest house. See HUL, DDLO 20/54b, *Pensiones et Feoda*; and WDA, Se/Ac/8c, 1421–22.
[29] He is described later in this section as page (*paiettus*) of the abbot's chaplain (see p.124).

And for 4 quires of paper purchased for writing rentals and other things with this year 2s.

And for the expenses of Brother John Crossethwayt, John Byrne,[30] and others with them for three weeks for making the rentals of Crowle, Luddington, Garthorpe, and Amcotts,...[31] for the expenses of John de Byrne, Stephen Yong,[32] and others at Crowle for 15 days for the aforesaid reason 60s.

And for the gift to the serjeant at Crowle taking care of the lord's animals within the manor there 12d.

And for the expenses of the aforesaid Brother John Crossethwayt, Stephen Yong, and others at Rawcliffe for making a rental there 13s.4d.

And for the gift to the serjeant of the manor at Monk Fryston this year 12d.

And to the serjeant of the manor at Stainer this year 12d.

And for one lined tunic (*tunica duplicata*) purchased for William Carter, page of the chaplain this year 3s.

And for one gown purchased for the same person 2s.

And for 6 pairs of shoes purchased for the same person 3s.

And for 4 ells of cloth of burnet purchased for making one cape for the said accountant 13s.4d.

And for one pair of boots purchased and given to *dominus* John Olif this year 4s.

And for one pair of boots purchased and given to Thomas 'from the stable' (*de stabulo*) 2s.6d.

Total £8 12s.3d.

Payments of cash (*Liberatio denariorum*)
And for the payment to John Duffeld, serjeant at Eastoft this year, 23s.4d.

And for the payment to John Wright, serjeant at Adlingfleet this year, 20s.

Total 43s.4d.

---

[30] Described as the clerk of the extern cellarer and bursar in 1402, he was the recipient of a fee of 66s.8d. from the abbey this year, the same fee that he had received in 1398–99. See British Library, Cotton Vit. E.XVI, f.140; HUL, DDLO 20/54b, *Pensiones et Feoda*; and above, p. 56.

[31] A word is illegible at this point.

[32] By 1416–17 he was receiving an annual fee of 26s.8d. from the abbey. See WDA, Se/Ac/9, *Feoda*.

Total of all expenses and payments £48 4s.5d.[33] And he exceeds (receipts by) £14 15s.5d.[33] And there is allowed to the same person £10 0s.2d., namely for (*ut in*) various repairs done in the manors this year as (appears by?)[34] the following details.[35] And thus he exceeds (receipts by) £24 15s.7d. now, which are owed to various creditors as appears.[36]

New chamber and chapel at Rawcliffe[37] (*Nova Camera et Capella apud Rouclif*)

And for the wage of John Undirwod shaping into posts and lopping 7 wagon-loads of timber in the *Westhag* of Hambleton for repair of the manor-house of Rawcliffe this year 16d.

And for transport of the said timber from the *Westhag* to the bank of the Ouse 4s.1d.

And for loading and unloading of the ship with the said timber 18d.

And for the expenses of Stephen Whyte at Hambleton and Selby to expedite the said work 3s.4d.

And for the gift to the workmen there for drink by courtesy 12d.

And for the service of Stephen Whyte working around the new chamber at Rawcliffe for 24 days before Christmas, receiving 4d. a day without food (being provided) 8s.

And for the service of the same person working there on the chapel in the manor-house between the festivals of Christmas and Pentecost (27 May) for 82 days, receiving 5d. a day without food (being provided) 34s.2d.

And for sawing the timber for the said work, collectively 14s.

And for 6 boards of sawn wainscot (*Waynscot*) purchased for the same work 3s.

And for 15 boards of wainscot purchased for making the doors and windows there (this year?)[38] 5s.4d.

And for large (spike-nails and?)[38] medium spike-nails (*mediis spyk-yng*) purchased for the said work 4s.

---

[33] These sums are also written in the margin of the manuscript.

[34] Two words virtually illegible at this point due to a stain.

[35] An extra piece of parchment has been stitched on to the main account at this point, which contains the required details of expenditure on repairs.

[36] Where the list of creditors is to be found is not specified, and it does not appear in the manuscript.

[37] Rawcliffe is on the River Aire some 11 kilometres south-east of Selby as the crow flies, but somewhat further by the winding river-route down the Ouse. It was evidently a place of recreation for the abbots of Selby earlier in the 14th century (see G. S. Haslop, 'The Abbot of Selby's Financial Statement for the year ending Michaelmas 1338', p. 161).

[38] The manuscript is stained and some words illegible.

And for 3,600 wall-tiles (*wallteghell*)[39] purchased from John Haynson for the said work ...[40]

And for 2 boat-loads of plaster purchased from John Addy at Crowle 20s.

And for transport of the same by water from Crowle to Rawcliffe 10s.

And for the gift to the workmen there for drink on various occasions 12d.

Total £6 8s. ...d.[41]

| New stable there (*Novum stabulum ibidem*) | And for the service of Stephen Whyte taking down the lord's old stable at Thorpe Willoughby[42] for 6 days 2s.6d. |

And for the transport of timber, thatch (*Damthak*), and stones by water from Selby to Rawcliffe on 2 occasions 3s.

And for loading and unloading the ship 18d.

And for the service of Stephen Whyte rebuilding the said stable at Rawcliffe for 6 weeks about the festival of Michaelmas (29 September), receiving 3s. a week 18s.

And for 360 stowers (*stovres*) purchased from Thomas Dilcok by the aforesaid Stephen 7s.6d.

And for carting of the same from Snaith to Rawcliffe 14d.

And for 10 beams purchased from the same Thomas Dilcok 2s.

And for 60 stowers purchased from Robert Courtnay 18d.

And for 240 spike-nails (*spikyng*), 3600 stowering-nails (*stovryng-nayll*) purchased 7s.

And for the service of the same Stephen making from timber the screen (*clausuram*) between the chamber and the kitchen at Rawcliffe, and making hedges and fences for 16 days and a half, receiving 6d. a day 8s.3d.

And for the sawing of the timber there for the said work 4s.
Total (56s.?)...[43]

More on the dorse[44]

---

[39] The long hundred of 120 is in use in this account, so that *iii m*[1] is translated 3600.

[40] The total is illegible in the manuscript.

[41] The pence total is illegible in the manuscript.

[42] Where the abbot of Selby also had a manor-house (see W. P. Baildon, *Notes on the Religious and Secular Houses of Yorkshire*, vol. I, YAS, RS 17, 1895, p. 201; and WDA, Se/Ac/9, *Custus Feni*).

[43] The manuscript is worn and creased, and the total illegible. The total should be £2 16s.5d.

[44] The account continues on the other side of the parchment at this point.

| The palisade with other things at Rawcliffe (*Palicium cum aliis apud Rouclif*) | And for the service of Stephen Whyte working and making a door between the kitchen and the stable of the lord abbot there, and making a palisade for 2 weeks and 2 days, receiving 2s.6d. a week 5s.10d. |

And for the service of the same person (working?)[45] on the palisade there in various places for 2 weeks 5s.

And for spike-nails purchased for the said work 3s.4d.

And for the service of the same Stephen repairing a postern-gate (*posticium*) at *Nesse* this year 10d.

Total 15s.[46]

Stock account of the extern cellarer for the time of the account as above (*ut infra*)

| Beans and peas (*Fabe et Pise*) | The same person answers for beans and peas coming from tithes of Hook. |

Total ( ) And they were sold as above. And quit (*eque*).

| Barley (*Ordium*) | And for 20 quarters of barley received from Robert Swylyngton, farmer of the rectory of Redbourne[47] this year. |

Total 20 quarters. And they were sold as above. And quit (*eque*).

| Dredge (*Dragetum*) | And for 42 quarters of dredge received from William Swalowe, serjeant at Crowle this year. |

Total 42. And they were sold as above. And quit (*eque*).

| Malt (*Brasium*) | And for 8 quarters of dredge-malt (*brasii drageti*) received from dominus John Oliff, serjeant at Reedness this year. |

Total 8 quarters. And they were sold as above. And quit (*eque*).

| Bullocks (*Boves*) | And for 3 bullocks purchased for fattening against the festival of Easter (8 April) this year. |

And for 12 bullocks purchased at Pontefract this year.

---

[45] The manuscript is worn and illegible at this point.
[46] At this point the added section giving details of the repairs for which the accountant received allowance finishes, and the account resumes its normal form with the stock account.
[47] The rectory, and its revenues, had long been appropriated to the abbey. See *The Coucher Book of Selby*, I, p. 347.

And for 24 bullocks purchased at Doncaster this year.

And for 12 bullocks purchased there by *dominus* John Oliff this year.

Total 51 bullocks.

From which he accounts for delivery to Brother Thomas Bolton, kitchener of the monastery this year, of 20.

And for the death (*morina*) of 1 and it was flayed.

Total 21. And 30 bullocks remain, for which the same accountant will be answerable next year in the office of kitchener.[48]

Sheep (*Multones*)	And for 70 sheep by purchase this year, as appears above.

Total 70.

From which he accounts for the delivery to Brother Thomas Bolton, kitchener of the monastery this year, of 69.

Total 69. And there remains 1 sheep, for which the same accountant will be answerable next year in the office of kitchener.[48]

Wool (*Lana*)	And for 26 stones of wool coming from parochial tithes of Whitgift this year.

Total 26 stones. And they were sold as above. And quit (*eque*).

Hide (*Corrium*)	And for the hide coming from one dead bullock (*de uno bove in morina*) as above this year.

Total 1. And there remains 1 bullock hide in the keeping of John Wright, serjeant at Adlingfleet, for which the same person will be answerable.

---

[48] Marginal note: 'Crossethwayt will answer as kitchener next year' (*r' Crosseth' Coquinar' in anno sequent'*).

(c) The office of Granger

After the extern cellarer it is logical to pass to the granger, for the sole purpose of both offices was to supply particular commodities of food to the monastic community, and with the kitchener they formed the trio of obedientiaries at Selby charged with victualling the abbey. The granger's responsibility was grain supplies, from which in particular the community's bread was baked and its ale brewed. Both bakery and brewery were part of his charge, with their staff receiving their wages from him. Virtually all the grain utilized within the monastery seems to have been channelled through his office, which also was generally responsible for distributing it to the appropriate quarters.[1] The stock account[2] which follows records the large quantities of grain consumed at Selby and the organization of supplies from its manors and other resources necessary to meet its needs. In order to satisfy the demands of a considerable community, the granger drew on a wide area reaching some 70 km to Stallingborough in Lincolnshire.

Bread and ale were staple items in the medieval diet, of course; and the figures for consumption of grain in baking and brewing are an indicator of the size of the establishment maintained at Selby. Whilst pittancers' rolls reveal the number of monks at any one time in the community, no one type of obedientiary account will provide a similarly complete and reliable guide to the number of servants, corrodarians, and guests maintained by the abbey.[3] However, the granger's rolls do provide data for estimating the total size of the community in particular years, if grain used in baking and brewing is converted into quantities of bread and ale and an average is set for individual levels of consumption. In his estimate of the size of the household at another northern religious house, Bolton Priory, I. Kershaw has suggested that for each person over the whole community an average allowance of one 2½ lb. loaf and one gallon of ale per day is reasonable; that one 2½ lb. loaf a day is equivalent to about 2½ quarters of corn in a year; and that a quarter of malt yields about 60 gallons of ale.[4] When these

---

[1] The kitchener's account for 1416–17 translated below does, however, show that official acting as an intermediate step between the granger and abbey servants, receiving grain from the former and accounting for its supply to the bakery and brewery. See below, pp. 178–179 (WDA, Se/Ac/10).

[2] Like the extern cellarer's and the kitchener's rolls translated here the granger's roll is comprised of two sections, a money account and a stock account. The latter records mainly the movement of grain in and out of the office.

[3] G. S. Haslop has suggested 50–60 servants, 10 corrodarians, and an indeterminable number of guests at Selby in the early 15th century, making a total community of 100 persons exclusive of casual workmen (G. S. Haslop, 'A Selby Kitchener's Roll of the Early Fifteenth Century', p. 122).

[4] I. Kershaw, *Bolton Priory: the economy of a northern monastery, 1286–1325*, OUP, 1973, pp. 132–133. A major problem, of course, is the distortion caused by short-term incomers,

figures are applied to the Selby granger's grain accounts, they produce an estimate of a total community in 1413–14 of rather more than 100 persons[5] which had changed very little sixty years later in 1474–75.[6]

Despite the many limitations of such calculations, it would be of value to the historian of Selby Abbey to have a good run of figures for grain consumption over a period of years. In fact, however, only five granger's accounts have survived and these are widely spaced, the earliest being 1349–50 and the latest 1500–01.[7] It appears that during the 40 years following this last account the granger's office was absorbed into the bursary, for it makes no appearance in the survey of Selby obediences made just prior to the Dissolution, and it is clear from this latter document that revenues previously assigned to the office were now paid to the bursar.[8]

The Granger's roll translated here covers the accounting period from Michaelmas 1404 to Michaelmas 1405, and is in excellent condition virtually throughout. It is the only account of its type surviving from the abbacy of John de Shirburn (1369–1408). Just six years separate this account from the bursars' roll of 1398–99 included above and its accountant, Brother Peter de Rouclif, also served as one of the two bursars of the earlier roll. The known facts of Brother Peter's career have already been outlined above and will not be repeated here;[9] but this present record does indicate in him a penchant for detail and self-justification that take his account briefly beyond the usual formal accounting style. In his efforts to justify large over-expenditure by his office, Brother Peter incidentally sheds a little light on the financial administration at Selby Abbey in these years that resulted by 1410 in alleged debts of £1040.[10] And whatever the prudence of his activities, his outlays cannot be characterized here as waste and maladministration.

---

such as workmen and guests, whose incidence cannot be calculated. The calculations here suggest a stability of numbers in the community that may well not have existed in reality.
[5] In 1413–14 283½ quarters of grain were baked into bread and 714 quarters of malt used for ale. At 2½ quarters of grain per person for the year, this produces a figure of 113. 714 quarters of malt would yield 42,840 gallons of ale; and at 1 gallon per person each day that produces a community of 117 persons. HUL, DDLO 20/54e.
[6] The granger's roll for 1474–75 provides no figures for malt brewed into ale, but shows 280 quarters baked into bread. Divided by 2.5 this gives the figure 112 persons. HUL, DDLO 20/46. Apart from the granger's roll of 1404–05 translated here, the kitchener's roll for 1416–17 below will also provide the required figures for this type of calculation.
[7] HUL, DDLO 20/43 and 47. The other three are for 1404–05, 1413–14, and 1474–75 (HUL, DDLO 20/44, 46, and 54e). In 1349–50 the quantity of grain delivered to the baker for bread appears to have been 475 quarters, but the manuscript is faded and difficult to read at this point.
[8] HUL, DDLO 20/60.
[9] See above, pp. 43–44.
[10] See above, p. 43.

The Granger's account of 1404–1405

Table of Contents

The account of Brother Peter de Rouclif, granger of the abbey of Selby, from the festival of St Michael (29 September) A.D. 1404 to the morrow of the said festival A.D. 1405.

Arrears (*Arreragia*)	No arrears are held (from the previous account) because (the expenditure and allowances of) this same accountant in his last account exceeded income.

Fixed rent (and?)[11] farms with profits of the court (*Redditus assisus ... Firme cum perquisitis Curie*)	The same person answers for 64s. from the fixed rent of the tenants of 8 bovates of land in Over Selby[12] yearly.

And for 6s.8d. yearly from the farm of one toft in *Midilthorp*[13] at (*de*) Selby, which Matilda de Bigging holds.

And for 12d. yearly from the farm of one selion of land lying in *le Longridding*, which Robert Fox holds.

And for 20s. yearly from the farm *del Couperland, Bondeker,* and *LangthWayt kerr*, newly leased to the tenants there.

And for 6s.8d. from the farm of the meadow of *les vyvers* minor (*minoribus*) yearly.

And for 26s.8d. from the farm of Peter Milner for the horse-mill leased to him in the town of Selby yearly.

And for 9s. from the tenants of 6 bovates of land in Hambleton for customary services of carrying wood thence for the use of the office yearly.

And for 10s.8d. from profits of the court of the office this year.[14]

Total £7 4s.8d.

---

[11] The edge of the manuscript is torn away here and *et* is surmised.

[12] Mr Haslop has commented on 'an interesting small manor called Over Selby, the 'ufer Seleby' of c.1030, the Minor Selby of Foundation time and in the fifteenth century referred to as 'alias Bondgate'. Its extents and boundaries are not known but separate courts were held there and the survey preceding enclosures of c.1800 shows all copyhold to be in this area.' *YAJ*, 44, 1972, p.159.

[13] According to Mr Haslop it was originally a hamlet between Selby and Over (Upper) Selby, then on the river bank. *YAJ*, 48, 1976, p.123.

[14] Records of the court of Over Selby for the years 1399–1415 survive. The heading for the first of these courts reads: 'The court of the lord abbot of Selby for his tenants in bondage in Over Selby, held in the office of the granger of the abbey of Selby on Saturday the 7th day of June A.D. 1399.' During this accounting year courts were held on Saturday 18 October 1404, and Tuesday 10 February 1405, and income was derived from fines for non-attendance and for entry to a holding. HUL, DDLO 18/1.

Profit of mills, tithe, etc. (*Proficuum molendinorum decime et cetera*) The same person answers for £11 6s.8d. from the profit of the water-mills at Selby this year, in addition to 75s.7d. for the wages of John Milner and his two men receiving the fourth penny; and no more (is accounted for) because of the smaller price of grains, loss of water in the dam and overflowing of the waters of the Ouse frequently happening in winter time.

And for 107s. from the profit of tithe sheaves at Selby from the fruits of the past year, that is 1 quarter 4 bushels of corn at a price of 5s.6d., 8 quarters of rye at a price of 16s., 15 quarters of barley at a price of 45s., 36 quarters of oats at a price of 54s., less (*unde*) for storage and threshing and winnowing 13s.6d. in addition to the fodder which he used for the monastery's needs.

And for 70s. from 42 quarters of beans sold as below (*ut extra*).

And for 66s.8d. from 5 bullocks sold.

And for 26s.8d. from the sale of the bark of 21 poor (*debilium*) oaks felled in the park of Thorpe Willoughby and 10 oaks felled in the north wood for fuel for the office.

Total £24 17s.

Sum total of receipts £32 1s.8d.

Excess (*Excessus*) From which the same person accounts for the excess of expenditure (over income) in the previous account, as it appears at the foot of the said account £87 1s.3½d.

Total £87 1s.3½d.

Cost of the cart with shoeing of horses (*Custus carette cum Ferrura equorum*) Likewise he accounts for one cart with untired wheels (*cum rotis nudis*) newly purchased 10s.8d.

And for the service of the smith fitting the aforesaid wheels with metal tires and nails of his own 33s.4d.

And for pitch purchased for smearing on the naves (*modiolis*) of the said wheels 3d.

And for the purchase of one horse hide, together with dressing (*dealbatione*) of the same, for repairing the harness of the cart 4s.

And for fitting the cart with axles, with 2 axles purchased for the same, 10d.

And for 18 clouts (*clutis*) purchased for the axles of the cart, with nails purchased for the same 20d.

And for traces and halters purchased 18d.

And for grease purchased for greasing the axles and wheels of the cart 2s.2d.

And for the purchase of 63 horse-shoes, with fitting of the same on the feet of the cart-horses 10s.6d.

And for removing 112 horse-shoes and fitting them again, at ½d. each 4s.8d.

Total 69s.7d.

Airing and Winnowing of grains and malt (*Ventatio et Vannatio bladorum et brasii*)	Likewise he accounts for the service of 2 men spreading (*iactantium*)[15] barley, dredge, and oats before malting (*ante fusionem*) for 15 days without food (being provided) 10s.

And for the service of the man winnowing 772[16] quarters of malt this year, at 1d. for each 20 quarters, in addition to the rye below (*extra*) 3s.2½d.

And for the service of the men helping the servants of the office to carry the grains from the ship to the cart and thence to the granary this year 3s.4d.

Total 16s.6½d.

Wages of servants (*Stipendia Famulorum*)	Likewise he accounts for the wage of John de Bliburgh serving the granger and taking care of and turning (*vertentis*) the corn in the office yearly 20s.

And for the wage of Robert Courtnay, baker and brewer, yearly 16s.

And for the wages of Thomas Rosell, brewer, and John Pin, carter, yearly 26s.8d.

And for the wages of the 2 men in the bakery and the brewery, and of one groom of the brewer, yearly 30s.

And for the wage of one page in the brewery yearly 3s.4d.

And for the service of Henry Milner assisting in making the brews from the festival of St Martin (11 November 1404) to the festival of

---

[15] The activity accounted for here may be the process in traditional malting in which steeped grain is spread on floors after draining in thick heaps to initiate germination. After about 24 hours the grain is spread more thinly to moderate the temperature. See *The New Encyclopaedia Britannica*, 15th edn, Chicago, 1974, vol. 3, s.v. Brewing.

[16] *DCIii*, translated as 772 because the long hundred of 120 is in use in the account.

Pentecost (7 June 1405) because of the infirmity of Thomas Rosell 6s.8d.

And for cloth purchased from the bursars for the livery (*pro vestura*) of the aforesaid John de Bliburgh, Robert Courtnay, Thomas Rosell, (and) John Milner, of John Adcok transporting grains from the manors to the office, and of Robert Brid looking after the turves of the office, of the type (*de secta*) of the servants of the lord abbot 38s.

And for cloth purchased from the same persons for John de Berlay, groom of the extern cellarer, William de Swilyngton, Robert Cloke, grooms in the bakery and brewery, Henry Milner, William Cut and John Pyn, of the type of the grooms of the said lord 25s.

Total £8 5s.8d.

Small expenses (*Minute*)	Likewise he accounts for 2 stones of paris candle purchased for the office this year 2s.8d.

And for cloth purchased for making sieves (*bultellis*) with 2s.

And for 60 ells of sack-cloth purchased 15s.

And for sewing together 19 sacks from it 6d.

And for 26 ells of hair-cloth (*cilicii*) purchased 12s.

And for thread purchased for sewing the same together 3d.

And for one cord purchased for hauling (*tractu*) *del Cath'*[17] 6d.

And for 2 sieves (*cribris*) purchased 9d.

And for victuals purchased for the provisions of the men receiving food (*ad mensam*) in the office within the time of the account 30s.

And for 20 stones of cheese purchased for the same reason, at 6d. a stone 10s.

And for gifts given to various persons during the year 6s.8d.

And for the service of the cooper putting 4 great hoops around the gyle-fat (*le Gilefat*)[18] in the brewery from his own timber 2s.8d.

And for the service of the same person putting 37 hoops on various vessels in the office and store-room, at ¼d. for each 9d.

And for the service of the same person renewing one cask and two scoops (*scopas*) and repairing another cask and felling ash-trees in the garden for making into hoops for 7 days with food (provided) 14d.

And for one empty wine-pipe purchased for the store-room 12d.

Total £4 5s.11d.

---

[17] Possibly the word 'cat', meaning a kind of boat. See J. Wright (ed.), *The English Dialect Dictionary*, London, 1898, s.v. *cat*.
[18] The vat in which the wort is left to ferment in the brewing process. (*OED*)

Purchase of grain with purchase and renewal of stock (*Emptio bladi cum emptione et Restauratione instauri*)

Likewise the same person accounts for 3 quarters of green peas purchased at Owsthorpe (*Ousthorp'*)[19] for the convent's pottage 14s.

And for one black horse purchased for the cart 20s.

And for 26 wagon-loads of hay purchased for the cart-horses and for the horses of the extern cellarer this year, in addition to half a mark from tithe hay of the fields of Newland 66s.8d.

Total 100s.8d.

Repair of buildings (*Emendatio domorum*)

Likewise the same person accounts for the service of John Wright, carpenter, working at his trade (*carpentantis*) and stopping up holes in the malt room for 2 weeks, without food (being provided) 5s.

And for the service of John de Binglay, carpenter, at the same (*ad idem*) and making one door in the bakehouse for 3 weeks without food (being provided) 7s.6d.

And for the service of John Bonde, carpenter, at the same works for 3 weeks without food (being provided) 6s.

And for the service of 2 men sawing boards from aspens for the aforesaid works 8d.

And for various nails purchased for the aforesaid works 5s.2d.

And for the service of Thomas Theker roofing and ridging the office's barn, with the service of his mate, for 2 days and a half with food (provided) 15d.

And for the purchase of 2 cart-loads of lime 5s.4d.

And for the purchase of a stable (*in stabulo empto*) 3s.

And for the service of Peter Geve pointing on the malt-house (*le Malthous*) for 12 weeks, in addition to bread and ale from the store-room 24s.

And for the service of Thomas de Preston, his mate for the said time, without food (being provided) 16s.

Total 73s.11d.

---

[19] In Howdenshire. A possible alternative is Ousethorpe, also in the East Riding of Yorkshire, but this appears to have been usually spelt with a 'U' (i.e. Ullesthorp etc.) until the 16th century. See A. H. Smith, *The Place-Names of the East Riding of Yorkshire and York*, English Place-Name Society Publications 14, CUP, 1937.

Renovation of mills (*Resumptio molendinorum*) Likewise the same person accounts for the service of John Wright searching in the woods and choosing timber for the mills, and renewing one inner wheel (*rotam interiorem*) for the upper mill in the town of Selby, and making mill-spindles (*fusillos*), cogs (*Cogges*), and other necessities for the same for 5 weeks in winter time, receiving 2s.6d. a week without food (being provided) 12s.6d.

And for the service of John Bonde, carpenter, at the same (work) for 9 days without food (being provided) 3s.

And for the service of Richard Fox, apprentice of John Wright, working on the same works for 9 days without food (being provided) 18d.

And for the service of the aforesaid John Wright and John de Binglay, carpenters, working and renovating the trough (*Alveum*) of the mills between the aforesaid mills and the stone bridge there, for emptying the water coming down from the same directly into the main channel (*canellum*), for one week in summer without food (being provided) 6s.

And for the service of John Bond, carpenter, at the same (work) for the said time without food (being provided) 2s.6d.

And for the service of Richard Fox, carpenter, at the same (work) for the said time without food (being provided) 18d.

And for the service of Robert de Bouland transporting clay to the aforesaid work for 2 days without food (being provided) 12d.

And for the service of 12 men working there on stopping up holes in the said work for 1 day without food (being provided) 4s.

And for breaking 4 cart-loads of stones called flagstones (*Flagges*) in Monk Fryston quarry and transporting (them) thence to the aforesaid mills 5s.

And for the service of John del Wod, mason, making one pavement under the bridge there for 1 week 3s.

And for the service of Peter Geve helping there at the aforesaid work, in addition to bread and ale from the store-room during the said time 2s.

And for the service of one man helping the same persons during the said time 18d.

And for one net purchased for catching fish there 6s.2d.

Total 49s.8d.

Renovation of the wharf, pavement, and enclosure (*Resumptio stathe, pavimenti, et inclusi*) — Likewise the same person accounts for the service of 12 men for 1 day digging and throwing earth upon the abbot's wharf and raising the same, without food (being provided) 4s.

> And for the service of Thomas Wake repairing defects in the pavement between the gates of the abbey and the malt-house (*le Malthous*) for 8 days without food (being provided) 3s.4d.

> And for the service of Roger Coke, his mate, during the said time 2s.8d.

> And for 2 cart-loads of stone purchased for the said work 12d.

> And for the service of 2 men cutting down willow wood in *Skaholm* marsh, and transporting the said wood thence by water to the turf-house (*le Turfhous*), and making two fences from it between the said house and the brew-house for 7 days, each receiving 3d. a day without food (being provided) 3s.6d.

> And for the service of the same persons taking up roots, earth, and dust (*pulverem*) near the banks of the ditch there for 2 days, with food (provided) 12d.

> Total 15s.6d.

Cost of turves and fuel (*Custus turbarum et focalis*) — Likewise the same person accounts for transporting by water 28 boat-loads of turves from Rawcliffe to Selby for the use of the office, at 8s. for each £11 4s.

> And for unloading the aforesaid turves from the ship, at 2s.3d. for each (boat-load) granted that they did not receive (*ut non caperent*) 12 full nets of turves to each boat-load for their payments as porters (*pro protagiis suis*) as have been customary before, 63s.

> And for the service of the men transporting the aforesaid turves by water by means of *le Cath*[20] to the turf-house (*le Turfhous*) on the said occasions, at 2d. for each occasion 4s.8d.

> And for the service of the women, as if (there had been) 40 for 1 day, stacking (*tossantium*) the aforesaid turves in the turf-house (*le Turfhous*) with food (provided) 6s.8d.

> And for making 10,800 faggots in the north wood and in the park of Thorpe Willoughby for the use of the office, at 5½d. for every hundred 41s.3d.

---

[20] See above n. 17.

And for the service of one man cutting down 31 poor (*debiles*) oaks in Thorpe Willoughby park and in the north wood, delivered to the office for fuel, by contract 6s.8d.

And for the service of the same person shaping one oaken post there 8d.

And for the service of 2 men lopping and splitting fuel for drying malt from the aforesaid oaks for 37 days, each receiving 4d. a day without food (being provided) 24s.8d.

And for making 1260 pieces of firewood from underwood in various places for the aforesaid office 21d.

And for transporting 66 cart-loads of the said wood from Thorpe Willoughby park to the abbey, at 5d. for each 19s.2d.

And for transporting 27 cart-loads of the said wood from the north wood to the abbey, at 4d. for each 9s.

And for transporting 2400 faggots from the aforesaid wood to the bank of the dam at Thorpe Willoughby 4s.

And for transporting the said faggots by water thence to the abbey 2s.

And for transporting 7200 faggots from the aforesaid wood to the abbey 18s.

Total £21 5s.6d.

Payments of money Likewise the same person accounts for the payment (*Liberationes denarii*) to the pittancer for the fulling-mill of Selby lately moved away (*nuper ammoto*), yearly 10s.

And to the same for the wind-mill called *Langelay*[21]*milne* lately moved away and sold, yearly 10s.

And to the keeper of the guest house for the farm belonging to his office, yearly 12s.

And to this accountant himself for his labour 13s.4d.

Total 45s.4d.

Total of all expenses and payments £139 9s.7d. And thus he exceeds (income by) £107 7s.11d. The which (sum) is charged to the same person in his account as granger for the year next following.

Whereof the causes of such an excess (of expenditure over income are the following): Repairs of houses, mills, and other things useful to the

---

[21] *Langelay* is lost, but was at Brayton (Yorkshire, West Riding). See A.H. Smith, *The Place-Names of the West Riding of Yorkshire*, English Place-Name Society Publications 30–37, CUP, 1961–63, IV, p. 25.

same in preceding accounts £40, in addition to the money received for the sale of the mill of *Langelay*.

Likewise the repair of the western end of the malt-kiln house, the buildings (*domorum*) of the horse-mill, the fuel-house, and the stables in the office, which were all threatened with ruin, £25, in addition to £25 from sale of the stock of the manor of Eastoft, 60s. from the gift of Robert Courtnays, and 20s. from the gift of John Milner of Brayton.[22]

Likewise the repair of the roof of the turf-house (*del Turfhous*) with reeds £4.

More on the dorse[23]

Likewise the renovation of the wharf and the crane (*le Crane*) £13 6s.8d.

Likewise because of the hay purchased for the horses of Brother Peter as extern cellarer now for 4 years past £6. The which (hay) the same person provided whilst he remained in the office of bursar, just as his predecessors as bursar had done, and the present bursar has not done so.

Likewise because of cloths purchased for the livery of the servants of the granger's office this year 63s., where formerly the same Brother Peter whilst he remained in the office of bursar and all his predecessors as bursars had provided (them) for 36 years.

Likewise because the profits of the mills (and) of the tithes of the town of Selby on the northern side of the town in the past and present years have been of smaller value than for the two preceding years, because of the cheaper price of grains and lack of water in the dam in summer time and overflowing of the waters in the Ouse on the eastern side, £29 4s.8d.

Total £120 14s.4d. The which (sums) exceed the abovesaid excess (by) £12 4s.3d.

Likewise where his predecessors as grangers have sold corn and malt for the common reprises of the aforesaid office, this accountant for the 6 years which he has remained in the same office has sold

---

[22] A Robert Courtenay is found in later accounts of the abbey as the purchaser of tithe wool, grain, hay, and timber (see HUL, DDLO 54c, e, and g, 1413–14; WDA, Se/Ac/9, 1416–17); and a Robert de Courtenay of Selby is known from a deed of 1400 (*Yorkshire Deeds*, ed. C. T. Clay, VII, p. 121). In 1416–17 a John Milner was lessee of the mills of Crowle for life and the miller at Selby this year had the same name (see above, p. 133, and WDA, Se/Ac/9, *Nove firme cum molendinis et operibus*). Both names are, however, common and these are not necessarily the same persons as the donors above.

[23] At this point the account continues on the dorse of the manuscript with the statement *In tergo plus*.

nothing, but rather keeps it together (*uniit*) and provides[24] for the needs of the office, as appears by his accounts till now for the 4 years since he retired as bursar (*recessit de Bursuria*).

Likewise where his predecessors have sold boards and timber coming from the oaks delivered to them for fuel, he has not made sales of this kind.

Likewise where his predecessors have had the whole rent and all payments (*oblationes*) belonging to the office of the fabric in the monastery, he has not had such things.

Likewise where his predecessors have had sums of money (*summas*) from the bursar by his own hands whilst he was bursar, for renewing lead vessels and the ovens in the office and for repair of houses and mills, he has had nothing to this end from the bursar.

Likewise note that Brother Peter himself as accountant for 5 years now has bought corn, barley, dredge and oats, and has afterwards sold it through his servants and from the profit taken from the same has spent on common uses and improvements (*ad communes utilitates et honores*) within the monastery and outside at least £50.[25]

| The grain account | The granger | A.D. 1404 |

Wheat (*Frumentum*) The same person answers for 52 quarters 5 bushels of wheat by the razed measure from the remainder (of the previous account).

And for 11 quarters derived from (*de exitude*) 4 skeps (*Skeppes*)[26] for the (rent?)[27] of the tenants of 4 bovates of land in Hillam (held) by the ancient farm this year, and not more because all the remaining bovates (there?)[27] are leased at penny farm (*Penyferm*) making (money) payment to the bursar.

And for 1 quarter 5 bushels from the rent of quarters (of grain) there, namely from the tenants of 6 (acres?)[27] (held) by the ancient farm this year, and not more because all the remaining acres there are leased at penny farm making (money) payment to the (bursar?)[27]. And you must know that the bursar has in money £16 19s.(0½d.?)[27] for 67

---

[24] The words that follow to the end of the sentence are written above to the right and down the right hand margin of the account.
[25] The explanation of the granger's excess ends here, and the account resumes its normal form with the grain account.
[26] i.e. baskets. See *OED*.
[27] The edge of the manuscript is frayed away here and a number of words have been surmised.

quarters of corn leased at penny farm, and thus the rent of corn is in grain and in money[28] just as it was for 80 years past, namely £20 2s.2¼d.

And for 57 quarters from the serjeant of Stallingborough by the razed measure.

And for 9 quarters 4 bushels from the serjeant of Crowle.

And for 14 (quarters?)[29] from the serjeant of Eastoft.

And for 47 quarters from the serjeant of Garthorpe.

And for 42 quarters from the serjeant of Adlingfleet.

And (for?)[29] 55 quarters from the serjeant of Reedness.

And for 15 quarters 6 bushels from the farmer of the tithe-barn of *Loune*.

And for 33 quarters from the tithe-barn of Hook.

And for 31 quarters 4 bushels from the serjeant of Stainer.

And for 42 quarters from the serjeant of Monk Fryston.

Total 412 quarters.

From which he accounts for delivery to the baker for baking into bread (*pro pane inde furniendo*), both for victuals in the abbey household and for the corrodarians' allowance, this year of 316 quarters 6 bushels.

And to the same person for baking into 'pain demaine' (*pane dominico*)[30] for victuals of the lord abbot and visitors (*extraneorum*) with him at (his) table, this year 3 quarters 3 bushels.

And to the same person for the same (bread) for victuals on the jubilee day (*die Jubileo*) of Brother Adam de Crosseby[31] 4 bushels.

And to the kitchener for pastry this year 7 quarters 4½ bushels.

And to the cook of the lord abbot for the same this year 4 quarters 6 bushels.

---

[28] A few words now largely illegible interlined: possibly *hic quarterius ...v...quia minus est quam standardum Regis per 1 busselum...*, an explanation of the size of the quarter here (one bushel smaller than the normal eight).

[29] The edge of the manuscript is frayed and some words are virtually illegible.

[30] Pain-demaine is white bread of the finest quality. (*OED*)

[31] Brother Adam appears in the Pittancer's roll for 1362, at which time he seems to have been a novice (WDA, Se/Ac/2, *Liberationes denarii*); and he was still alive in 1416 (HUL, DDLO 20/15, *Liberatio denarii*). He received a large legacy of 56s.8d in 1408 by the will of William, son of John de Escryk, priest of Selby, (*North Country Wills*, ed. J. W. Clay, pp. 2–5). In 1410 he and Brother Thomas Allerton complained to the Archbishop of York of certain actions against them by other members of the community, which involved in Brother Adam's case forcibly preventing him from attending matins by shutting him in his cell. Brother Thomas seems to have been the real object of attack in the episode (Borthwick Institute of Historical Research, Archbishop's Register 18, Henry Bowet pt 1, fos 274v–275).

And to the sacrist for baking into 'pain demaine' for the convent in Lent in the customary fashion 4 bushels.

And for the multure[32] of 20 quarters at Knottingley this year because of the lack of water in the dam 1 quarter.

And for bread baked for distribution to the poor on Maundy Thursday (16 April) because of the lack of rye 2 quarters 4 bushels.

And for bread baked for victuals in the office this year 7 quarters.

And to the friars of the mendicant orders for charity's sake, by order of the lord abbot 4 quarters.

And for the gift to Henry the painter (*Pictori*) of York, by order of the same lord 1 quarter.

And to William the painter by order of the said lord 4 bushels.

And to Richard de Holdrenesse of Cawood by order of the same lord 1 quarter.

And to Walter Coke of Thorpe Willoughby by order of the said lord 1 quarter.

And to John de Brighton[33] by order of the same lord 4 bushels.

And to Thomas de Munkton[34] by order of the said lord 4 bushels.

And to Alice Coke by order of the same lord 4 bushels.

And to Isabella de Cawod by order of the said lord 4 bushels.

And to Ellen de Dunstan and her sister by order of the same lord 4 bushels.

And to various servants of the monastery and poor persons by order of the said lord 2 quarters.

And to John de Bliburgh for taking care of and spreading (*iactanti*) the wheat in the office this year 4 bushels.

And to the baker and brewer of the office 4 bushels.

And to the two grooms in the brew-house, the two grooms in the malt-house (*le Malthous*), and the carter of the office 5 bushels.

And to the brewer and his 2 grooms and the carter of the office, because of the poor quality (*debilitatis*) of their allowances of rye 1 quarter.

---

[32] i.e. payment for grinding.

[33] In the bursars' account roll for 1398–99 John de Brighton received payment for boots and other things received from him for the abbot's use (see above, p. 66).

[34] The Patent Rolls record a grant of pavage for 5 years for the town of Selby to William Malet, John de Byrne, John Dawncer, Robert de Santon, Thomas Monkton, and John Alas, dated 5 March 1410 (*CPR, 1408–13*, p. 171). Malet, Byrne, and Santon are known from other evidence to have been servants of the abbey.

And to John de Ledsam and William Carter for spreading the grain in the office before malting, as a gratuity (*ad bonitatem*) 2 bushels.

And to 2 servants of the brewer for carrying the wheat into the upper granary, so that they would not refuse the said work 4 bushels.

And for the gift to John Wright[35] by order of the lord abbot 1 quarter.

And to Peter Geve[36] by order of the same person 2 bushels.

And to John de Binglay and John Bond, carpenters working with John Wright, 4 bushels.

And to William Marshall 2 bushels.

And for (loss by) drying up in the granary 2 quarters 4 bushels.

And for chaff thrown out (*in crapinis eiectis*) 1 quarter 4 bushels.

Total 365 quarters 2½ bushels. And there remain 46 quarters 5½ bushels of wheat.

Rye with maslin (*Siligo cum mix- tilione*)   Likewise the same person answers for 2 quarters 4 bushels of maslin by the razed measure received from the serjeant of Reedness.

And for 38 quarters 2 bushels of rye by the razed measure received from the serjeant of Carlton.

Total 40 quarters 6 bushels.

From which he accounts for the excess of consumption (*expensarum*) in the preceding account 4 quarters 6 bushels.

And for the allowances of the 2 brewers, the carter in the office, 1 clerk in the church, 2 workmen in the pool, 1 forester in the north wood, 1 forester of the Haggs (*Hogarum*), (and) 1 forester of Hambleton yearly, each receiving 4 quarters 2 bushels yearly, 38 quarters 2 bushels.

And for the allowance of Henry Milner for assisting with making malt for 30 weeks within the time-span of the account because of the ailments (*infirmitatum*) of Thomas Rosell,[37] 2 quarters 4 bushels.

And to the man winnowing 772 quarters of malt as below this year 6½ bushels.

Total 45 quarters 2½ bushels. And thus he exceeds (his receipts by) 4½ quarters of rye.

---

[35] A carpenter employed on various repairs (see above, pp. 136–137).
[36] Employed on pointing the malt-house (see above p. 136).
[37] Described as 'brewer' above, p. 134, where his wage of 13s.4d. p.a. is accounted for.

Beans and peas
(*Fabe et Pise*)
The same person answers for 1 quarter 6 bushels of beans and peas from the remainder (of the previous account).

And for 25 quarters by the razed measure received from the serjeant of Garthorpe.

And for 21 quarters 4 bushels[38] from the serjeant of Reedness.

And for 22 quarters 4 bushels[38] from the tithe-barn of Hook.

And for 12 quarters from the serjeant of Stainer.

And for 3 quarters of green peas by purchase.

Total 85 quarters 6 bushels.

From which he accounts for delivery to the kitchener for the pottage of those present (*existentium*) at table within the abbey this year of 13 quarters.

And he has delivered to the almoner for common distribution (as alms) 21 quarters.

And to the stable of the lord abbot for the horses' fodder there 5 quarters 6 bushels.

And for sale as above (*ut infra*) 42 quarters.

And given to the buyer for heaped measures (*pro cantellis*) 2 quarters.

Total 83 quarters 6 bushels. And there remain 2 quarters of green peas.

Barley
(*Ordium*)
The same person answers for 21 quarters of barley by the razed measure received from the serjeant of Stallingborough.

And for 42 quarters from the serjeant of Redbourne.

And for 82 quarters from the serjeant of Crowle.

And for 23 quarters from the serjeant of Eastoft.

And for 171 quarters from the serjeant of Garthorpe.

And for 69 quarters from the serjeant of Reedness.

And for 10 quarters 4 bushels from the tithe-barn of Hook.

And for 22 quarters from the serjeant of Carlton.

And for 30 quarters from the serjeant of Stainer.

And for 42 quarters from the serjeant of Monk Fryston.

Total 501 quarters 4 bushels.

---

[38] *iiii bussellos* interlined.

From which he accounts for the chaff and dross-corn thrown out (*eiectis*) of the 140 quarters of the aforesaid grain spread (*iactatis*) in the office before malting (*fusionem*), at 4 bushels from every 20 quarters, 3 quarters 4 bushels.

And for oats thrown out of the same, at one quarter from every 20 quarters, 7 quarters.

And mixed with dredge and oats below for improvement of the dredge-malt (*pro melioratione brasii drageti*) 60 quarters.

And for wort (*Brasio fuso*) 431 quarters.

Total as above. And quit (*eque*).

Dredge (*Dragetum*)	The same person answers for 21 quarters of dredge by the razed measure received from the serjeant of Eastoft.

And for 40 quarters from the serjeant of Garthorpe.

And for 51 quarters from the serjeant of Adlingfleet.

And for 66 quarters 4 bushels from the serjeant of Reedness.

And for 84 quarters from the farmer of the tithe-barn of *Loune*.

And for 126 quarters from the tithe-barn of Hook.

And for 23 quarters from the serjeant of Stainer.

And for 60 quarters of barley received (as) above.

And for 180 quarters of oats received (as) below and mixed for malt.

Total 651 quarters 4 bushels.

From which he accounts for the chaff and dross-corn thrown out of 160 quarters of the said grain spread in the office before malting, at one quarter from every 20 quarters, 9 quarters.

And for oats thrown out for fodder because of poor quality (*causa debilitatis*) 99 quarters.

And for wort 543 quarters 4 bushels.

Total as above. And quit.

Oats (*Avena*)	The same person answers for 8 quarters 6 bushels of oats from the remainder (of the previous account).

And for 4 quarters by the razed measure from the serjeant of Eastoft.

And for 161 quarters 2 bushels from the serjeant of Adlingfleet.

And for 63 quarters from the serjeant of Reedness.

And for 80 quarters from the serjeant of Carlton.

And for 84 quarters from the serjeant of Stainer.

146

And for 106 quarters received (as) above, thrown out from the barley and dredge.

Total 507 quarters.

From which he accounts for chaff and dross-corn thrown out of 200 quarters of the aforesaid grain 12 quarters.

And for flour made for pottages for provisions within the abbey this year 24 quarters.

And for the fodder of the cart-horses of the office, in addition to beans and other things from tithe 18 quarters.

And for the fodder of the horses of Brother Peter, extern cellarer,[39] 22 quarters.

And[40] he has delivered to John Palfrayman for the fodder of the horses in the lord abbot's stable and of visitors' horses, for feeding the hunting dogs of the warren (*cuniculariae*) and fattening the swans, 155 quarters.

And for the fodder of visitors' horses, by means of (*per manus*) Thomas Rosell and John de Berlay[41] in the absence of the aforesaid John Palfrayman 24 quarters.

And for the maintenance of the swans in the dam and in the ditches of the abbey, of the peacocks (*pavonum*) and capons 13 quarters.

And mixed with barley and dredge (as) above for malt 180 quarters.

And for (loss by) drying up in the granary and waste (*consumptione*) through rats and mice 10 quarters.

Total 458 quarters. And there remain in the granary 49 quarters of oats.

Malt (*Brasium*)	The same person answers for 17 quarters 6 bushels of dredge-malt from the remainder (of the previous account)

And for 431 quarters from as many quarters of malted barley as above.

And for 543 quarters 4 bushels from as many quarters of malted dredge as above.

Total 992 quarters 2 bushels.

---

[39] Presumably Brother Peter de Rouclif, the accountant in this account (see above, p. 140), though there was another Brother Peter in the convent at this time, Brother Peter de Sutton (see HUL, DDLO 20/14, *Liberatio denarii*).

[40] *Et* repeated in the manuscript.

[41] Thomas Rosell was paid a wage as a brewer in this account, whilst John de Berlay appears earlier in the account as the groom of the extern cellarer (see above, pp. 134–135).

From which he accounts for loss in the malting (*in decremento fusionis*) of two hundred and seventy-eight quarters of barley-malt not spread before malting, at two quarters from every twenty quarters, 31 quarters 7 bushels.

And for loss in the malting from 111 quarters of barley-malt spread before malting, at 3 bushels of London from every 20 quarters, 2 quarters half a bushel.

And for loss in the malting of three hundred and forty-two quarters of dredge spread before malting, at one quarter from every twenty quarters, 20 quarters half a bushel.

And for loss in the malting of one hundred and thirty quarters four London bushels of low-grade (*debilis*) dredge not spread before malting, at three quarters from every twenty quarters, 22 quarters 4 bushels.

And for loss of amount (*mensure*) in a hundred and eighty quarters of the aforesaid malt dried a second time on account of softness, at 2 quarters and a quarter bushel of London from every 20 quarters, 25 quarters.

And for dross-corn thrown out of the malt delivered to the brewer this year in sifting 16 quarters.

And for (malt) thrown out with *les Cummes*[42] in winnowing 16 quarters.

And for destruction (of malt) by worms called weevils (*Wyvels*) and by rats and mice this year 20 quarters.

And for gifts to various servants of the monastery and to poor persons by order of the lord abbot 4 quarters.

And for gifts to John Wright and the carpenters working with him on various monastery jobs, and to other workmen and servants of the office for a gratuity 3 quarters.

And he has delivered to the brewer for brewing ale both for provisions within the abbey and for the corrodarians' allowance, on 52 occasions this year 752 quarters.

And for ale brewed for provisions in the office and for provisions of those transporting grains by water from the manors to the office, and for provisions of the workmen and rewards of servants within the office and outside, and visitors, in addition to the seven quarters by purchase of the granger himself 20 quarters. For this reason, then, (such an amount has been necessary) because he has taken nothing

---

[42] 'Coom' is dust, and the word is used of the waste from corn-milling among other usages. (*OED*)

from the store-room as his predecessors took; and where his predecessors had one carter and one wagoner and those transporting grains by water from the manors (were) receiving food (*ad mensam*) in the lord abbot's hall daily, he himself has had no such persons and has taken little or nothing for his other workmen from the store-house and kitchen.

Total 931 quarters 4 bushels. And there remain in the granary 60 quarters 6 bushels of malt.

Chaff (*Crapine*)	The same person answers for 1 quarter 4 bushels of chaff thrown out of the wheat.

And for 16 quarters thrown out with *les Cummes* of malt, as above.

And they are accounted for in maintenance of the peacocks, capons, and pigeons (*columbarum*) of the lord abbot and prior. And quit.

Horses (*equi*)	The same person answers for 7 horses from the remainder (of the previous account).

And for 1 by purchase.

Total 8. And there remain 8 horses.

Oxen (*Boves*)	The same person answers for 5 oxen from the remainder (of the previous account).

And they are accounted for by sale as above (*ut infra*). And quit.

(d) The office of Kitchener

The kitchener completes the trio of officials at Selby responsible for provisioning the abbey. His name, of course, describes his basic function well enough: he was the official in charge of the kitchen, receiving provisions of all kinds from a variety of suppliers and superintending its preparation as food for the various tables of the monastic community. His staff included the convent's cook;[1] his expenditure the maintenance of the equipment for preparing food.

Like the extern cellarer, however, his was an office that expanded and contracted in its functions and responsibilities, presumably in response to circumstances now lost to our view. At one stage early in the abbacy of William Pygot (1408–29) it appears that there was even a brief experiment with two kitcheners dividing the office between them.[2] In all surviving rolls the kitchener has the task of accounting for the items purchased from day to day for the community's needs, and expenses here vary relatively little over time.[3] But the office also maintained more long-term stores, and its store-room was stocked not only by deliveries from manorial servants and other resources of the house, but also by bulk purchases of such items as fish and cattle. Such buying necessitated considerable money expenditure; and the extent to which it was undertaken by the kitchener himself, as distinct from the extern cellarer (for cattle) or the bursar, determined the size of the income allocated to his office which thus varied widely: £196 in 1416–17; £134 in 1438–39; and £120 in 1475–76.[4] The kitchener of 1438–39 spent about £41 on purchasing animals and other stock; his predecessor in 1416–17 spent £114. Similarly, the kitchener of 1475–76 purchased no cattle himself, where his predecessor of 1416–17 had bought more than 400 cattle, pigs, and sheep. Stock still needed to be purchased, of course, in the later fifteenth century; but other obedientiaries like the extern cellarer were now more active in this regard.[5]

The basic income of the kitchener's office, permanently assigned to its needs, seems to have been well below its actual expenditure in the later middle ages, totalling less than £100 for an office that spent in excess of

[1] The abbot had his own cook for his household, who received his stipend from the bursar. See above, bursars' roll 1398–99, p. 56.
[2] The surviving kitchener's roll for 1413–14 has Brother Thomas Crull as accountant, but he catered only for the prior and convent (HUL, DDLO 20/54d). Other evidence shows that there was another kitchener this year, Brother Thomas Bolton (HUL, DDLO 20/54 a and c). For the previous year, 1412–13, Brothers John Anlaby and John de Gaynesburgh are both described as kitchener in different documents (HUL, DDLO 20/54d and DDX 145/1).
[3] £78 in 1416–17; nearly £75 in 1438–39; and nearly £66 in 1475–76 (WDA, Se/Ac/10; and HUL, DDLO 20/50 and 51).
[4] WDA, Se/Ac/10; HUL, DDLO 20/50 and 51.
[5] For example, the cellarer of 1479–80 delivered more than 650 oxen, bullocks, bulls, cows, sheep, and pigs to the kitchener (HUL, DDLO 20/56).

£200 in 1416–17. A budget of 1372 shows an anticipated expenditure by the kitchener of £160, out of which his expected income was to provide £90;[6] and a survey of the Selby obedientiaries in 1535 has the kitchener's gross income from all sources as £74 15s.3½d.[7] However, given that the purchasing functions of the office varied so widely in different years, no permanent extra sources of income could be assigned to it to make up the difference. Instead there were temporary diversions of particular revenue-sources, notably tithes, or direct transfers of money from the bursary. Thus spiritual revenues varied in surviving accounts between less than £50 and £120;[8] whilst the bursar contributed cash payments to the office of £108 in 1398–99 and £103 in 1431–32.[9] Considerable flexibility seems to be indicated in the financing of a highly important contributor to the monastery's welfare.

Conclusions about the kitchener's office at Selby are necessarily somewhat tentative because here, as in other areas concerned with victualling the house, few records have survived. Just 5 accounts for a full year remain, with one account for 23 weeks; and they are widely spread in date, the earliest dating from the time of Abbot Heslington (1335–42) and the latest 1475–76.[10] Of these the latter account appears never to have been completed, lacking the stock account which usually accompanies the record of money income and expenditure; and the earlier is only a large fragment. A further account, that for 1413–14, belongs to the same problematical group of accounts as the extern cellarer's roll translated above, and seems to represent the record of activities of one of two kitcheners operating the office at this time.[11] Expenditure on food here was only slightly more than £64, where other fifteenth century accounts exceed £100; no purchases are recorded for the store-room, and there is no stock account.

This leaves just two kitcheners' rolls, of which by far the most comprehensive and best preserved is that for 1416–17, the one translated here.[12] The kitchener is seen operating at the widest level of responsibility, purchasing stock on a scale that made the extern cellarer's office of minor importance to provisioning, and managing an income that exceeded £196

---

[6] See G. S. Haslop, 'A Selby Kitchener's Roll of the Early Fifteenth Century', p. 120.

[7] HUL, DDLO 20/60.

[8] The earlier figure is for 1475–76 (HUL, DDLO 20/51) and the later for 1416–17 (WDA, Se/Ac/10).

[9] For 1398–99 see above, p. 84, and for 1431–32 HUL, DDLO 20/1.

[10] The accounts are as follows: between 1335 and 1342, WDA, Se/Ac/6; Easter to Michaelmas 1413 and 1413–14, HUL, DDLO 20/54d; 1416–17, WDA, Se/Ac/10; 1438–39, HUL, DDLO 20/50; 1475–76, HUL, DDLO 20/51.

[11] For a discussion of this composite bundle of accounts, see above p. 116.

[12] The roll has already been edited and translated by G. S. Haslop in the *Yorkshire Archaeological Journal*, volume 48 for 1976, pp. 119–133. For this volume a new translation has been made which conforms to the editorial practices used throughout; but my great indebtedness to Mr Haslop both in this regard and in respect of these notes on the office is very gratefully acknowledged.

yet was overspent by £34. The roll is not undamaged, about 20 cm of its head being holed and fragile, with some damp stains elsewhere; but it remains the most impressive single piece of evidence for the provisioning and dietary lifestyle of Selby Abbey that has survived. With the granger's roll it evidences the monks' exploitation of their manorial and other resources over a wide area for supplies of provender. Yet at the same time it records a bill for purchased foodstuffs equal to nearly a quarter of the money income of the house,[13] and buying activities that included not only the major northern trading centre of York but also London in the south. Altogether there is something irresistibly Chaucerian about the range of food commodities that found their way into the stock account of the Selby kitchener.

Only the bursars of Selby Abbey controlled a larger income than that managed by Brother John Anlaby as kitchener in 1416–17, and the confidence in his administrative abilities that this perhaps suggests is indicated too by his regular employment as an obedientiary in the early years of Abbot William Pygot's rule. He is known to have been almoner 1413–14 and 1415–17, and pittancer 1414–16.[14] Apart from this, however, there is little evidence of a career at Selby that had begun at least as long ago as 1388, when he appears in a court roll.[15] The last discovered reference to him is in 1418, when he represented the abbot in the Selby court.[16]

[13] Even so this total does not include all items of expenditure on food by the monks. Wine expenditures are to be found in the bursars' accounts; and in 1398–99 the sum involved was nearly £37 (see above, p. 73).
[14] HUL, DDLO 20/54e and 21/19; WDA, Se/Ac/10, for almoner. HUL, DDLO 20/15, for pittancer.
[15] HUL, DDLO 21/13.
[16] HUL, DDLO 21/20.

The Kitchener's account of 1416–1417

Table of Contents

Money Account

Grain and Stock Account

Wheat	294 quarters 2 bushels	178
Malt	625 quarters	178
Beans and peas	16 quarters 6 bushels	178
Oats	29 quarters	179
Bulls (and) oxen	21 oxen, 2½ shoulders	179
Cows	51 carcases, 2 quarters, half a shoulder	180
Bullocks and heifers	25, 1 quarter, 2½ shoulders	180
Calves	21	181
Boars, pigs, and piglets	86	181
Piglets	37	182
Sheep	396	182
Lambs	66, 2 quarters, and 1 shoulder	183
Swans and Cygnets	27	183
Coneys and young rabbits	45	184
Partridges with pheasants	20	184
Herons	33	185
Geese and ducks	105	185
Capons	36	185
Cocks and hens	181	186
Chickens	24	187
Pigeons	731	187
Eggs	2760	187
Hides	99	188
Wool-fells, with pelts and wool	455 fells and pelts	188
Lambs' fells	67	189
Red and white herrings	41,470	189
Salted fish	477¼	190
Dried fish	869	190
Salmon	104½ salmon, 2½ sprents, 1 *cokke*	190
Large (and) small eels and a tench	1221	191
Pikes and Pickerels, Roach and Perch	4519	191
Milk and cheese	173 gallons of milk, 7½ stones of cheese	191
Salt, pepper, and saffron	17 quarters 4 bushels of salt 19 pounds of pepper 5¼ pounds of saffron	192

Almonds, rice, and sanders	8 dozen and 2 pounds of almonds 113½ pounds of rice 2 pounds of sanders	192
Cumin, honey, and oil	2 pounds of cumin 20½ gallons of honey 7 gallons and 1 quart of oil	192
Figs and raisins	3 baskets and 13 pounds	193
Tallow	49½ stones	193

(The Account?)[17] of Brother John Anlaby, kitchener of the kitchen of the lord abbot and the convent of Selby from Thursday namely (the first?) of October and the festival of the Burial of St German A.D. 1416 to the morrow (of the same festival of St German?) A.D. 1417, namely for one whole year and one day.

(Arrears?)[17]

(No arrears?) because Brother John Milling-ton,[18] his immediate predecessor of the year preceding, (exceeded income?) in his last account.

Total nothing.

(Fixed rents and?) farms

(... *Firme*)

... he answers for £43 ...[19] from fixed rents yearly of the town of Selby and elsewhere belonging to the office of the kitchen for the terms of ... and Pentecost according to the new rental.

And for 66s.8d. from the farm of John Babthorp for the toll of Selby, (leased to him?) for a term of seven years, this year being the fifth.

And for 100s. received from Robert Courtenay and Walter del Sartryn for draff, dregs, and lees (*lotione*) of the brew-house, leased for this to the same persons for the term of 9 years, this year (being) the fourth.

---

[17] There is considerable damage to approximately the first 20 cm. of the roll, which is fragile and holed in places and has lost a section torn off at the left side.

[18] Brother John Millington became a full member of the community in December 1388, when he was ordained a priest. As well as kitchener he is known to have served as pittancer 1402–04 and chamberlain 1413–14. See Borthwick Institute of Historical Research, Archbishop's Register 14, Thomas Arundel, f.11b; HUL, DDLO 20/14 and 54c, 21/19.

[19] 10s.4d. (*xs.iiiid.*) has been crossed out and a new sum added above, which is now lost. It presumably read: £43 14s.6d.

And for 40s. received from Roger Stansfeld[20] for his allowance (of food) from the kitchen this year; and he has died.

And for 6s. from the *Wethirsilver* of Hillam and (Monk Fryston?) yearly, and not more because one toft there which used to pay 12d. yearly has been leased at money-rent (*ad firmam denarii*).[21]

Total . . .[22]

Altar-dues of churches and chapels with mortuaries (*Alteragium ecclesiarum et Capellarum cum mortuariis*)

The same person answers for £11 9s.11d. received from lenten tithes of the town of Selby this year, as shown by check of individual items.

And for £7 12s.5d. received by means (*per manus*) of Thomas Wentworth this year from the profit of the minor church of Selby, as from small offerings and mortuaries in cloths.

And for 4s.4d. from money for the blessed bread this year, at (*prout*) 1d. each Sunday.

And for 10s. received this year for one ox deriving from the mortuary of the wife of the late William Thomson, sold for this to a certain butcher of York.[23]

And for 10s. this year from one mortuary cow of Alice, wife of the late John de Brend, sold for this to Richard Heworth.

And for 20s. this year for tithe flax and hemp from Selby, sold for this to Alice de Burn and others.

And for £11 6s.8d. received from altar-dues of the chapel of Hook this year.

And for £6 13s.4d. from John Clerc, farmer of the altar-dues of the chapel of Carlton this year; whereas he used to pay £8 previously.[24]

And for 100s. from John Selby, farmer of the altar-dues of the chapel of Rawcliffe this year.

---

[20] The grant of a corrody to Roger de Stansfield for life in return for 40s. p.a. is recorded in an abbey register with the date 10 June, 1407 (British Library, Cotton Vitellius E.XVI, f.141v).

[21] *Wethirsilver*, presumably a money payment in lieu of a wether, was one of several such dues (cocks, hens, and eggs) attached to villein tenure on these manors (see WDA, Se/Ac/24, Rental of Monk Fryston of c.1400). The toft had evidently now been leased for money rent in place of all other dues.

[22] The total is lost, but should read £54 7s.2d.

[23] *carni* is written in the manuscript, with *fici Ebor'* interlined.

[24] *cum solebat reddere in preced' viii li'* interlined.

And for 24s.[25] from offerings of the chapel of Turnbridge[26] (received) by means of Robert Forman for the past year.[27]

And for 10s.5d. by means of Richard Glover from offerings coming to the said chapel of Turnbridge in the present year; and not more because allegedly[28] it is so damaged by John Joce.

And for 2s.7d. deriving from the money-box (*stipite*) of St Zita[29] (*Cithe*) in the minor church of Selby this year.

And for 22s. received this year from 2 bullocks sold for this to a certain butcher of York.

And for £27 13s.4d. this year from tithes of sheaves and hay deriving from two thirds of the parish of Brayton,[30] sold for this to Geoffrey Baxter, Richard Broun, and others.

And for 30s. received this year from 15 stones of tithe-wool deriving from two thirds of the aforesaid parish.

And for 32s. received from 16 stones of wool shorn from 120[31] sheep purchased for the victuals of the household (*ad expensas hospitii*) this year.

And for £17 10s. received this year from William Pulter and his partner, farmers of the tithe-barn and tithes of Snaith.

And for £6 this year from Thomas Dilcok, farmer of the tithe-barn and tithes of Balne.

And for £18 10s. this year from John Went and his partners, farmers of the tithe-barn and tithes of Heck.

And for 2s.[32] this year from one stone of wool from the tithes of Selby, sold for this to Agnes Bernard.

---

[25] *vii* crossed out and *xxiiii* interlined.

[26] Mid-way between Snaith and Rawcliffe.

[27] *de anno preterito* interlined, replacing the following deleted statement: 'as part of 24s. for the past year, leased for this to John Joce by surety of John Gledehogh, Henry Bond and William Schipwright' (*in parte de xxiiiis. pro anno preterito sic dimiss' Johanni Joce per plegium Johannis Gledehogh Henrici Bond et Willelmi SchipWright*).

[28] *ut dicitur* interlined.

[29] Perhaps, as Mr Haslop suggests, St Zita of Lucca, said to be the patron of servants (see *YAJ*, 48, 1976, p.123 n.21).

[30] As noted above (see Bursars' Account, p.50 n.38) the division of the tithes of Brayton into fractions was an ancient one. In 1218 Archbishop Gray included a third of the church of Brayton among the endowments of the prebend of Wistow in York Minster.

[31] *C* interlined. The long hundred of six score is in use in this account.

[32] *xviiid.* has been crossed out and iis. interlined.

And for 6s.8d. received this year from one gown[33], the mortuary of Beatrice wife of the late Peter Porter,[34] sold for this to the wife of Robert Courtenay.

Total £120 9s.8d.

Sale of hides, skins, and offal, with the (profits of the) court and deficiencies in the account (*Venditio corriorum pellium et exitus bestiarum cum Curia et venditionibus super compotum*)

The same person answers for 32s.8d. received this year from the hides of 14 oxen slaughtered as below (*ut extra*) sold for this to John Barneslay, *barker*, at 2s.4d. a hide.

And for 70s.10d. received this year from the hides of 49 cows and one heifer slaughtered as below, sold for this to the same John at 17d. a hide.

And for 25s. received this year from the hides of 15 bullocks slaughtered as below, sold for this to the said John at 20d. a hide.

And for 2s.8d. this year from 16 calf-skins, sold for this to the said John as below.

And for 39s. this year from 156 wool-fells, sold for this to John Pulter at 3d. a fell.

And for 31s.8d. from 223 pelts containing 19 dozen and 1 skins, sold for this to the same John at 19d. a dozen plus in all 9½d.[35]

And for 7s.5d. from 67 lamb-skins, sold for this to the said John at 16d. a dozen.

And for 32s.11d. this year from intestines of animals slaughtered as below, sold for this to Agnes Bernard at 5d. each.

And for 32s.11d. this year from 41½[36] stones of fat from beasts killed as below, sold for this to the chandler of Riccall at 8d. a stone less 1d. in all.[37]

---

[33] *una toga* interlined.

[34] During this same accounting year Beatrice wife of the late Peter Porter was paying off to the bursar 20 marks due for her corrody, possibly under the terms of a grant made in 1399. (See WDA, Se/Ac/9, *Forinsecum Receptum*; British Library, Cotton Vitellius E.XVI, fos 144v–145; and above, p. 52).

[35] *ixd. ob. plus toto* interlined. The figures given in this entry have more than one error.

[36] *et di'* interlined.

[37] *id. minus toto* interlined. The figure of 32s.11d. is the value of the total fat recorded below in the Stock Account (p. 193).

And for 53s.4d. received by means of Brother Thomas Crull,[38] bursar, in respect of (*de*) Katherine Dring[39] for her livery from the kitchen this year.

And for 6s. received this year from William Pinne[40] for a certain black horse (called) *Stray*, sold to the same for this.

And for 49s.3d.[41] from fines and amercements of 48 courts held at the gates of the abbey this year.

And for 29s.2d. from fines and amercements of the brewsters in the town of Selby for Michaelmas and Easter terms this year.

And for 20d. received this year from charcoal sold for this to a certain friend of Brother John Hales.[42]

And for 6s.4d. this year from 2 pigs sold for this.

And for 18s.1¼d. for various deficiencies in the account as shown below.

Total £21 18s.11¼d.

Sum total of receipts £196 15s.9¼d.[43]

Daily food expenses (*Expense Dietariorum*) From which the same person accounts for the expenses of the households of the lord abbot, the convent, and others visiting, as shown by the daily

---

[38] Brother Thomas Crull had an active career as an administrator at Selby. In the period from 1413 when he became a full member of the community, to 1457 when he was still receiving a pittance, he is known to have served as bursar 1416–17 and 1441–42, kitchener 1413, 1413–1414, and 1436, granger 1421–22 and 1423–25, and almoner 1431–32, and 1433–34. (See Borthwick Institute of Historical Research, Archbishop's Register 18, Henry Bowet pt.I, f.39d; HUL, DDLO 20/1, 5, 21, 54d, 55, and 66, 4/3; WDA, Se/Ac/8a & 8b, 9, and 18; B. Dobson, 'The Election of John Ousthorp', p. 38. He received a legacy of a gold ring and a pair of ivory tablets under the will of a Selby corrodarian, Isabella Hamerton, in 1433 (*Testamenta Eboracensia*, II, pp. 22–23).

[39] She had been granted the corrody by the abbey in March 1399 (see British Library, Cotton Vitellius E.XVI, f.143v; and Bursars' Account 1398–99, above, p. 51).

[40] Pinne received a wage of 12s. as poulterer in this account (see p. 165).

[41] *iiid.* interlined.

[42] Having joined the abbey about 1404, Brother John Hales was very active in its administration during the second decade of the 15th century, when he served as bursar 1411–12, Easter-Michaelmas 1413, 1413–14, and 1415–16, and kitchener 1418. But he then disappears from the abbey records. (See Borthwick Institute of Historical Research, Archbishop's Register 16, Richard Scrope, f.310; HUL, DDLO 20/54a and 54d, 21/20; WDA, Se/Ac/9; Lincolnshire Archives, CM 1/56).

[43] A small strip of parchment has been attached to the left margin at this point. It contained three lines of writing, but most is now lost because the strip is torn and worn. The three lines survive as follows:

'De ..bus ...
exam' videlicet ...
li' iiis viid ...'

accounts of the households and of the recreations[44] examined, namely by purchase £78 13s.7¼d. And thus he has spent each week 30s.3d. plus 7¼d. in all.

Total £78 13s.7¼d.

Purchase of stock and sheep (*Emptio stauri et multonum*)   The same person accounts for 2 oxen purchased from Richard Pulter this year, 40s.8d.

And for one bull purchased from William Raufmell and 20 cows purchased from the same person this year, at 7s.3d.[45] a head, £7 19s.3d.

And for 2 bullocks purchased from the same 19s.

And for 22 bullocks purchased from Thomas Dilcok this year, at 10s.2d. a head less 4d. in all, £11 3s.4d.

And for one heifer purchased from Richard Goldale 8s.

And for 5 pigs purchased from Walter del Sartryn and Peter Milner 16s.8d.

And for one pig purchased from John Hamond 3s.8d.

And for 120 sheep purchased by John Hoperton about the festival of St Michael (29 September), at 14¾d.[46] a head plus 14¾d.[47] in all, £7 8s.8d.

And for the expenses of John Hoperton (going) to Craven in order to buy the said sheep 2s.

And for 3 sheep purchased from William Pulter of Snaith 3s.9d.

And for 20 sheep purchased by William Courtenay[48] before Lent 30s.

And for 120 unshorn sheep purchased from Richard Marschall at 19d. a head, £9 10s.

And for 120 shorn sheep purchased from Nicholas Tupper at 15d. a head, £7 10s.

Total £49 15s.

---

[44] A reference, no doubt, to the system by which the monks of a house visited one of the abbey manors in the neighbourhood of the monastery for a short period each year, enjoying there a relaxation of the normal monastic regime. The Selby manor for this purpose seems to have been at Stainer, a mile from the abbey. See D. Knowles, *The Religious Orders in England*, II, pp. 245–246.

[45] The figure should be 7s.7d. in order to get the sum recorded.

[46] The figure should be 14d. only in order to get the sum recorded.

[47] *ob.qª* interlined.

[48] He was serjeant at Stainer, an office that he occupied as early as 1411 and still held in 1424 (see p.180; B.Holt (ed.), *Two Obedientiary Rolls of Selby Abbey*, p.40; and HUL, DDLO 20/66).

Purchases (*Emptiones*)

Red and white herr- The same person accounts for 30,000 red herrings
ings (*Allecia rubea et* purchased from William Muston[49] this year at
alba) 12s.10d. for 1200, £16 10s.[50]

> And for 6,000 red herrings purchased from the same person at 8s. for 1200, 40s.
>
> And for 1200 red herrings purchased from the same person 10s.
>
> And for 600 red herrings purchased from the same person 6s.8d.
>
> And for 480 red herrings purchased from the same person 6s.
>
> And for 1440 white herrings purchased from the same person and from Thomas Freman in one barrel and 1 firkin (*Ferthekin*) 16s.8d.
>
> Total £20 9s.4d.

Salted fish The same person accounts for 30 salted fishes called
(*Pisces salsi*) lobs (*lobbes*) purchased at Scarborough from Henry
Acclombe at 16½d. a fish 41s.3d.

> And for 26[51] salted fish purchased from the same person at 8d. a fish 24s.
>
> And for 336 salted fish purchased from the same person at 7d. a fish £9 16s.
>
> And for 2 salted fish called ling (*leng'*) purchased from William Benyngholm this year 3s.
>
> And for 3 salted fish purchased from the same person 21d.
>
> And for 7 salted fish called ling purchased from John Wright, shipman, at 14d. a fish 8s.2d.
>
> And for 15 salted fish called lobs (*lobbes*) purchased from William Muston at 16d. a fish 20s.
>
> And for 20 salted fish purchased from Richard Sutton at 7d. a fish 11s.8d.
>
> And for 2 salted fish called keeling (*keling*) purchased from the same person 2s.
>
> And for 6 salted fish purchased from William Muston 7s.6d.
>
> Total £15 15s.4d.

---

[49] Fishmonger and freeman of York. He purchased a corrody for the lives of himself and his wife Margaret, with a pension of £6 p.a., in June 1402; and left the abbot and convent of Selby a pipe of red wine in his will in 1418. (See British Library, Cotton Vitellius E.XVI, f.137v; *Testamenta Eboracensia*, I, p.390).

[50] The sum should be £16 0s.10d.

[51] The figure should be 36 in order to achieve the sum given.

Dried fish
(*Piscis durus*)

The same person accounts for 120 dried fishes purchased at Hull from Robert Percy by John Barlay[52] at 3d. a fish 30s.

And for 60 dried fish purchased at York from William Muston, at 2¾d. a fish less 2½d.[53] in all, 13s.4d.

And for 120 dried fish purchased at York from Robert Hayn, at 2¾d. a fish plus 6d. in all, 28s.

And for 360 dried fish purchased there from William Muston at 3d. a fish £4 10s.

And for 20 dried fish purchased from William Benyngholm 6s.8d.

And for 120 dried fish purchased at York from William Muston at 2½d. a fish 25s.

And for 54 dried fish purchased from Thomas Freman at 2½d. a fish 11s.3d.

Total £10 4s.3d.

Salmon
(*Salmones*)

The same person accounts for 9 salmon and 2 *sprentz*[54] purchased from John Babthorp at 18d. a fish 14s.6d.

And for 7 salmon and 2 *sprentz* purchased from Robert Pulayn at 13d. a fish 8s.4d.

And for 3 salmon purchased from John Rughsthagh at *Ayr*'[55], at 2s.1d. a fish plus 1d. in all, 6s.4d.

And for 12 salmon purchased from the same person at 17d. a fish 17s.

And for 7 salmon purchased from Robert Pulayn at 17d. a fish 9s.11d.

And for 1 salmon purchased at Turnham Hall[56] for the lord abbot's provisions at Rawcliffe 2s.

And for one salmon purchased from John Babthorp about the festival of Easter (11 April) 4s.

And for one salmon purchased afterwards from the said John 3s.4d.

---

[52] John Barlay received a wage of 20s. in this account as the convent's cook (see p. 165).

[53] The figure should be 5d. in order to obtain the sum recorded.

[54] i.e. young salmon, which cost one third the price of the grown fish. John Babthorp from whom they were purchased is presumably the same person who was leasing the toll of Selby from the abbey at this time (see above, p. 155).

[55] Presumably Airmyn.

[56] As Mr Haslop has noted, it is some 2 miles downstream from Selby (*YAJ*, 48, 1976, n. 32).

And paid to John Babthorp for his share of 8 salmon from the Selby fishery[57] from the festival of Easter to the festival of Pentecost (30 May) this year 12s.

And for 8 salmon and 1 *sprent* from the Selby fishery purchased from the same person from the festival of Pentecost to the festival of the Nativity of St John the Baptist (24 June) this year 19s.8d.

And for 15 salmon of the said fishery purchased from the same person from the festival of the Nativity of St John the Baptist to the festival of St Peter Advincula (1 August) this year 30s.

And for 4 salmon purchased from Thomas Freman this year at 17d. a fish 5s.8d.

Total £6 12s.9d.

Purchases of spices, salt, and other things (*Emptiones specier-um, salis et aliorum*)

The same person accounts for 6 quarters of salt purchased from Richard Sutton at 3s.8d a quarter 22s.

And for 11 quarters of salt purchased from John Wright, mariner (*maryner*), at 4s. a quarter 44s.

And for 4 bushels of salt purchased from John Adcok 2s.4d.

And for 7 pounds of pepper purchased from William Benyngholm, Robert Waynflet and others this year at 2s. a pound 14s.

And for 7 pounds of pepper purchased at London by Brother Thomas Bolton[58] at 21d.[59] a pound 12s.10d.

And for 2 pounds of pepper purchased from John Bouche[60] 3s.4d.

And for 1 pound of pepper purchased by John Totty[61] 18d.

---

[57] *de Selby piscaria* interlined.

[58] He was abbot's chaplain this year and active in securing provisions for the abbot's household. He had joined the house about 1404 and become a priest in 1406. In 1413–14 he had served as kitchener and keeper of the guest house (Borthwick Institute of Historical Research, Archbishop's Register 16, Richard le Scrope, f.311, and Register 5A, *Sede Vacante* 1405–07, f.100; HUL, DDLO 20/54a; WDA, Se/Ac/8 & 9). It is clear from this present account that Brother Thomas Bolton was closely involved in the hunting activities of the abbey (see p. 183).

[59] The figure should be 22d. in order to secure the sum recorded.

[60] In 1406 the abbot and convent of Selby had granted to John Bouche and his wife Mary an annual pension of £10 for life, presumably for cash or other financial consideration (though none is specified in the grant). He was a spicer of York. His wife left to Selby Abbey a tenement in York by her will of 1422. (See British Library, Cotton Vitellius E.XVI, fos 117–117v; and W. Dugdale, *Monasticon Anglicanum*, re-ed. J. Caley, H. Ellis, and B. Bandinell, 6 vols in 8, London, 1817–30, III, p. 495).

[61] He received a fee of 26s.8d. as receiver of the house in the bursar's account for 1416–17; and was appointed as one of three proctors of the abbot to the parliament of November 1417 (WDA, Se/Ac/9; PRO, SC 10/46/2278).

And for 2 pounds of pepper purchased from Robert Holm of York 3s.4d.

And for 1 pound of saffron purchased from John Nesse[62] 9s.6d.

And for 3 pounds of saffron purchased from the same person 30s.10d.

And for 3 quarters of a pound of saffron purchased at York from Roger Selby 8s.3d.

And for half a pound of saffron purchased from John Nesse 6s.8d.

And for 4 dozen almonds purchased at York from Roger Selby at 2s.8d. a dozen 10s.8d.

And for 4 dozen almonds purchased from John Nesse and William Benyngholm 12s.

And for 2 pounds of almonds purchased from John Nesse 7d.

And for 44 pounds of rice (*Rys*) purchased from William Benyngholm at 1¼d. a pound 4s.7d.

And for 69½ pounds of rice purchased from John Bouche, Roger Selby, and others, at 1¼d. a pound 7s.2½d.

And for 2 pounds of sanders (*Saundrez*)[63] purchased from William Benyngholm 2s.5d.

And for 2 pounds of cummin (*cumin*) purchased from the same person 4d.[64]

And for 13 pounds of figs purchased from John Nesse 13d.

And for one measure (*secta*) of figs and raisins purchased from Robert Tupper of Hull 15s.

And for 20 gallons and 1 pottle of honey purchased from various persons this year at 10d. a gallon 17s.1d.

Total £11 9s.6½d.

| Transfer of rent (*Resolutio redditus*) | The same person accounts for the transfer (of rent) to the keeper of the fabric of the monastery yearly for the toft in Micklegate which Walter del Sartryn holds 3s. |

And to the pittancer yearly for the land formerly (in the possession) of Denis Marays 5d.

---

[62] By 1431–32 he was receiving an annual pension of 40s. from the abbey. He seems from various references to have been a Selby man (see HUL, DDLO 20/1; 21/23; and this account p. 175).
[63] 'A flavouring derived from sandal wood' (G. S. Haslop, *YAJ*, 48, 1976, n. 34).
[64] *x* has been crossed out and *iiii* interlined.

And to the keeper in the guest house yearly for land formerly (in the possession) of the said Denis 4d.

And to John Ricall yearly for land formerly (in the possession) of the said Denis near the site of the *Langlay* mill 2d.

And to the keeper of the infirmary yearly for the toft called *Stokbrig* 4d.

And to Thomas de Berlay yearly for the toft in Micklegate which William Hwet holds 3s.

And to William Kemp yearly for the land in *le longridding* formerly (in the possession) of John Escrik 2d.

And to the pittancer of the monastery for the rent belonging to his office issuing from the dwelling-house of the parish chaplain of Selby, because the church with the house (is) in the lord's hand this year, 26s.8d.[65]

Total 34s.1d.

| Salaries, with wages and clothing (*Salaria cum stipendiis et vestura*) | The same person accounts for the salary of John Bulkyn, parish chaplain of Selby this year, £4 13s.4d. |

And for the salary of the same for collecting the Lenten tithes of Selby this year, by agreement 13s.4d.

And for the fee of the clerk, the scribe of the Selby court this year, 3s.4d.

And for the wage of Robert Santon, barber, for collecting the rents and farms of this office this year 13s.4d.

And for the wage of John Barlay, cook of the convent this year, 20s.

And for the wage of William Pinne, poulterer this year, 12s.

And for one pair of boots purchased for the same person, by agreement 2s.6d.

And for the wage of Thomas Ripon, scullion (*Squiller*) this year, 10s.

And for the wage of Robert Bernard, page in the kitchen this year, 6s.8d.

---

[65] For repairs done to the chaplain's house this year, see *House repairs*, pp.171–172. The statement that the church was in the lord's hand this year may mean simply that its revenues had not been leased for a fixed farm, as with other chapels contributing to the office's income (see above, *Altar-dues of churches and chapels with mortuaries*, pp.156–157). That there was a parish chaplain is indicated by the *Salaries* section below; and there is no indication here that John Bulkyn received his salary for only part of the year.

And for the wage of Agnes Bernard, preparer of animal intestines this year, 6s.8d.

And for the wage of Robert de Aland, page in the kitchen this year, 6s.8d.

And for 3 ells of russet cloth purchased from John Hull for a gown for William Pinne 3s.4d.

And for 3 ells of russet cloth purchased from the said John for one gown for Robert de Aland 2s.9d.

And for 2 ells of cloth purchased for a gown for Robert Bernard 2s.2d.

And for 2 ells of russet cloth purchased from John Hull for a gown for Richard Maunsell, page of the kitchen, 12d.

And for the making of the same 3d.

And for 2 pairs of shoes purchased for the same person 7d.

Total £9 17s.11d.

Small expenses and sundries (*Minute cum variis*)   The same person accounts for 8 pounds of wax purchased for lighting in the refectory this year at 6½d. a pound 4s.4d.

And for wick purchased for the same, with the service of Henry Clerc making candles therefrom, 3d.

And for hire (*conductione*) of one horse from William Martin for transport of geese from Reedness to Selby about the festival of Michaelmas 4d.

And for 2 girths purchased for the horses' saddles 3d.

And for 3 girths (*Wambtyes*) purchased from William Roper 9d.

And for 11 ells (of cloth)[66] for horses' girths purchased from William Benyngholm 6½d.

And for 2 strainers (*Streignours*) purchased 6d.

And for one great knife purchased from Robert Smith for dressing (*dirigenda*) meat 2s.

And for one knife called a *lechingknyf*[67] purchased from the same person 3d.

And for the service of the same person repairing 2 *Skoinours*, making 1 hasp (*hesp*) and staple for the vat for soaking fish (*pro piscibus adaquandis*), and repairing other faults in the utensils, 11d.

---

66 The nature of the material is not specified in the document.
67 'A knife for slicing meat' (G. S. Haslop, *YAJ*, 48, 1976, n. 38).

And given to the king (*Regi*) of the pages of the kitchen this year 8d.[68]

And for one basket purchased for carrying turves this year 3s.

And for 2 hampers (*cartallis*) purchased for the poulterer 10d.

And for 4 ells of canvas purchased from William Benyngholm for making sacks for the poulterer with, 10d.

And for the service of a certain man from York repairing the grinding stones for grinding mustard, by agreement 16d.

And for 2 bushels of mustard seed purchased from John Wright, serjeant at Adlingfleet this year, 3s.6d.

And for transport of the same from Adlingfleet to Reedness by Henry Olive[69] 2d.

And for 3 pecks of mustard seed purchased by William Pinne[70] 15d.

And for the service of 8 women washing and shearing 120 sheep of the office this year, 20d. with food provided (*ad mensam domini*).

And for cabbages and leeks purchased from Amyas Spaldyng and others this year by William Pinne 5s.4½d.

And for 48½ pounds of lard (*albi pinguedinis*) purchased from John Hoperton this year at 2d. a pound 8s.1d.

And for the service of Thomas Sadeller repairing faults in the saddle-pads this year 11d.

And for 1 halter purchased from William Roper for leading animals from the office pasture to the abbey 16d.

And for 3 hanging-locks purchased for the office and for the money-box of the blessed Mary at Turnbridge this year 8d.

And for the service of Roger Cooke repairing the ranges (*lez Raungez*) in the kitchen for one day 2d.

And for the service of the same person digging in the garden called *Herynghousgarth* for 3 days in order to plant and sow herbs there, 6d. with food provided (*ad cibum domini*).

And for shoeing the office horses this year on different occasions (*per vices*) 4s.7d.

---

[68] Presumably this entry refers to a similar kind of activity as the election of a boy-bishop by the cathedral choristers of York Minster about the festival of Holy Innocents (28 December). The York boy-bishop received a regular payment of 6s.8d from Selby Abbey in connexion with his 'visitation' of his diocese (see above, Bursars' Account, p. 53; and G. S. Haslop, *YAJ*, 48, 1976, n. 39).

[69] He received a wage as a door-keeper of the abbot's hall in the bursar's account for this year (see WDA, Se/Ac/9, *Stipendia Famulorum*).

[70] He received a wage as poulterer in this account (see above, *Salaries*, p. 165).

And for 1 brass ladle purchased at York this year 10d.

And for the service of one man making 20 quarters of charcoal in the woods of Hambleton, by agreement 5s.

And for 80 wooden dishes, plates, and saucers, purchased from Thomas Turnour this year 18d.

And for 3 ells of linen cloth purchased and given to the cooks of the lord duke of Gloucester[71] this year 12d.

And for the service of Nicholas Couper repairing various vessels in the kitchener's office with hoops from the granger's office this year, collectively (*in grosso*) 2s.

And for tar purchased for sheep-salve (*pro multonibus unguendis*) this year 2d.

And for 2 earthenware jars purchased for carrying milk from Stainer this year 3d.

And for one net called a *Tramaill*[72] purchased for taking fish in the dam 2s.

And for garlic purchased this year 12d.

And for onions purchased from John Wright this year 3s.

And for 7 gallons and 1 quart of oil purchased from W. Benyngholm and others this year at 20d. a gallon 12s.1d.

And for 1 quarter and 1 bushel of white and green peas purchased from Cecil Smith and others this year 7s.6d.

And for paper and parchment purchased for the writing of the daily accounts of the kitchen (*dietariis Coquine*), (the records of) the court of Selby, the account, and the rental this year, 3s.4d.

And for 6 stones of paris-candle purchased for lighting in the office this year at 14d. a stone 7s.

Total £4 11s.8d.

External expenses   The same person accounts for his own expenses as
(*Forinsece expense*) accountant and those of others (going) with him to

---

[71] Humphrey of Lancaster, born 1390 and created duke of Gloucester in May 1414, the youngest son of Henry IV and brother of Henry V (*Complete Peerage*, V, pp. 730–737). Preparations for his arrival at Selby were being made about 25 March 1417; and 7 gallons of Rhenish wine were purchased at York on his account (see WDA, Se/Ac/9, Bursar's Account 1416–17, *Minute cum Variis* and *Emptio Vini*).
[72] The trammel is a long, narrow fishing net set vertically with floats and sinkers. The fish pass through the outer coarse net to be held by an inner finer one. (*OED*)

Scarborough on one occasion[73] and Hull twice[74] in order to buy fish, and to Pontefract twice[74] to buy animals, at various times this year 13s.4d.

And for transporting 120 dried fish by water from Hull to Selby this year 6d.

And for carrying fish purchased at York to the boat there and transport of the same by water thence to Selby this year 20d.

And for the expenses of John Barlay[75] at York in order to buy herrings and ox-feet (*ped' bovium*) there this year, with transport of the same to Selby by water, 2s.4½d.

And for the expenses of William Pinne[76] (going) to York, Marshland,[77] Monk Fryston, Pontefract, and Howden on office business this year at various times 3s.11d.

And for the expenses of John Wotton and William Pinne (going) to Stallingborough to drive 80 sheep taken from stock (*multonibus extractis*) to Selby, with the ferry-toll at Burton on Stather,[78] 3s.8½d.

Total 25s.6d.

Running-costs of the church (*Resumptio ecclesie*)	The same person accounts for 9 pounds of wax purchased for the making of candles in the minor church of Selby this year at 7d. a pound, 5s.3d. in addition to 16 pounds from stock.

And for the service of Henry Clerc making tapers with it and wax-candles for *le Rowell*[79] this year 16d.

And for 480 wafers purchased for celebration of masses this year 4d.

And for wine purchased for the same reason 2s.2d.

And for incense purchased 4d.

And for one stone of paris-candles purchased for lighting at dawn (*Auroris*) on festival days in winter 15d.

Total 10s.8d.

---

[73] *una vice* interlined.
[74] *ii vic'* interlined.
[75] The convent's cook (see above, p. 165).
[76] Poulterer in the kitchener's office (see above, p. 165).
[77] 'once the large area of marshy land along the south side of the Ouse, chiefly the parish of Whitgift' (A. H. Smith, *The Place-Names of the West Riding of Yorkshire*, II, p. 2).
[78] Across the River Trent from Garthorpe, co. Lincolnshire.
[79] Mr Haslop suggests a wheel-shaped chandelier (*YAJ*, 48, 1976, n. 43).

Cost of ditches
(*Custus fossatorum*)

The same person accounts for the service of John Croxdale cleaning-out 100 rods of ditch around the office pastures across the Ouse, receiving 4s.2d. for 50 rods and as above for the other 50 rods, 8s.4d.[80]

And for the service of the same person cleaning-out the horse-pond (*le Wayhour*) there 6d.[81]

And for the service of John Dobbe cutting-down 3 cart-loads of thorns in the Northwoods (*lez NorthWoddes*) 4d.

And for the service of the same person carting these to the house which Agnes del Grene holds in *le Cowelane* 12d.

And for the service of one man making a hedge there near the said house for 4 days, 16d. without food (provided).

Total 11s.6d.

Maintenance of the fishery[82]
(*Resumptio Piscarie*)

The same person accounts for the service of John Copyn and two others for 3 days pulling up and taking out (*trahentium et suscipientium*) the timbers of the old office fishery, each receiving 2d. a day, 18d. and bread and ale from the monastery store-room.

And for the service of John Osgodby felling 8 oak saplings with which to make piles for repair of the new office fishery 4d.

And for the service of the same person stripping the said oak saplings and cutting them to a point (*decortantis dictos querculos et acuentis eosdem*) for one day 4d.

And for the service of John Dobbe carting the said piles from Spark Hagg[83] to Selby in 3 trips (*per iii vices*) 15d.

And for the service of 3 men working on the repair of the new fishery for 4 days, each receiving 2d. a day, 2s.

And for the service of Robert Bird[84] transporting the boat (*batellam*)

---

[80] The peculiar form of this entry is due to an alteration in the manuscript. Originally Croxdale was to receive 9s.4½d., made up of 4s.2d. for 50 rods and 5s.2½d. for the other 50 rods. The alteration presumably followed a marginal instruction to measure the rods (*Mensurentur rod'*).

[81] ¾d. (*ob. q*[a]) has been crossed out.

[82] Near Rosscarrs, about 2.5 kilometres down the Ouse from Selby (G.S.Haslop, *YAJ*, 48, 1976, n.45).

[83] About three kilometres north-west of Selby.

[84] In a granger's account of 1413–14 he received a wage of 26s.8d. as master of the abbey's ship (HUL, DDLO 20/54e, *Stipendia Famulorum*).

for the said fishery by water from *Donemouth*[85] to Selby, by agreement 12d.

And for one rope purchased from William Roper for securing the said boat 6d.

Total 6s.11d.

House repairs (*Emendatio domorum*)

The parish chaplain's (*Capellani parochialis*) The same person accounts for the service of John Ledsham carting 2 waggon-loads of stone from the Monk Fryston quarry to Selby for the repair of the house in the tenure of the parish chaplain 20d.

And for 1680 bricks (*Walletighell'*) purchased from Roger Barker for the same work 7s.

And for 2 waggon-loads of lime bought for the same work at Sherburn[86] 3s.

And for carting of the same from Sherburn to Selby 20d.

And for 6 quarters of sand purchased from John Huglot and John Wayt for the same work 2s.

And for the service of Peter Geve making one wall from the said stones and bricks between the minor church of Selby and the dwelling-house of the said chaplain, and repairing the foundations of other walls there, by agreement 6s.

And for 9 oak timbers purchased from Robert Courtenay for repair of the said house 2s.

And for 8 timbers and 8 oak boards of five feet purchased from John Nelleson for the same work, 22d. in addition to 600 laths from the abbey store.

And for the service of 2 men sawing the said timber 14d.

And for 5 boards of wainscot (*Waynscot*) purchased from John Nesse for repairs there at 3½d. a board 17½d.[87]

And for 7 wainscots purchased from the same person 2s.4d.

And for sawing the said wainscot and part of the timber, by agreement 14d.[88]

---

[85] At Adlingfleet, 'where the old south course of the Don joined the Trent' (G. S. Haslop, *YAJ*, 48, 1976, n. 46).
[86] Some thirteen kilometres west of Selby.
[87] *xviid. ob.* interlined.
[88] *xiiiid.* interlined.

And for the service of John Orwell, carpenter, working on repair of the said house, by agreement 10s. in addition to the expenses incurred by John Bulkyn, parish chaplain.

And for 1680 brad-nails purchased for repair of the said house 2s.4d.

And for 900 medium spike-nails (*Middelspykyng*) purchased for the same work at 3d. for 120, 22½d.

And for 720 stowering-nails (*stouryngnaill*) purchased for the same 12d.

And for 14 brags purchased from John Smith for the same 4d.

And for carting 7 waggon-loads of mud for daubing the said house[89] 8d.

And for the service of John Orwell, carpenter, making and strengthening the top of a certain porch over the exit (*supra portam ad egressum*) there, by agreement 8d.

And for 1 lock with a key purchased for the same from John Nesse 4d.

And for 40 thraves of *Dryvyngthak*[90] purchased from John Hamond for roofing the said house 13s.4d.

And for the service of one man collecting withies for roofing the said house 4d.

And for the service of Patrick the thatcher and his mate thatching the said roof by agreement 9s.

And for various expenses incurred through John Bulkyn, parish chaplain, as shown by the detailed bill (*per billam de parcellis*), 11s.6½d.

Gowthorp (*Goukthorp*)

Henry Joynour And for carting of 17 waggon-loads of stone from Monk Fryston quarry to the house in the tenure of Henry Joynour at 9d. a waggon-load 12s.9d.

And for 4 waggon-loads of stone purchased for the kiln-house there, with carting of the same 3s.

And for 480 bricks (*Walletighell*) purchased for the said kiln 2s.

And for 2 waggon-loads of lime purchased at Sherburn for repair of the said house, with carting of the same 4s.8d.

And for the service of one mason making *le kilnehorn* and footing (*bassantis*) the lean-to (*le Tofall*) in the garden there for 3 days 15d.

---

[89] *domus* interlined.
[90] Thatch, but of what particular kind is not clear.

And for the service of his assistant for the same time 12d.

And for the service of one man from Sherburn making the stone foundation (*fundum*) around the kitchen and brew-house there for 4 days without food provided (*sine mensa*) 20d.

And for timber purchased for repair of the kiln and the lean-to (*le Tofall*) there by Henry Joynour, with 2d. for carting thence to the said house, 6s.10d.

And for sawing of the same in part (*pro parte*) for the said work 6½d.

And for the service of John Orwell, carpenter, building and repairing the said house for 15 days, receiving 5d. a day without food provided, 6s.3d.

And for 9 tumbrell loads of mud for daubing the walls there carted by William Pyper 9d.

And for 60 daubing stowers[91] (*Doubyng stoures*) purchased from William Bower for the said work 18d.

And for 240 medium spike-nails purchased for the same, and 180 stowering-nails and brad-nails, 2s.9d.

And for 60 laths purchased from Robert Courtenay 6d.

And for the service of John Croxdale and his mate daubing the walls of the brew-house and kitchen there for 5 days, each receiving 4½d. a day, 3s.9d.

And for the service of 2 men daubing the walls of the kiln-house and the lean-to (*le Tofall*) there for two days 16d.

And for 400 slates purchased at Sherburn, with carting thence to Selby, 2s.

And for the service of one man roofing and slating the house there for 8 days 3s.4d.

And for the service of his assistant for the said time 2s.

And for 34 thraves of thatch (*Damthak*) purchased for thatching the aforesaid kiln-house and the lean-to (*le Tofall*) at 3d. a thrave 8s.6d.

And for the service of the woman drawing the said thatch 6d.

And for the service of John Croxdale thatching the said houses for 5 days 2s.1d.

And for the service of his assistant 20d.

And for staples, crooks (*crokez*), and 4 iron bars purchased for strengthening the doors and windows there 12d.

---

[91] Mr Haslop has noted that stowers were 'the upright timbers on which twigs and branches, and in later times laths, were fixed prior to daubing.' (*YAJ*, 48, 1976, n. 47).

Thomas Sadeller's   And for 60 laths purchased from John Spencer for repair of the house in the tenure of Thomas Sadeller 3d.

And for nails purchased for the same 2½d.

And for 1 iron bar purchased from John Smith for the door of the said house 4d.

And for the service of John Orwell, carpenter, working on repairing the faults in the said house for 2 days 8d.

And for the service of William Pyper carting 2 tumbrell-loads of mud for daubing the said house 2d.

And for the service of Richard Belman daubing the walls there for one day 4d.

Micklegate (*Mikelgate*)

Richard Goldale's   And for expenses incurred on repair of the house in Micklegate in the tenure of Richard Goldale, according to his own bill:

For carting timber given by the lord from Spark Hagg to Selby 4d.

And for daubing stowers purchased from John Burton 8d.

And for the service of one carpenter working there for 3 days 15d.

And for one threshold purchased 1d.

And for nails purchased from William Benyngholm 7½d.

And for 20 thraves of thatch (*Damthak*) purchased for thatching the said house 5s.

And for the service of the thatcher for 3 days, with the assistance of the woman drawing (the thatch) and serving him, 21d.

And for withies purchased for the same 1d.

And for 15 tumbrell-loads of mud carted to the said house 15d.

And for the service of John Stag daubing and repairing faults there, by agreement 19d.

(Walter del Sartryn's) And for the expenses incurred on the repair of the house in the tenure of Walter del Sartryn:

For the service of Patrick the thatcher, thatching the said house for 12 days with thatch acquired in the time of Brother John Millington[92] 4s.

And for the service of his assistant for the said time 3s.

---

[92] For whom see above, p. 155 n. 18.

And for the service of the women carrying the said thatch from the water-mills in Selby to the said house 6d.

Total £8 16s.5d.

Office maintenance (*Resumptio officii*)	The same person accounts for the service of William Plummer melting and working afresh with office lead one lead vessel in the kitchen weighing 32 stones for cooking meat, with the repair of another lead vessel there for the scullery, by agreement 5s.

And for the service of Peter Greve strengthening and repairing the said lead vessel in the furnace there 6d.

And for the service of John Osgodby felling and squaring (*postantis*) one ash-tree in *le Schaghgarth* for the dressers (*lez dressourz*) in the kitchen 20d.

And for sawing the same 9d.

Total 7s.11d.

Allowances (*Allocationes*)

Gowthorp	The same person asks that he be allowed 16d. for decrease in the rent of one stall near the gates of the abbey lately in the tenure of William Benyngholm, because (it was) in the lord's hand this year for lack of tenant.

And 4s. for loss of rent of three stalls in the market-place lately in the tenure of John Nesse, Thomas Lowe, and John Crowebane, because (they were) in the lord's hand for lack of tenants this year.

And 10s. for decrease of rent of one house in Gowthorp in which John Litster lives, because (it is) totally ruinous.

Micklegate	And 10s. for the rent of one toft in Micklegate lately in the tenure of Emma Turnour, because (it was) in the lord's hand this year for lack of tenant.

And 6s. for the rent of one toft lately in the tenure of Agnes Grayngham, because (it was) in the lord's hand this year for lack of tenant.

Ousegate	And 16s. for loss of the rent of one messuage in Ousegate lately in the tenure of John Babthorp, because (it was) in the lord's hand this year for lack of tenant.

Middlethorp   And 2s.6d. for decrease of rent of a certain assart
called *Nueland* formerly (the property) of John
Barneby (and) lately in the tenure of John Dobbe,
because (it was) in the lord's hand for Pentecost term
for want of tenant. And at that time it used to return
yearly 7s.6d. as of old (*de antiquo*). And it newly
returns 5s.

And to this accountant himself for his diligence in the said office as a
gratuity this year 10s.

And 3s. for loss of the rent of one cottage lately in the tenure of John
Yharom, because (it was) in the lord's hand for the Martinmas term
this year for lack of tenant.

And 13s.4d. for tithe of the barn at Balne in the hands of Thomas
Dilcok junior,[93] because the same Thomas has paid the aforesaid
money to Brother Thomas Crull, bursar this year,[94] as shown by a
bill (made) between the lord abbot and the said bursar.

Court of Selby   And 16s.8d. from a certain fine of John Plummer
pardoned to him by the lord abbot, namely out of
20s.

And 5s. from a certain fine of John Pacok pardoned to him by the
lord abbot (but) charged to John Babthorp, collector of the proceeds
of the court, namely out of 10s.

And 4d. from the amercement of John Barker, lately living in New
Lane (*le Nuelane*), because distraint could not be found.

And 2d. from the amercement of Thomas Wherldale charged to the
aforesaid John, for the aforementioned reason.[95]

Total £4 18s.4d.

Settlement of debt   The same person accounts for payment to William
(*Acquietatio debiti*)   Pulter of Snaith of 57s., as part of the sum of 65s.
owed to him from the time of Brother John Milling-

---

[93] The Thomas Dilcoks, senior and junior, were associated with the tithes of Balne as early as
1398–99 at least; and a Thomas Dilcok was still farmer of the tithes there in 1432 (see above,
p.50, Bursars' Roll 1398–99; and HUL, DDLO 20/1, *Firme (Decim)arum*, Bursar's Roll
1431–32).

[94] For whom see above, p. 159 n. 38.

[95] Following this another entry has been crossed out, with the explanation 'because (entered)
above' (*quia supra*). It reads: 'And to this accountant himself for his diligence in the said office
as a gratuity this year 10s.' (*Et sibi ipsi computanti pro diligentia sua in dicto officio ex
curialitate hoc anno xs.*)

ton his predecessor, as shown at the end of his account.[96]

Total 57s.

Total of all expenses, allowances, and settlements £228 17s.8¾d. And he exceeds (income by) £32 1s.11½d.[97] And the same person is allowed 53s.4d. for the livery from the kitchen of Katherine Dring[98] this year, with which he was charged above under the heading 'Sale of hides'. And he now exceeds (income by) £34 15s.3½d. Of which excess the sums written below are owed to sundry creditors as follows, namely:

to William Muston of York for sundry herrings and fish purchased from him this year 23s.[99] Quit.[100]

to Roger Selby of York, spicer, for sundry spices purchased from him this year 7s.3d. By Crull. Quit.

[101]to Richard Holme of Selby from a loan 6s.8d. Quit.

[102] And to Brother John Anlaby for money received from the almoner's office this year £8.

to Nicholas Couper of Selby for sundry works in the office of the kitchen this year 2s.6d. By Crull. Quit.[103]

to William Ferrour for shoeing of the kitchen horses this year 2s.8d. By Crull. Quit.

[104]to Robert Santon, barber, collecting the rents and farms of the office this year 13s.4d.

Total £10 15s.5d.

---

[96] William Pulter and his partner were farmers of the tithe-barn and tithes of Snaith (see above, p. 157).

[97] A few words have been crossed out at this point and others erased at the end of the sentence: 'Of the excess the sums written below are owed to his sundry creditors ...' (*excessu debentur summe subscripte diversis creditoribus suis ...*).

[98] See above, p. 159.

[99] See above p. 161 n. 49.

[100] *Quietus* has been entered in the margin. Notes recording the acquittance of debts and by whom have been added in a different hand, presumably at a later time than the compilation of the account.

[101] This entry has been deleted in the manuscript with the explanation: '(Settled) By the accountant himself' (*per ipsum computantem*).

[102] This entry has been deleted in the manuscript with the explanation: 'because the said accountant received (the money) for the use of the kitchen. And they are owed to the said office.' (*quia dictus computans recepit ad opus Coquine. Et debentur dicto officio*). Brother John Anlaby was, of course, the accountant himself and apparently almoner as well as kitchener this year.

[103] *Quietus* has been written in the margin, and *per Crull* added in a different hand.

[104] This entry has been deleted in the manuscript, with the explanation: 'because (settled) by the accountant' (*quia per computantem*).

The account of grains and stock of the time of Brother John Anlaby, kitchener, during the time (of the account?)[105]

Wheat	Firstly the same person answers for 10 quarters of
(*Frumentum*)	wheat received from Brother Robert Selby,[106] granger of the monastery this (year?).

And for 2 quarters 2 bushels received from the same granger by means of John Hazand, cook of the lord abbot,[107] (this year?).

... the same granger for the provisions of the household this year, by 4 tested tallies.

Total 294 quarters 2 bushels.

From which he accounts for 282 quarters in bread baked for the provisions of the lord abbot, the convent, (the corrodarians?) and other visitors, ... tested ...

And for 12 quarters 2 bushels delivered to John Hazand, cook of the lord (abbot?) ... cook of the convent, (for the provisions?) of the lord abbot, convent, and other visitors this year.

(Total?) as above. (And quit?).

Malt	The same person answers for 625 quarters of malt
(*Brasium*)	received from Brother Robert Selby, ..., by tested tallies.

Total 625 quarters.

And he accounts for this as brewed for consumption by the lord abbot, convent, and other visitors this year, as shown by the daily accounts of the store-room examined.

Total as above. And quit.

Beans and peas	... and peas received from the said Brother Robert,
(*Fabe et Pise*)	granger of the monastery this year.

And for 1 quarter 1 bushel of white and green peas purchased for pottage (in Lent?) this year as above.[108]

Total 16 quarters, 6 bushels.

From which he accounts for 3 quarters 5 bushels in kitchen expenses of the lord abbot and convent for making pottage with this year.

---

[105] Part of the right hand side of the dorse of the manuscript has been torn off, and a number of words are lost.
[106] One of the bursars of the 1398–1399 account roll (see above, p. 44).
[107] He was appointed in 1399 (see above, Bursars' Account 1398–99, p. 57).
[108] For the purchase see above, p. 168.

And for 12 quarters in feeding and sustenance of pigs in the office this year.

And for 1 quarter 1 bushel in pottage made for consumption by the lord abbot and convent in Lent this year.

Total as above. And quit.

Oats (*Avene*)	The same person answers for 29 quarters of oats received from the aforesaid Brother Robert Selby, granger of the monastery this year.

Total 29 quarters.

From which he accounts for 22 quarters in flour made for the making of the pottage in the kitchen of the lord abbot and convent this year.

And for 1 quarter 4 bushels in ...[109] of the horses of the office this year.

And for 5 quarters 4 bushels in feeding and sustenance of the swans and poultry (*pullalii*) this year in the office.

Total as above. And quit.

Bulls (and) oxen (*Tauri Boves*)	The same person answers for 2 oxen purchased this year as above.[110]

And for 5[111] received from John Whyteheued, serjeant at Monk Fryston this year.

And for one bull and one ox received from William Courtenay, serjeant at Stainer this year.

And for 10 oxen received from the extern cellarer this year.

And for one ox received from the mortuary of the wife of the late William Thomson.

And for one bull by purchase this year as above.[112]

And for 2½ shoulders found at the making of this account.

Total 21 oxen, 2½ shoulders, of which 2 (were) bulls.[113]

From which he accounts for 14 carcases, 1 shoulder and half a shoulder in slaughtering for consumption by the lord abbot both in the household within the abbey and external expenses, as shown by the daily accounts examined.

---

[109] The word is faded and illegible.
[110] See above, p. 160.
[111] *iiii* has been crossed out and *v* interlined.
[112] See above, p. 160.
[113] The manuscript has in the margin the accounting dots by which this calculation was made.

And for 1 shoulder of ox delivered to the keepers of the ferry at Carlton in the customary fashion.

And for 1 sold as above this year.[114]

Total 15 carcases, 2½ shoulders. And 6 oxen remain.

Cows
(*Vacce*)

The same person answers for 14 cows received from John Wright, serjeant at Eastoft this year.

And for 1 received from William Courtenay, serjeant at Stainer this year.

And for 1 coming under the heading (*nomine*) of the mortuary of the wife of the late John del Brend.

And for 20 by purchase this year as above.[115]

And for 13 received from Brother John Crossethwayt, extern cellarer this year.[116]

And for 1 from the mortuary of John Hanson this year.

And for 1 quarter 2 shoulders and half a shoulder found at the making of this account.

Total 51 carcases, 2 quarters, half a shoulder.[117]

From which he accounts for 49 carcases in slaughtering for consumption by the lord abbot, convent, and other visitors this year, as shown by the daily accounts examined.

And for 1 sold this year as above.[118]

Total 50 carcases. And 1 carcase, 2 quarters, half a shoulder remain.

Bullocks and heifers
(*Bovetti et Juvence*)

The same person answers for 24 bullocks by purchase this year as above.[119]

And for one heifer by purchase this year as above.[120]

And for 1 quarter, 2 shoulders, and half a shoulder found at the making of the account.

Total 25, 1 quarter, 2 shoulders and half a shoulder.[121]

From which he accounts for 2 bullocks sold as above this year.[122]

---

[114] See above, p. 156.
[115] See above, p. 160.
[116] For Brother John Crossethwayt, see above p. 117.
[117] The manuscript has accounting dots in the margin for this calculation. The total should read 50 carcases, 1 quarter, 2½ shoulders.
[118] See above, p. 156.
[119] See above, p. 160.
[120] See above, p. 160.
[121] The manuscript has accounting dots in the margin for this calculation.
[122] See above, p. 157.

And for 15 bullocks and 1 heifer in slaughtering for consumption by the lord abbot, convent, and other visitors, as shown by the daily accounts of the households and of external expenses examined.

Total 18. And 7 bullocks, 1 quarter, 2½ shoulders remain.

Calves
(*Vituli*)
The same person answers for 3 calves received from William Courtenay, serjeant at Stainer this year.

And for 17 calves received from *dominus* John Olive, serjeant at Rawcliffe this year.

And for 1 found at the making of the account.

Total 21.

And he accounts for these in victuals of the lord abbot, convent, and other visitors this year, as shown by the daily accounts of the households and of external expenses examined.

Total as above. And quit.

Boars, pigs, and
piglets (*Apri, Porci, et Porculi*)
The same person answers for 1 boar, 2 pigs, and 10 piglets received from John Whyteheued, serjeant at Monk Fryston this year.

And for 6 piglets received from William Swalowe, serjeant at Crowle this year.

And for one boar, 12 pigs and piglets, received from John Wright, serjeant at Eastoft this year.

And for 1 boar, 4 pigs, and 9 piglets, received from John Wright, serjeant at Adlingfleet and Garthorpe this year.

And for 1 boar, 11 pigs, and 6 piglets received from William Courtenay, serjeant at Stainer this year.

And for 16 piglets received from *dominus* John Olive, serjeant at Rawcliffe this year.

And for 6 pigs by purchase this year as above.[123]

Total 86.

From which he accounts for 19 pigs, 2 quarters, and 1 shoulder, in slaughtering for consumption by the lord abbot, convent, and other visitors, as shown by the daily accounts of the households and of external expenses this year examined, as for bacon.

And for 57 pigs and 2 shoulders in slaughtering of this kind for consumption as above.

And for 3 boars in slaughtering of this kind for the same reason.

[123] See above, p. 160.

And for 1 boar given to Brian de Stapleton, knight,[124] by order of the lord abbot.

And for 1 pig delivered to Brother John Crossethwayt, extern cellarer this year.

And for 1 shoulder of pork in external expenses because of the court.

And for 1 shoulder of pork delivered for consumption by the archdeacon of Richmond in the house of W. Pecton.[125]

And for 2 pigs sold as above.[126]

And he asks to be allowed 1 pig from Stainer charged to him above, because diseased (*leprosus*) and of no use for consumption.

And 1 pig charged to him above from Rawcliffe for the same reason.

And 1 shoulder of pork valued at ( )[127] debited to the accountant because wanting.

Total as above. And quit.

Piglets (*Porcelli*)	The same person answers for 22 piglets deriving from tithes of Selby this year.

And for 4 received from John Sutcliff, serjeant at Eastoft this year.

And for 11 received from William Courtenay, serjeant at Stainer this year.

Total 37.

From which he accounts for 28 in victuals of the lord abbot, convent, and other visitors, as shown by the daily accounts of the households and external expenses examined this year.[128]

Total 28. And 9 piglets remain.

Sheep (*Multones*)	The same person answers for 383 sheep by purchase this year from various persons for sundry prices as above.[129]

---

[124] Sir Brian de Stapleton of Carlton near Snaith, who served with Henry V in France and died in Normandy in 1418. For a brief biography, see *The Parliamentary Representation of the County of York*, 1258–1832, ed. A. Gooder, I, YAS, Record Series 91, 1935, pp. 176–177.

[125] William Pecton or Pekton was the servant of the keeper of the guest house in 1421–22, and presumably also at this time (see WDA, Se/Ac/8c, account of the keeper of the guest house). The archdeacon was Stephen le Scrope (died 1418), who sent game to the abbot this year (WDA, Se/Ac/9, *Dona*).

[126] See above, p. 159.

[127] There is a blank in the manuscript, but the margin supplies the valuation figure: '3¼d.' (*iiid.q*ᵃ).

[128] *Et in* has been crossed out in the manuscript.

[129] See above, p. 160.

And for 13 received by means of Richard Glover this year.

Total 396.

From which he accounts for 383 carcases, 1 quarter, 2 shoulders and half a shoulder in slaughtering for consumption by the lord abbot, the convent, and other visitors, as shown by the daily accounts of the households and external expenses examined this year.

And for 1 carcase delivered to the keeper of the ferry at Carlton by custom.

And for 3 quarters of mutton in victuals of Brothers John Crossethwayt and Thomas Bolton on account of the court and of sundry hunts this year.

And he asks for allowance to him of 10 totally torn apart by the dogs of Brother Thomas Bolton, William del Malthous,[130] and others within the abbey this year.

Total 395 carcases, 2½ shoulders. And 3 quarters, half a shoulder[131] remain.

Lambs (*Agni*)	The same person answers for 3 lambs deriving from tithes of the town of Selby this year.

And for 60 by means of Richard Glover this year.

And for 3 carcases, 2 quarters, and 1 shoulder found at the making of this account.

Total 66, 2 quarters, and 1 shoulder.[132]

From which he accounts for 66 carcases, 2 quarters and 1 shoulder in slaughtering for consumption by the lord abbot, convent, and other visitors, as shown by the daily accounts of the households and the recreations examined this year, with 1 for the victuals of Brother Thomas Bolton by reason of the hunt in the North Woods (*lez North-Wodd*).

Total as above. And quit.

Swans and Cygnets (*Cigni et Cignetti*)	The same person answers for 20 swans and cygnets deriving from issue of the swans of Crowle this year.

And for 7 from issue of the swans on the Selby dam this year.

Total 27.

---

[130] An account roll of 1426–27 describes William del Malthous as keeper of the malt-house and keeper of the rabbit-warren of Thorpe Willoughby (HUL, DDLO 20/68, account of the serjeant of Carlton).

[131] *di' spaud'* interlined.

[132] The manuscript has accounting dots for this calculation in the margin.

From which he accounts for 8 in victuals of the lord abbot, convent, and other visitors, as shown by the daily accounts of the households examined.

And 2 given to William Lodington.[133]

And 2 to Thomas Burnham, steward of Crowle.[134]

And 2 to William Gascoign.[135]

And 2 to the archdeacon of Richmond.

And 2 to Brian de Stapleton, knight.

And 9 by disease (*in morina*) this year.

Total as above. And quit.

Coneys and young rabbits (*Cuniculi et rabetti*)	The same person answers for 45 coneys deriving from the warrens of Crowle and Thorpe Willoughby this year, of which 4 (were) from Thorpe Willoughby.

Total 45.

From which he accounts for 39 in victuals of the lord abbot, convent, and other visitors this year, as shown by the daily accounts examined.

And 6 given to Brian de Stapleton, knight, this year.

Total as above. And quit.

Partridges with pheasants (*Perdices cum Phasianis*)	The same person answers for 18 partridges coming from the lord's warrens this year.

And for 2 pheasants coming from the warren of Acaster Selby this year.

Total 20.

And he accounts for these in victuals of the lord abbot, convent, and other visitors, as shown by the daily accounts of the households and the recreations examined this year. And quit.

---

[133] Presumably the judge of the Common Pleas of that name, who previous to his appointment as a judge in 1415 had received fees from Selby Abbey of 20s. in 1398–99 and 26s.8d. in 1413–14 (see above, Bursars' Account p. 55; DDLO 20/54b, List of Pensions and Fees 1413–14; E. Foss, *The Judges of England*, 9 vols, 1848–64, IV, s.v. Lodington, William).

[134] He had been appointed steward of Crowle in 1390 (British Library, Cotton Vitellius E.XVI, f.123).

[135] Presumably William Gascoigne of Gawthorpe, chief justice of King's Bench, who died in 1419. William de Gascoigne had received a fee of 26s.8d. from Selby Abbey in 1398–99 (see above, Bursars' Account, p. 55; and R. Somerville, *History of the Duchy of Lancaster*, I, pp. 373, 386, and 468).

Herons
(*Ardee*)

The same person answers for 33 herons coming from issue of *Schaghgarth* this year.

Total 33.

From which he accounts for 9 as gifts to the lord archbishop of York this year.[136]

And 24 in victuals of the lord abbot, convent, and other visitors, as shown by the daily accounts of the households and recreations examined this year.

Total as above. And quit.

Geese and ducks
(*Auce et Anates*)

The same person answers for 16 geese received from William Haliday, proctor and serjeant at Reedness this year.

And for 16 geese deriving from the lake-rent (*de laco*)[137] of Acaster Selby this year.

And for 2 from tithes of Selby this year.

And for 10 ducks received from William Haliday, proctor and serjeant at Reedness this year.

And for 61 ducks from gifts of sundry tenants at Crowle this year.

Total 105.

From which he accounts for 26 geese in victuals of the lord abbot, convent, and other visitors, as shown by the daily accounts of the households and the recreations examined this year.

And 8 valued at ( )[138] debited to the accountant because lacking.

And for 71 ducks in victuals of the lord abbot, convent, and other visitors, as shown by the daily accounts of the households and the recreations examined this year.

Total as above. And quit.

Capons
(*Capones*)

The same person answers for 6 capons coming by gift of John Gaytford this year.[139]

And for 6 by gift of Thomas Gibson this year.

And for 2 by gift of William Courtenay this year.[140]

---

[136] Henry Bowet, archbishop of York 1407–1423.

[137] A rental of Monk Fryston of circa 1400 also speaks of cocks, hens, and eggs *de lake* (WDA, Se/Ac/24).

[138] There is a blank in the manuscript, but the margin supplies the valuation figure of 2s. (*iis.*).

[139] He was farmer of the tithes of Carlton in 1411–12 and 1413–14 (HUL, DDLO 20/54e; B. Holt (ed.), 'Two obedientiary rolls of Selby Abbey', p. 39).

[140] He was serjeant at Stainer (see above, p. 181).

And for 22 by gift of the rector of Stanford on Avon and others this year.

Total 36.

And he accounts for these in victuals of the lord abbot, convent, and other visitors this year, as shown by the daily accounts of the households and the recreations examined.

Total as above. And quit.

Cocks and hens
(*Galli et Galline*)
The same person answers for 16 cocks and 64 hens coming from a certain lake-rent of 16 bovates of land in Acaster Selby for the Christmas term this year.

And for 7 cocks and hens from the lake-rent of 7 bovates of land in Bondgate this year.

For the lake-rent of 8 bovates of land there he does not answer, because (they are let) at money rent.

And for 24 hens from the lake-rent of 11 bovates of land in Hambleton this year.

And for 2 cocks and 2 hens from lake-rent of Brayton coming from 2 bovates of land there this year.

And for 11 cocks and 11 hens from lake-rent of Thorpe Willoughby coming from 11 bovates of land there this year.

And for 24 cocks and hens from lake-rent of Monk Fryston, as shown by the rental this year.

And for 12 cocks and hens coming from lake-rent of Hillam, as shown by the rental this year.

And for 8 hens coming from lake-rent of Rawcliffe, as shown earlier (*ut patet in precedente*).

Total 181.

From which he accounts for 100 cocks and hens in victuals of the lord abbot, convent, and other visitors, as shown by the daily accounts of the households and the recreations examined this year.

And 1 cock and 2 hens are allowed to him for the rent of one toft and one bovate of land in Hillam formerly in the tenure of John Heton and now (let) at money rent payable to the bursar.

And 1 cock and 2 hens (are allowed) to him for the rent of one toft and one bovate of land lately in the tenure of Richard Parlebien of Hillam, because (it was) in the lord's hand for lack of tenant this year.

And 1 hen given to William Pinne, poulterer, for his diligence about the collection of the said lake-rent this year.

And 8 as dead by disease (*in morina*).

And 1 hen given to John Webster.[141]

And 65 debited to the accountant because lacking, of which 10 (were) cocks and 55 hens, valued at ( )[142] (in all) at 2d. a hen and 1½d. a cock.

Total as above. And quit.

Chickens (*Pulcini*)	The same person answers for 24 chickens coming from lake-rent of Hambleton from 11 bovates of land there yearly, as shown by the rental.

Total 24.

From which he accounts for 22 in victuals of the lord abbot, convent, and other visitors this year, as shown by the daily accounts examined.

And 2 as dead by disease. And quit.

Pigeons (*Columbelle*)	The same person answers for 244 pigeons received from John Whyteheued, serjeant at Monk Fryston this year.

And for 207 from issue of the lord's cote at Selby this year.

And for 200 pigeons received from William Courtenay, serjeant at Stainer this year.

And for 80 from issue of the cotes of Thorpe Willoughby this year.

Total 731.

And he accounts for these in victuals of the lord abbot, convent, and other visitors this year, as shown by the daily accounts of the household and of the recreations examined.

Total as above. And quit.

Eggs (*Ova*)	The same person answers for 640 eggs coming from lake-rent of Acaster Selby this year.

And for 520 eggs coming from tithes of the town of Selby this year.

And for 160 eggs coming from lake-rent of Monk Fryston this year.

And for 1440 tithe[143] eggs received from William Haliday, serjeant at Reedness this year.

Total 2760.

---

[141] *Johanni Webster i gallin'* interlined.
[142] There is a blank in the manuscript here, but the margin supplies the valuation figure of 10s.5d. (*xs.vd.*).
[143] *decim'* interlined.

From which he accounts for 2240 in victuals of the lord abbot, convent, and other visitors this year, as shown by the daily accounts of the households examined.

And 120 in expenses about the collection of the said eggs this year.

And 400 thrown-out because bad.

Total as above. And quit.

Hides
(*Corria*)

The same person answers for 14 hides produced by slaughter of that many oxen this year.

And for 49 produced by slaughter of that many cows this year.

And for 16 produced by slaughter of that many bullocks and heifers this year.

And for 20 skins from that many calves slaughtered this year, as shown above.

Total 99.

From which he accounts for 79 hides of 94 oxen, cows, bullocks, heifers, and calves, by sale this year, as shown above.

And one ox-hide and 1 cow-hide given to the tanner, purchaser of the said hides, by agreement.

And 3 cow and bullock hides valued at ( )[144] debited to the accountant because lacking.

Total as above. And quit.

Wool-fells, with pelts and wool
(*Pelles lanute, cum pellettis et lana*)

The same person answers for 156 wool-fells coming from that many sheep slaughtered from the festival of St Michael (29 September) to Lent[145] this year.

And for 300 fells and[146] pelts coming from that many sheep slaughtered as above from the festival of Easter (11 April) to the festival of Michaelmas (29 September) this year.

And for 120 fleeces weighing 16 stones of wool coming from that many sheep shorn this year as above.

Total 455[147] fells and pelts.

---

[144] There is a blank in the manuscript here, but the margin supplies the valuation figure of 4s.3d. (*iiiis.iiid.*).
[145] Lent in 1417 began on 24 February.
[146] *pellibus et* interlined.
[147] The figure should be 456.

From which he asks that he be allowed 10 from that many sheep destroyed and savaged by dogs.

And 446 in sale as above.[148]

And quit.

Lambs' fells (*Pelles Agnorum*)[149]	The same person answers for 67 fells coming from that many lambs for the victuals of the households this year, as shown above.

Total ( )[150] And sold this year as above.[151]

Red and white herrings (*Allecia rubea et alba*)	The same person answers for 38,520 red herrings purchased this year at various prices this year,[152] as shown above.[153]

And for 1510 red herrings found at the accounting (*repertis super compotum*).

And for 1440 white herrings purchased this year as above in one barrel and 1 firkin.[154]

Total 41,470.[155]

From which he accounts for 38,590 red herrings, 1440 white herrings, in victuals of the lord abbot, convent, and other visitors this year, as shown by the daily accounts examined.

And 1200 red herrings for the distribution to the poor on Maundy Thursday this year (8 April).

And 112 red herrings for the distribution to the poor on All Saints Day (2 November) and the two days following.

And 128, valued at ( ),[156] debited to the accountant because lacking.

Total as above. And quit.

---

[148] See above, p. 158.
[149] This whole entry has been crossed out in the manuscript, with the explanation above: 'because (recorded) above under the heading Wool-fells and Pelts' (*quia superius in titulo pelles lanute et pellette*).
[150] Blank in the manuscript.
[151] See above, p. 158.
[152] *Sic.*
[153] See above, p. 161.
[154] See above, p. 161.
[155] There are accounting dots for this calculation in the margin.
[156] There is a blank in the manuscript here, but the margin supplies the valuation figure 14d. (*xiiiid.*).

Salted fish
(*Piscis Salsus*)

The same person answers for 457 salted fish purchased from sundry persons for various prices this year as above.[157]

And for 20 and 1 quarter salted fish found at the accounting.

Total 477 and 1 quarter.

From which he accounts for 474 salted fish and 1 quarter in victuals of the lord abbot, convent, and other visitors this year, as shown by the dietaries of the households and the recreations examined.

And for 1 salted fish delivered to the keepers of the ferry at Carlton in the accustomed manner.

And for 2 to the Prioress of Gokewell[158] by order of the lord abbot this year.

Total as above. And quit.

Dried fish
(*Piscis Durus*)

The same person answers for 842 dried fish purchased from sundry persons at various prices this year, as shown above.[159]

And for 27 found at the making of this account.

Total 869.

From which he accounts for 869 in victuals of the lord abbot, convent, and other visitors this year, as shown by the daily accounts of the households and the recreations examined, with 8 in victuals outside the house because of hunts and courts.

Total as above. And quit.

Salmon
(*Salmones*)

The same person answers for 76 salmon coming by purchase this year at various prices, as shown above.[160]

And for 5 sprents (*sprentz*) purchased this year as above.[161]

And for 16 salmon and a half coming from the office fishery this year, receiving[162] half a fish for the lord.

---

[157] See above, p. 161.
[158] Gokewell was a small priory for Cistercian nuns in Lincolnshire, with 8 nuns and a revenue of £10 p.a. in 1440 (see D. Knowles and R. N. Hadcock, *Medieval Religious Houses*, pp. 272–273; *VCH*, Lincoln, II, London, 1906, pp. 156–157). Selby Abbey made a number of gifts to the priory during Abbot William Pygot's rule; and in 1431–32 Lady Joan Pygot, former prioress of Gokewell, is listed in a bursar's roll as the recipient of a pension of 26s.8d. p.a. from the abbey (HUL, DDLO 4/3, 20/1, and 20/54e; WDA, Se/Ac/9).
[159] See above, p. 162.
[160] See above, pp. 162–163.
[161] See above, pp. 162–163.
[162] *capiend'* is repeated in the manuscript.

And for 8 salmon, 1 *cok*, 2 sprents and a half, found at the accounting.

Total 104½ salmon, 2 sprents, 1 *cokke*, and half a sprent.[163]

And he accounts for these in victuals of the lord abbot, convent, and other visitors this year, as shown by the daily accounts of the households and the recreations examined.

And quit.

Large (and) small eels and a tench (*Anguille grosse minute et Tencha*)

The same person answers for 5 great eels, 810 small eels, and 1 tench coming from the lord's fishery at Crowle this year.

And for 406 small eels coming from the Selby dam this year.

Total 1221.[164]

And he accounts for these in victuals of the lord abbot, the convent, and other visitors this year, as shown by the daily accounts of the households and the recreations examined.

And quit.

Pikes and pickerels, roach and perch, (*Pykes et Pikerelli, Rochie et Perche*)

The same person answers for 8 pikes, 49 pickerels, 840 roach and perch, coming from the lord's fishery at Crowle this year.

And for 4 pikes, 18 pickerels, 3600 roach and perch coming from the Selby dam this year.

Total 4519 pikes, pickerels, roach, and perch.

And he accounts for these in victuals of the lord abbot, the convent, and other visitors this year, as shown by the daily accounts of the households and the recreations examined.

And quit.

Milk and cheese (*Lac et Caseus*)

The same person answers for 173 gallons of milk, 7½ stones of cheese, coming from the dairy at Stainer this year.

Total 173 gallons of milk, 7½ stones of cheese.[165]

And (all) as above (used) for victuals.

---

[163] The figures actually add up to 100½ salmon, 1 *cokke*, and 7½ sprents.
[164] The same figure is written in the margin of the manuscript, but it does not include the tench.
[165] *vii petr' et di' casei* interlined.

Salt, pepper, and saffron (*Sal, Piper, et Crocus*)   The same person answers for 17 quarters and 4 bushels of salt purchased from sundry persons this year at various prices, as shown above.[166]

And for 19 pounds of pepper purchased this year from sundry persons at various prices, as shown above.[167]

And for 5¼ pounds of saffron purchased this year from sundry persons at various prices, as shown above.[168]

Total 17 quarters, 4 bushels of salt; 19 pounds of pepper; 5¼ pounds of saffron.[169]

And he accounts for this in victuals of the lord abbot, the convent, and other visitors this year.

Total as above. And quit.

Almonds, rice and sanders (*Amigdale, Rys et Saundrez*)   The same person answers for 8 dozen and 2 pounds of almonds purchased from sundry persons at various prices this year, as above.[170]

And for 113 pounds and half a pound of rice purchased from sundry persons at various prices this year, as above.[171]

And for 2 pounds of sanders purchased this year, as above.[171]

Total 8 dozen and 2 pounds of almonds; 113 pounds and half a pound of rice; 2 pounds of sanders.

And he accounts for this in victuals of the lord abbot, the convent, and other visitors this year.

Total as above. And quit.

Cumin, honey, and oil (*Ciminum, Mel, et Oleum*)   The same person answers for 2 pounds of cumin purchased this year as above.[171]

And for 20½ gallons of honey purchased this year as above.[171]

And for 7 gallons and 1 quart of oil purchased this year as above.[172]

Total 2 pounds; 20½ gallons; 7 gallons and 1 quart.

And he accounts for this in victuals of the lord abbot, the convent, and other visitors this year.

Total as above. And quit.

---

[166] See above, p. 163.
[167] See above, pp. 163–164.
[168] See above, p. 164.
[169] *v lib' et 1 quarteron' croci* interlined.
[170] See above, p. 164.
[171] See above, p. 164.
[172] See above, p. 168.

Figs and raisins (*Ficus et rasinus*)	The same person answers for one basket (of figs) with raisins, 2 baskets and 13 pounds of figs purchased from sundry persons this year as above.[173]

Total 3 baskets and 13 pounds.[174]

And they are used as above.

Tallow (*Cepum*)	The same person answers for 49½ stones of tallow derived from (*provenientibus de exitu*) beasts slaughtered this year; and not more because (they were) too lean.

Total 49½ stones.

From which he accounts for 41½ stones by sale as above.[175]

And for 2 stones provided for the needs (*ad expensas*) of the lord prior for light.

And 4 stones to the keeper in the store-room for light there.

And 2 stones to the keeper in the refectory for light in the same.

Total as above. And quit.

---

[173] See above, p. 164.
[174] *et xiii lib'* interlined.
[175] See above, p. 158.

(e) The office of Keeper of the Refectory

As custodian of the monks' dining-hall the keeper of the refectory was the official responsible for maintenance of facilities in the room where the community received its daily meals. He purchased necessary equipment, like the towels for use at the lavatorium where the monks washed their hands before meals; he paid a laundress for her services in keeping table-linen clean. Necessarily with an annual income of around 27s.[1] he could not be responsible for the fabric of the building, and small items of expenditure are all that were within this official's competence. In fact income was more than adequate to cover expenses in all surviving accounts, which show surpluses carried forward to the next year in every case.[2] The minor nature of the office is also indicated by the fee paid to its occupant: 2s. p.a., as compared with 40s. for the bursars of 1398–99 or 10s. for the kitchener in 1416–17.[3]

Just four accounts have survived from this office, two from the abbacy of William Pygot (1408–29) and two from that of John Ousthorp (1436–66).[4] The earliest account has been chosen for inclusion here because, like the latest of the four, its condition is excellent; the other two have both suffered some damage and loss. It may once have had another document attached to it, as four small holes and a small piece of thread survive at the bottom of the single piece of parchment.

The accountant, Brother John Grayngham, is a somewhat obscure figure. He entered the house about 1406,[5] and served frequently in the office of keeper of the guest house during the 1420s.[6] Apart from this little is known about his career at Selby, not even the approximate date of his death. In view of the minor nature of the offices he held, perhaps the emphasis of his career was rather on his duties in the abbey church as a choir-monk than on the business affairs of the house; but this is mere speculation that the available evidence can neither confirm nor disprove.

[1] Income from rents and farms was £1 7s.1d. in all four surviving accounts, and the only other income recorded was the arrears carried forward from the previous account. Just before the Dissolution the revenues of the office were assessed at £1 0s.4d. See WDA, Se/Ac/11, 13, 15, and 19; and HUL, DDLO 20/60.

[2] The surplus was 47s.3½d in 1423–24, 40s.2¼d in 1436–37, and 3s.2½d in 1459–60, and in all cases arrears were brought forward from the previous account. WDA, Se/Ac/13, 15, 19.

[3] For the bursar's and kitchener's fees in 1416–17, see WDA, Se/Ac/9, and above p. 176.

[4] All these accounts are to be found in the Westminster Diocesan Archives. They cover the years 1421–22, 1423–24, 1436–37, and 1459–60. WDA, Se/Ac/11, 13, 15, 19.

[5] Borthwick Institute of Historical Research, Archbishop's Register 5A, Sede Vacante 1405–07, f.100.

[6] He was keeper of the guest house in 1420–21, 1422–25, and 1426–27 (WDA, Se/Ac/8 and 14).

The Keeper of the refectory's account of 1421–22

Table of Contents

The account of Brother John Grayngham, keeper of the refectory of the monastery of Selby from the festival of St Martin in Winter (11 November) A.D. 1421 to the same festival of Martin A.D. 1422, for one whole year.

Arrears (*Arreragia*)	Firstly the same person answers for 26s.4½d. from arrears of the last account of Brother Richard Athelingflet,[7] his predecessor in the said office in the preceding year.

Total 26s.4½d.

Rents and farms (*Redditus et Firme*)	Likewise the same person answers for 27s.1d. from rents and farms belonging to the said office this year according to the rental.

Total 27s.1d.

Total of receipts with arrears 53s.5½d.

---

[7] He entered the house in 1408 and was ordained a priest in 1413. He served as keeper of the guest house 1421–22 and as kitchener 1421–25, 1431–32, and in 1433. The pittancer's roll for 1441–42 is his last known appearance in the Selby records. See HUL, DDLO 20/1, 21, and 66; 21/21 and 22; and 4/3; WDA, Se/Ac/8c, 11 and 12; Borthwick Institute of Historical Research, Archbishop's Register 18, Henry Bowet, fos 39 & 39v.

Small expenses (*Minute*)
From which the same person accounts for 9 yards (*virgis*) of linen cloth purchased from Juliana Raghton for long towels in the refectory this year, at (*prout dat'*) 4½d. a yard 3s.4½d.

And for 4 yards of linen cloth purchased from Alice Ughtreth for napkins (*Napkyns*) 16d.

And for 4 yards of linen cloth purchased from Juliana Raghton for the cupboard (*le Coppebord*) in the refectory 16d.

And for the service of Thomas Goldsmith repairing one maple-wood cup (*ciphum murreum*) formerly (the property) of Brother William Lathom[8] 4d.

And for the service of William Pyper making 2 mats for the benches in the refectory from his own reeds (*Damthak*) 16d.

And for the service of Adam Smith repairing the handle (*le Stert*) of one vessel (*Amphore*) for ale 4d.

And for the wage of the laundress of the office this year 16d.

And given to the clerk of the refectory as a Christmas present (*ex curialitate ad Natale Domini*) this year 6d.

And for the service of Henry Clerc making candles for distribution in the convent this year 2d.

Total 10s.0½d.

Cost of ditches (*Custus fossatorum*)
Likewise he accounts for the service of Alan Lindezay newly making and digging 12 rods (*rodas*) of ditch on the east part of the assart called *Hundlund* this year, receiving 2d. a rod, 2s.

And for the service of the same cleaning out 24 rods of ditch on the south side of the said assart 2s.

And for the service of Richard Chast digging and making 24 rods around the assart near *Hirdyhate* 2s.

Total 6s.

Allowances (*Allocationes*)
Likewise he asks that 5d. be allowed to him this year from the rent of one garden lying on the bank of the dam in the tenure of Stephen Whallay, because no distraint could be found for the rent and also it has lain empty.

---

[8] A former prior of Selby, who appears in the first surviving pittancer's roll for 1362, and makes his last appearance there in 1404 (HUL, DDLO 20/14, 21/14; WDA, Se/Ac/2).

And to this accountant himself for his diligence in the said office this year as a gratuity (*ex curialitate*) 2s.

Total 2s.5d.

Total of expenses and allowances 18s.5½d.

And thus the accountant owes 35s.

From which he has paid to Brother John Haldenby,[9] his successor, on account (*super compotum*) 26s. And he owes 9s.[10]

---

[9] He entered the abbey in 1421 and served in a large variety of offices: keeper of the refectory 1422–24; keeper of the guest house 1427–29; sacrist 1431–32 and 1446–48; bursar 1432–33; granger and keeper of the spiritualities of Snaith 1436. By 1465 he was prior of Selby, an office he held until 1468. HUL, DDLO 20/1, 27, and 28; WDA, Se/Ac/11, 13, 14, 17; *The Coucher Book of Selby*, II, pp. 348–349; B. Dobson, 'The Election of John Ousthorp as Abbot of Selby in 1436', p. 38; British Library, Additional Charter 45854; Borthwick Institute of Historical Research, Archbishop's Register 18, Henry Bowet, f.412r.

[10] The last three sentences have been added later in a darker ink.

(f) The office of Infirmarer

The infirmarer, like the keeper of the refectory, was a minor official in charge of a particular part of the monastic complex of buildings, in this case the infirmary. His fee for his services of 2s. ranks him with the refectorian; whilst the assigned income of his office was of a similar order of magnitude. The infirmarer received from rents and farms less than 50s. p.a., a sum that was not nearly adequate even for his modest expenses in the four surviving accounts of the office; and sales of turves and wood brought in more than rents in two of those four accounts.[1] Just prior to the dissolution of the house a survey of 1535 records the income of the office, derived from rents and farms, as 41s.8d.[2]

There is very little information to be obtained from the Selby Abbey archives about the infirmary building or the services that were provided within it. Just a single document has survived to record the activities of its obedientiaries, containing four accounts for the period Pentecost (6 June) 1400 to Martinmas (11 November) 1403, three for a full year and the last for approximately six months.[3] They appear to represent the record of office of a single accountant, Brother Thomas de Howeden, who was certainly responsible for the last three accounts; but the roll has suffered damage that renders the heading of the first account and some of its early entries illegible.[4] Of the two remaining full year accounts the earlier has been chosen for inclusion here, as form and content are virtually the same in both.

The details contained in these accounts very largely record the minor but necessary expenses of running a small household: the provision of lighting, utensils, and fuel, for example. They tell us nothing about the specific functions of the infirmary or its layout; and the situation at Selby can only be suggested in broad outline from the evidence of better documented houses. Fundamentally, of course, the infirmary was for sick monks; but the old were also retired there and, in earlier days at least, all monks went

---

[1] Rents and farms brought in 49s.4d. in 1402–03 and 22s.2d. for the approximately half year period in 1403 from Pentecost to Martinmas. In the earlier year sale of turves brought in 53s., and in the later year sale of wood 26s.8d. HUL, DDLO 20/53.
[2] HUL, DDLO 20/60.
[3] The four accounts are written one after the other on both face and dorse of the roll. There is some doubt about the dating of these accounts because the heading of each states the year only once (e.g. 1401 for the second account), situating this statement at the end of the heading, although the accounts run from Pentecost to Pentecost. I have interpreted this statement of the year as applying to the commencement of the account rather than its close, because only thus can the final account Pentecost-Martinmas 1403 be made to follow from the previous account. HUL, DDLO 20/53.
[4] The parchment roll is decayed and fragile, and the first few inches have suffered particular damage on the left side of the face of the manuscript.

there for the regular blood-letting or phlebotomy for medical reasons that was also an occasion for a few days of holiday and relaxation.[5] It provided on a small scale the facilities for sleeping, eating, and worship, that were supplied for the bulk of the community in the dormitory, refectory, and abbey church; but because of the condition of its charges, the infirmary had long been the place where the monastic regime was relaxed, a richer diet provided, and greater freedom from the round of services enjoyed.

At contemporary Durham cathedral priory, a Benedictine community of about 70 monks of whom some 40 were normally resident at Durham itself,[6] the infirmary contained nineteen private rooms with their own fireplaces. Most were occupied by the old and sick, but senior obedientiaries and doctors of divinity also had their sleeping quarters there instead of in the common dormitory. There was a hall in which the residents of the infirmary were expected to eat together when possible; and spiritual needs were catered for by provision of a chapel.[7] Probably Selby Abbey would not have been very different from the larger northern house in its provision of infirmary facilities.

The infirmarer in the account which follows, Brother Thomas de Howeden, was a local man like so many of his fellow-monks. His local origins are suggested by his name,[8] although placenames used as surnames do not necessarily indicate place of origin of the individual at this late date in the medieval period.[9] There is confirmatory evidence in his case, however, in the fact that the proctor of the abbot of Selby at Whitgift and Reedness supplied wheat and barley to his mother in 1397–98, both these places being about 8 km south-east of Howden on the banks of the Ouse.[10] Brother Thomas had become a full member of the community at Selby in 1375, and in 1380 he was named as kitchener.[11] He held the same office in 1410–11.[12] With his term as infirmarer this is the sum of his known offices,

---

[5] For a general discussion of monastic infirmaries, see L. Butler and C. Given-Wilson, *Medieval Monasteries of Great Britain*, London, 1979, pp. 71–72. The normal position for the infirmary was east of the eastern range of the cloisters. Professor Knowles has suggested that in the later middle ages blood-letting may have declined with changes in hygienic fashions and provision of other forms of recreation, like visits to one of the monastery's manors (see D. Knowles, *The Religious Orders in England*, II, pp. 245–246).

[6] B. Dobson, *Durham Priory 1400–1450*, p. 54.

[7] B. Dobson, *Durham Priory 1400–1450*, pp. 78 and 88.

[8] Howden is some 15 km south-east of Selby.

[9] For a discussion of the problems involved in using such surnames at Durham Cathedral Priory, see B. Dobson, *Durham Priory 1400–1450*, pp. 56–58. At Selby two-thirds of the monks listed in the 1403–04 Pittancer's roll had surnames derived from places within 50 km of the abbey (for this roll, see above pp. 95–100).

[10] HUL, DDLO 20/65.

[11] Borthwick Institute of Historical Research, Archbishop's Register 12, Alexander Neville, f.122; HUL, DDLO 21/11.

[12] HUL, DDX 145/1.

though he is found in 1412 and 1413 acting as representative of the abbot in the court of Selby.[13] As one of the senior monks of the abbey he accompanied Brother William Pygot to London in 1408, in order to secure royal licence to elect a new abbot on the death of John Shirburn;[14] and he was evidently dead before the pittance list for 1415–16 was compiled, since his name does not appear in it.[15]

The Infirmarer's account of 1401–02

Table of Contents

The account of Brother Thomas de Howeden for the office of the infirmary from the festival of Pentecost A.D. 1401 (22 May) to the same festival (14 May) a year later (*Anno revoluto*)

Firstly he accounts for 4s.4d. from the farms of Selby, Brayton, and Menthorpe.

And for 12s. from Balne.

And for 5s. from Osgodby-in-Lindsey.

And for 26s.8d.[16] from Hambleton for the land called *Grekerland*.

Sum total of receipts 48s.0½d.[17]

From which the same person accounts for the excess of expenses (over income) in the preceding account 4s.6d.

---

13 HUL, DDX 145/1.
14 PRO, C.84/39/4.
15 HUL, DDLO 20/15.
16 *s.* and *d.* interlined.
17 The total should be 48s.0d. There is an erasure after the first sum in this section (4s.4d.), which may have been the missing *ob'*.

And for the wage of Robert Barbour[18] 10s.

And for the wage of the laundress 2s.

And for the wage of the servant of the infirmary 5s.

And for the livery of the said servant 3s.4d.

And for 3 stones and 3 lbs of candle purchased 4s.4d.

And for cups (*ciphis*) purchased 13d.

And for rushes and strewing (*strewyng*) 14d.

And for one embroidered cover (*cooperculo depincto*) purchased 4d.

And for the service of one carpenter making one window in *le Gannow* for one day without food (being provided) 4d.

And for nails purchased for the said window 2d.

And for loading of the boat with turves at Rawcliffe 3s.2d.

And to John Hippeswel for his ship for transporting the turves from Rawcliffe to Selby 7s.6d.

And for the wage of 18 women carrying turves for one day from the ship to the turf-house 4s.6d.

And for the service of 8 women carrying for half a day 12d.

And for bread purchased for the aforesaid reason 10d.

And for ale purchased 18½d.

And for beef (*in carne bovis*) 8d.

And for 1 sheep 14d.

And for cheese 5d.

And for herrings and codling (*codlyng*) 6d.

And for expenses at Balne at times 8d.

And for gifts (*oblationibus*) 12d.

And he asks that he be allowed 5s. from the farm of Osgodby, because (it is) in the hands of Gerard Suthill.[19]

And to the accountant for his labour 2s.

Total of all expenses with allowances 62s.2½d. And thus he overspends (income by) 14s.2d.

---

[18] His surname presumably indicates his occupation, which would include attending to the monks' tonsures. But the barber was also a regular practitioner in surgery and dentistry at this time.

[19] The Suthills were a considerable Lincolnshire family, holding among other possessions half a knight's fee in Redbourne, whose church was appropriated to Selby Abbey (see *Feudal Aids*, III, p.247). In the bursars' account roll of 1398–99 Sir Gerard de Suthill was said to hold Stainton Waddingham, also in Lincolnshire, for life (see above, p.87).

III

THE ABBEY CHURCH

(a) The offices of Sacrist and Keeper of the Fabric

Like the offices of pittancer and chamberlain the two departments considered in this section originally had separate monk-officials in charge of them; and as in the former case they were permanently united under one obedientiary during the first half of the fifteenth century, possibly in the course of a single reorganization. No account from the office of sacrist alone has survived, though stray references, as for example in 1355, name the occupant of the office and hence demonstrate its existence.[1] For the keeper of the fabric alone there is a single isolated account for the year 1413–14. The office was functioning in 1434–35, when the keeper of the fabric was named as Brother John de Ousthorp;[2] but no further records have been preserved until 1446–47, by which time fabric and sacristy had been united under a single monk-official. For this joint office eight accounts have come down to us, four for the fifteenth century and four from the last twenty years of the abbey's existence.[3]

As his name would suggest, the keeper of the fabric was plainly charged with the maintenance of the abbey buildings in good order; and his accounts record repairs to windows, walls, and gutters. His income from assigned rents and other sources, however, was not large: less than £14 in 1413–14 after transfers of rents to other monk-officials have been deducted. When, as in this latter year, he was engaged in extensive building operations, his regular income had to be heavily supplemented, on this occasion by payment from the bursar of rather more than £32. After the two offices had been combined, their joint income was still only £40–£50

---

[1] British Library, Cotton Vitellius E.XVI, f.147v.
[2] HUL, DDLO 20/55, s.v. *Resolutiones Redditus.*
[3] For the years 1446–47, 1447–48, 1494–95, 1497–98, 1522–23, 1523–24, 1524–25, and 1537–38 (WDA, Se/Ac/17 and 22; British Library, Additional Charter 45854; HUL, DDLO 20/37, 38, 39, 40, and 42).

Selby Abbey, west front, 1855 (Lithograph by W. Richardson; photograph by Dianne Tillotson)

and appears to have fallen to around £30 by the end of the fifteenth century.[4] Even so, much the larger proportion of expenditure in surviving accounts was undertaken on behalf of the sacrist's office.[5]

The conclusion seems to follow that the normal responsibility of the office was intended to be the minor repairs constantly needed in a complex of buildings like medieval Selby Abbey. If more extensive reconstruction was envisaged, the money had to be secured from the central treasury as in 1413–14; and plainly one alternative to this was to have the work funded directly by the office at Selby that commanded adequate resources. Thus the rebuilding of the cloisters under Abbot John de Shirburn (1369–1408) was not undertaken through the fabric office at all, but by the bursary.[6] Some less important works within the abbey can also be found in early fifteenth century bursars' accounts, like those of 1416–17 and 1431–32,[7] showing that the fabric office had no exclusive control in matters of maintenance of buildings as its name might at first suggest. No doubt as elsewhere the competence of particular officials, or some other factor now lost to view, determined the degree of responsibility of the keeper of the fabric in any year.

By the time that fabric office accounts survive for Selby Abbey, major new building on the abbey church had become a thing of the past. After the complete reconstruction of the choir in the Decorated style of the fourteenth century, the Perpendicular style of the late middle ages added no more than one chantry chapel to the northern transept, known as the Lathom chapel, a large west window, and a seven-light window in the northern transept.[8] This is not to say, however, that extensive reconstruction had ceased at Selby. Because only the church is now standing, we do not have the evidence in stone to indicate what rebuilding of the monastic complex was undertaken, and too few accounts remain for certainty. Yet there are indications in these rolls that here, as at Durham,[9]

---

[4] Income in 1447–48 was £50 19s.0d., of which £11 7s.2½d. was 'arrears' brought forward from the previous year (British Library, Additional Charter 45854). In 1494–95 receipts were £31 5s.4½d. and in 1497–98 £30 19s.6½d. (HUL, DDLO 20/37 and 38).

[5] In 1447–48, for example, the sacrist's office spent nearly £24, whilst repairs to the fabric accounted for less than £1 (British Library, Additional Charter 45854).

[6] See above, pp. 74–76.

[7] In 1416–17 repairs to the abbot's rooms and stables and to the chaplain's chamber were undertaken (WDA, Se/Ac/9, s.v. *Emendatio Domorum infra Abbatiam*); whilst in 1431–32 £29.2s.1d. was spent on the stonework and woodwork of the abbey, including extensive work on the abbot's quarters (HUL, DDLO 20/1).

[8] See N. Pevsner, *The Buildings of England: Yorkshire, West Riding*, 2nd edition, Harmondsworth, 1967, pp. 435–442, and *The Coucher Book of Selby*, II, pp. xxx–xxxii. John Lathom, secretary of Archbishop Kempe and canon of Beverley, wrote his will in June 1470 but it was only proved in 1476 (B. Dobson, 'The Election of John Ousthorp as Abbot of Selby in 1436', p. 38). For post-medieval changes to the abbey church, see G. Cobb, *English Cathedrals: The Forgotten Centuries. Restoration and Change from 1530 to the Present Day*, London, 1980.

[9] See R. B. Dobson, *Durham Priory*, pp. 292–296.

there was a remodelling of domestic buildings in conformity with contemporary standards of comfort and privacy that included cloister, abbot's lodgings, and guest house. Perhaps the monks of Selby had not in fact ceased to devote resources to new building in the early fifteenth century. Certainly the fabric roll for 1413–14 which follows has its own importance for understanding medieval monastic life. With the rebuilding of the cloisters detailed in the bursars' account of 1398–99 it brings us as close as is now possible to the constant activity of masons and carpenters that was a feature of medieval monasteries.

The workshops and stores attached to the fabric keeper's office have disappeared in the general destruction of the monastery's buildings; but for the other office considered in this section the survival of the abbey church has provided a happier fate. On the south side of the eastern arm of the church is still to be found the sacristy, where vestments and valuables in the care of the sacrist were stored. His was a position of vital importance in the monastic community, for his duties centred on the interior of the monastic church and the daily round of services that it was the prime duty of the monks to recite.[10] His staff kept the community's vestments clean and repaired, provided candles and lamps for lighting the church, maintained the clock that regulated the monastic day, and saw to the abbey's peal of bells. He supplied the hosts and wine for the many masses, the incense for the censers, and saw to the repair of the organs. It must have been an office busy with a mass of detail for the smooth running of the great church, and its occupant as sacrist and keeper of the fabric received a commensurately large fee of 10s. p.a., the same as the kitchener. As well another monk acted as his deputy, the sub-sacrist, receiving for his pains another 5s. a year.

Through the sacrists' rolls the modern reader can approach as near to the heart of the monastic life at Selby, service of God in the abbey church, as financial records will allow. They will not much aid an estimate of the diligence of the Selby monks, and less still of their fervour; but something of the character and atmosphere of their worship and intercession for souls clearly emerges from the details of money received and expended. The many altars and shrines, with their images, candles, and boxes for offerings; the masses being said for the souls of the dead; the rich

---

[10] The timetable at Selby can only be reconstructed from that of other houses. At Durham Priory, which probably corresponded closely to St Mary's abbey York in this regard, the monks' daily routine began with Matins at midnight. Matins may have lasted an hour. In summer Prime followed at 6 a.m. or 6.30 a.m., probably occupying about 30 minutes. Mass was then sung at 9 a.m., followed by the daily chapter meeting, and High Mass at 11 a.m. At 2 p.m. was Nones; at 4 p.m. Vespers; and Compline and the *Salve Regina* ended the day sometime after 6 p.m. or 7 p.m. As well there were demands on the monks for masses at the various altars and chantries of the church. See B. Dobson, *Durham Priory: 1400–1450*, pp. 69–73.

vestments of the celebrants, the music and chanting; these are some of the features of the scene in the early fifteenth century abbey church that must have been apparent to any visitor. The evidence for them will be readily found in the sacrist's roll translated below.

Two accounts follow these introductory remarks, illustrating respectively the operation of the fabric office as a separate department, and the functioning of the office of the sacrist with which it was combined. In the one case the account of the keeper of the fabric for 1413–14 is the sole surviving record of its kind; whilst in the other the sacrist and fabric keeper's roll for 1446–47 is the earliest of the small series of accounts recording the sacrist's activities.[11] Fortunately both are complete accounts which have suffered only minor damage, mainly some damp stains that have rendered a few words illegible in the earlier account. It should be noted that the keeper of the fabric's record is taken from the unique and problematical bundle of obedientiary accounts for 1413–14 that also supplied the extern cellarer's roll included above.[12] However, only the high level of expenditure on the fabric this year appears to make this account unusual by comparison with the later records of the combined offices of fabric and sacristy, not the nature of its activities.

The two accountants in these records present an obvious contrast in the character of their careers. Brother John Passelewe, the keeper of the fabric in 1413–14, is a quite obscure member of the community. The earliest known reference to him is in the pittance list for 1403–04, when he was already a full member of the community.[13] His only other known office was as paymaster of pensions and fees sometime before 1416, and he is not found in the abbey records after that date.[14] His origins may have been relatively humble, for there is a reference in his fabric account below to a relative acting as a plumber's assistant.[15]

The sacrist and keeper of the fabric of 1446–47 was Brother John Haldenby, who had entered the house in 1421.[16] Ultimately he rose to be prior of Selby, certainly by 1465 and possibly as early as 1436 after the then prior, Brother John Ousthorp, became abbot (1436–66).[17] He held the

---

[11] They are preserved respectively in Hull University Library as DDLO 20/54a, and Westminster Diocesan Archives as Se/Ac/17.

[12] For some discussion of the problems connected with this bundle of documents, see above p. 116.

[13] See above, p. 99.

[14] HUL, DDLO 20/15 and 45; WDA, Se/Ac/9.

[15] See p. 210.

[16] Borthwick Institute of Historical Research, Archbishop's Register 18, Henry Bowet pt 1, f.410v.

[17] Whilst the pittance paid to the prior is accounted for in these documents, his name is rarely given. He is mentioned as prior in 1465 in *The Coucher Book of Selby*, II, pp. 348–49.

office until 1468, when he was succeeded by Brother Walter Cotyngwith;[18] and this is also the probable date of his death. His career as an administrator was a busy one: keeper of the refectory 1422–24;[19] keeper of the guest house 1427–29;[20] sacrist 1431–32 and sacrist and fabric keeper 1446–48;[21] bursar 1432–33;[22] granger and keeper of the spiritualities of Snaith in 1436.[23] Finally he is known also to have had a prominent role in proceedings at the abbatial election in 1436, when he acted as scrutator of votes with two other monks.[24]

The Keeper of the Fabric's account of 1413–14

Table of Contents

---

[18] HUL, DDLO 20/28, s.v. *Solutiones denariorum.*
[19] WDA, Se/Ac/11 and 13.
[20] WDA, Se/Ac/14.
[21] HUL, DDLO 20/1; WDA, Se/Ac/17; British Library, Additional Charter 45854.
[22] HUL, DDLO 20/1.
[23] B. Dobson, 'The Election of John Ousthorp as Abbot of Selby in 1436', p. 38.
[24] *Ibid.*, pp. 34–35.

The account of Brother John Passelewe, keeper of the fabric of the monastery of Selby, from the festival of St Martin in winter (11 November) A.D. 1413 to the same festival A.D. 1414 for one whole year.

Arrears
(*Arreragia*)

No arrears are held because the same accountant in his last account exceeded income.

Receipts
(*Receptum*)

Firstly the same person answers for £8 3s.1d. from rents and farms belonging to the aforesaid office yearly, as appears by the rental.

And for 58s.11½d. from offerings coming to the chapel of Stainer[25] this year.

And for 20s. received from the keeper of the spirituality of Selby[26] this year, and not more because it is not fixed for certain.[27]

And for 40s. from the mills of Thorpe Willoughby this year.

And for 10s. issuing from the gift of William Muston and Margaret his wife[28] for the benefit of the office this year.

And for 6s.8d. issuing from the bequest of Katherine Basset this year.

And for £32 4s.7d. received from Brother John Hales,[29] bursar, by indenture this year.

Sum total of receipts £47 3s.3½d.

Excess
(*Excessus*)

From which the same person accounts for the excess of expenditure (over income) of his last account of the year next preceding, as it appears at the foot there, 19s.6½d.

Total 19s.6½d.

[25] Selby Abbey had a manor-house here, less than two kilometres from the abbey. In 1442 a papal grant of indulgences spoke of a painted picture of the blessed Virgin Mary at Stainer Chapel, and of its being frequented by the local faithful because of the miracles worked there by the Virgin. See *CPL*, IX, 1431–1447, p.253.
[26] The function of this official was presumably linked with the spiritual revenues of the abbey, as distinct from its temporal possessions. But no surviving account roll for the office has been discovered. The abbot of Selby's spiritual jurisdiction in Selby included probate of wills, and matrimonial and testamentary cases. See W. Dugdale, *Monasticon Anglicanum*, III, p.493n.k, for a description of this jurisdiction in 1409.
[27] *et non plus quia non ponitur in certo* interlined.
[28] They had purchased a corrody for both their lives from the abbey in 1402. William Muston was a fishmonger of York; and on his death in 1418 he left the abbey one pipe of red wine 'for one pittance'. See British Library, Cotton Vit. E.XVI, f.137v; and *Testamenta Eboracensia* I, p.390.
[29] Brother John Hales, a novice in the community in 1404, was bursar in 1411–12 and 1415–16 as well as this year. He was kitchener in 1418, but does not appear in the abbey records thereafter. See Borthwick Institute of Historical Research, Archbishop's Register 16, Richard le Scrope, f.310; WDA, Se/Ac/9; HUL, DDLO 21/20; Lincolnshire Archives, CM 1/56.

Transfer of farms[30]   Likewise he accounts for the repayment to Brother
(*Resolutio firmarum*)   Thomas Bolton,[31] kitchener of the monastery this
year, in respect of the old farm due to his office
yearly, 13s.4d.

And to Brother Thomas Warnefeld,[32] keeper of the infirmary, in
respect of the farm belonging to his office yearly, 2d.

Total 13s.6d.

Repair of the monas-   Likewise he accounts for the service of one glazier
tery   glazing 3 lights (*luminaria*) in the west gable (*le
(*Resumptio monas-*   *Westgavell*) of the monastery with new glass con-
terii)   taining 49 feet in length and breadth, at 9d. a foot,
36s.9d.

And for 3 stones of Spanish iron purchased for making bars out of it
21d.

And for the service of Adam Smith manufacturing the said bars 12d.

And for pitch purchased for smearing on the said bars 3d.

And for 200 brad-nails purchased for securing the glass 4d.

And for the service of William the plumber melting 191 stones of lead
from lead ash (*ex cineribus*), at 2½d. a stone, 33s.1½d.[33] in addition
to 6s.8d. pardoned by the said plumber.

And for the gift to the same person for drink 4d.

And for 2 quarters of charcoal (*charecoll*) purchased for the same
work 20d.

And for the service of the said plumber soldering (*consolidantis*) the
gutters of the cloister and the seams (*les semys*) for 5 days without
food (being provided) 3s.4d.

And for 8 lbs of solder purchased for the same 3s.

And for the service of the same plumber searching for faults in the
roof and gutters around the choir and soldering defects there for 2
weeks 8s.

---

[30] As the entries make clear, this section records the transfer to other monk-officials of rents
belonging to their offices which had been initially paid, presumably for convenience of
collection, to the office of keeper of the fabric.

[31] For Brother Thomas Bolton, see above p. 121 n. 20.

[32] Brother Thomas Warnefeld appears in the Selby records more than 30 years before this
time in 1380, when he was described as cellarer. He was serving as abbot's chaplain in 1389,
and pittancer in 1412–13; and he was still a member of the community in 1416. See
Lincolnshire Archives, CM 1/34; WDA, Se/Ac/7; HUL, DDLO 20/15; British Library,
Cotton Vit. E.XVI, f.149v.

[33] *viid.* crossed out and *1d.ob.* interlined.

And for 17 lbs of solder purchased for the same work 6s.4½d.

And for the service of the same person taking down the old lead roof of the vestry on the north side, repairing, soldering, and replacing the same, by contract 10s.

And for 4 lbs of solder purchased for the same 18d.

And for 960[34] lead nails purchased for the same work 2s.8d.

And for 240 medium-sized spike-nails (*middelspykyng*) purchased for the same 6d.

And for the gift to John Skott, relative of the said keeper of the fabric, assisting the said plumber for 3 weeks 3s.4d.

And for the service of one glazier repairing defects in the windows of the church, cloister, chapter-house, and dormitory, by contract 5s.

And for the service of the same glazier repairing one window in the nave of the church on the north side 12d.

And for the service of 2 masons taking down the stone chimney of the guest house's old hall for one week 5s.4d.

And for the service of 2 men helping them for the same time 3s.4d.

And for 18 stowers (*stoures*) purchased from John Wright for making scaffolding of them 14d.

And for the service of 2 workmen collecting and stacking stones in the cemetery of the monks for 2½ days 20d.

And for the service of the same persons knocking down 2 stone walls of the guest house's old hall, and carrying the said stones to the outer courtyard of the abbey, by contract 12s.

And for the service of the same persons sifting and cleansing the sand of the said walls and taking the same to the said courtyard for 9 days without food (being provided) 6s.

And for the service of the said workmen taking down the joists (*les gystes*) of the aforesaid hall and carrying the same to the royal hall (*Aulam regiam*)[35] for 3 days 2s.

Total £7 11s.5d.

---

[34] *DCCC* has been reckoned as 960, since the long hundred of 120 is in use in this account.

[35] Joists are the timbers on which the boards of a floor or the laths of a ceiling are nailed. They stand on edge parallel to each other stretching horizontally from wall to wall, or resting on supporting beams or girders. (*OED*)

There was also a Royal Hall at St Albans abbey, rebuilt in the later fourteenth century; whilst at Durham the most sumptuous guest apartment, the King's Chamber, was rebuilt during John Wessington's priorate (1416–1446). See L. F. Salzman, *Building in England down to 1540. A Documentary History*, p. 399; and R. B. Dobson, *Durham Priory*, p. 294.

Repairs of houses (*Emendationes domorum*)	Likewise he accounts for the carrying of 2 cart-loads of clay for repairing the walls of one shop at the corner near the cross[36] in the market place 2d.

And for the service of one man repairing the said walls for one day without food (being provided) 4d.

And for the service of Robert Sklater repairing the chamber (*cameram*) of the said shop with his own tiles for half a day 6d.

And for one ladder[37] purchased for entry to the said chamber 3d.

And for a lock with key purchased for the door of the said shop 6d.

And for the service of Robert Bouland carrying 2 cart-loads of clay to the new building in Gowthorpe for the walls and floor (*area*) of the chamber in which John Taillour is staying 3d.

And for the service of John Dyker repairing the walls of the said house and floor of the chamber there for one day without food (being provided) 4d.

And for 17 thraves of thatch (*Damthak*) purchased for the malt-house in the garden of John Wilkynson at 3d. a thrave 4s.3d.

And for the service of the thatcher putting a roof of the said thatch (*Damthak*) over the said house for 2 days without food (being provided) 10d.

And for the service of his mate for the same time 8d.

Total 8s.1d.

Repair of the mills (*Resumptio molen-dinorum*)	Likewise he accounts for the carrying of 5 cart-loads of stones from the quarry of Monk Fryston to the mills of Thorpe Willoughby 3s.4d.

And for 3 cart-loads of lime purchased from Richard Devias for the same work[38] at 16d. the cart-load 4s.

And for the carrying of the said lime from Hillam to the aforesaid mill 2s.

And for 9 quarters of sand purchased from John Inglot 3s.

And for the service of John Wilkynson carrying the said sand from Selby to the said mill 16d.

And for the service of the said John carrying one cart-load of timber from the West Hagg (*le Westhagg*) of Hambleton to the said mill 5d.

Total 14s.1d.

---

[36] *in cornera iuxta crucem* interlined.

[37] Marginal note: 'There remain 1 ladder, 1 lock with key' (*Remanent 1 scala 1 serura cum clave*).

[38] *ad idem opus* interlined.

Small expenses
(*Minute*)

Likewise he accounts for one pound of wax purchased for making and lighting the small tapers before the likeness (*Ymagine*) of the blessed Mary in the chapel of Stainer[39] 6d.

And for rations purchased for consumption by the brethren and clerks singing (*psallentium*) in the said chapel at the festivals of the Assumption (15 August) and the Nativity (8 September) of the blessed Mary 3s.5d.

And for the service of one man cleansing the passages (*aluras*) around the said chapel yearly 6d.

And for the service of one man cleansing the passages (*aluras*) of the church, cloister, chapter house, and dormitory yearly 5s.

And for paper and parchment purchased for indentures and accounts 6d.

And for the service of collecting the farms of the office yearly 12d.

And for the service of Adam Smith making one chain for the bell in the cloister called *Chyme* 4d.

And for 34 ropes called *Heltirstall* 17d.

And for 4 ropes containing 24 fathoms 12d.

And for 2 little cords containing 67 fathoms at 1d. for 3 fathoms 22d.

And for 4 *Quernyrens*, 1 *bitfer*, 1 *goris* and 1 *fourmer*[40] purchased from Adam Smith 18d.[41]

And for one axe purchased for the masons 12d.

And for 2 boards of wainscot (*Waynscot*) purchased for making mason's moulds with 8d.

And for tackets (*takettis*)[42] purchased for joining together the boards (*pro tabulis conjungendis*) 2d.

And for the service of Adam Smith sharpening the tools of the masons yearly 3s.1d.

Total 21s.11d.

---

[39] See above, p. 208 n. 25.

[40] A former is a kind of chisel or gouge, used by carpenters and masons (*OED*). The meaning of the remaining words, other than that they seem to be tools, is obscure.

[41] Marginal note: 'There remain iron tools from the past and present years, as in the indenture' (*Remanent instrumenta ferrea de annis preterito et instanti ut in indentura*).

[42] A tacket is a nail; in later use, a small nail, a tack. (*OED*)

212

Renovation of 2 walls, with 2 gates and 1 arch built of stone
(*Renovatio ii murorum cum ii portis et 1 arcu ex lapide constructis*)

> Likewise he accounts for 420 alder stakes purchased from John del Bakhous at 2s. for 120, 7s.
>
> And for 180 stakes purchased from John Nelson at 2s.6d. for 120 3s.9d.
>
> And for 28 stakes purchased from John Hamelton 16d.
>
> And for the service of 2 men digging the soil and extracting the roots[43] of hazel trees in the monks' cemetery for 2½ days 20d.
>
> And for the service of 2 men sharpening and fixing 497 stakes in the foundation of the stone wall on the eastern side of the church, by contract 8s.
>
> And for fixing 131 stakes, with 300 stakes received from the park of Stainer, for constructing the foundation of the stone wall and stone arch between the cemetery of the town and the monks' cemetery, with the service of the two workmen helping the said masons, (he accounts for) nothing here because done by the masons as in the indenture.[44]
>
> And for the service of 3 men hired to help the said masons to fix the said stakes on account of expediting the work and shortness of time for 3 days 3s.
>
> And for the service of William Pyper carrying 28 cart-loads of clay for putting on the tops of the aforesaid stakes (*pro capitibus predictorum pilorum argillandis*) 2s.4d.
>
> And for the service of the men breaking and taking up stones in the quarry of Monk Fryston, as (paid) by the bursar 68s. by indenture.[45]
>
> And for the carrying of 319 cart-loads of stone from the quarry of Monk Fryston to the monastery of Selby, paid by (*per manus*) the bursar at 9d. a cart-load £11 19s.3d. by indenture.[45]
>
> And for the carrying of 8 cart-loads of stones from the quarry of Monk Fryston to the said monastery in autumn time, at 10d. a cart-load 6s.8d. by indenture.[45]
>
> And for the service of Robert Bouland carrying stones from the abbey to the monks' cemetery for 15 days for the walls and arch

---

[43] *radices* interlined.
[44] *nichil hic quia per cementarios ut in indentura* interlined, replacing the following deleted words: *non respondet hic quia per expensas cementariorum ut patet per indenturam* ('he does not answer here because at the cost of the masons, as appears by the indenture').
[45] *per indenturam* interlined.

aforesaid, receiving for him and his son helping him 10d. a day, 12s.6d.

And for 32 cart-loads of lime purchased from Richard Devias at 21d. a cart-load 56s. by indenture.

And for 29 cart-loads of lime purchased from the same person at 11d. a cart-load 26s.7d. by indenture.[45]

And for the carrying of the same nothing, because it is pardoned by agreement.

And for 3 cart-loads of lime purchased from John Inglot 8s.

And for 3 boat-loads of sand purchased from William Duffeld of York 18s.

And for one boat-load of sand purchased from William Marshall, servant of the lord archbishop, 4s.

And for the carrying of the said cart-loads (*dictarum plaustratarum*) from the bank of the Ouse to the cemetery of the monastery 6s.9d.

And for the service of William Pyper carrying 37 cart-loads of sand from the abbey to the said cemetery 18d.

And for the service of 2 masons preparing the stones for 2 stone gates for 6 weeks before Christmas 32s.,[46] each receiving 2s.8d. a week.[47]

And for the service of the same persons preparing the stones for the said gates before the festival of Easter (8 April) for 4 weeks 21s.4d., receiving as above.[48]

And for the service of the same persons constructing a stone gate at the northern side of the monastery after the festival of Easter for 4½ weeks 24s., receiving as above.[48]

And for the service of 2 men helping the same persons for the same time 15s., each receiving 20d. a week.[49]

And for the service of the said masons constructing one stone wall on the eastern side of the monastery and another stone wall, one gate and one arch of stone between the cemetery of the town and the monks' cemetery, by contract made by indenture between William the lord abbot and the said masons £4 6s.8d.

And for gifts to the same persons by courtesy on the lord abbot's order 3s.4d.

---

[46] *viiid.* crossed out.
[47] *quolibet capiente iis.viiid. in septimana* interlined.
[48] *cap' ut supra* interlined.
[49] *quolibet capiente xxd. in septimana* interlined.

And for (the service of the said masons?)[50] raising the stone wall with the said arch, by order of the lord abbot, in addition to the contract previously made by indenture 3s. ...[51]

And for the service of 2 men helping the same persons for 25½ weeks £4 5s.

And for 9 stones of Spanish iron purchased from William Martin for the making of (hooks?) and bars for the said gates 5s.3d.

And for the service of Adam Smith making the said hooks and bars 3s.

And for half a stone of lead purchased for fixing the said hooks 3½d.

And for 12 great[52] nails purchased from John Nelson 4s.

Total £37 17s.6½d.

Allowances (*Allocationes*)	Likewise he asks that he be allowed 2d. from the farm of one acre of land in *le Claycroft* formerly John Rayner's, attached to the manor of Stainer in perpetuity.

And 5s. from the rent of one shop in the market place on the corner,[53] for want of a tenant this year.

And 3s.4d. from another shop there on the corner,[53] for the same reason.

And 20d. from one tenement in Monk Fryston formerly in the tenure of Selyman,[54] for Pentecost (27 May) term for want of a tenant.

And to this accountant himself for his diligence[55] this year 6s.8d.

Total 16s.10d.

Total of all expenses and allowances £50 2s.11d. And he exceeds (income by) 59s.7½d. And there is allowed to the same person 8s. from the farm of the mills of Thorpe Willoughby this year, because the said mills have been leased to William Rakes,[56] as appears in the indentures dated 20th day of the month of September A.D. 1413, for

---

[50] A stain extends over several lines at this point and some words are partly conjectural.
[51] The remainder of the sum is illegible, but an addition of the other individual items in this section indicates that the full sum should be 3s.4d.
[52] *grossis* interlined.
[53] *in cornera* interlined.
[54] *nuper in tenura Selyman* interlined.
[55] *feodo* ('fee') crossed out and *diligencia* substituted above.
[56] *dimissa sunt Willelmo Rakes* interlined, replacing the explanation: '(because the said mills) had not been repaired on account of the lord's default, as in provision of timber and other things for the repair of the same' (*non fuerunt reperati ob defectum domini ut in liberatione meremii et aliorum ad reperationem eorumdem*).

24s. annually to be paid, the term of the first payment beginning at the festival of Pentecost (27 May) this year, where previously (the mills) used to return 40s. a year, as appears on the receipts side (*in onere*) of the preceding account. And henceforth up to the end of 20 years (next?)[57] following (the mills will be) returning annually 24s. And thus he now exceeds (income by) 67s.7½d.[58]

The Sacrist and Keeper of the Fabric's accounts of 1446–47

Table of Contents

---

[57] Word obscured and conjectured here.
[58] *lxviis.viid.ob.* interlined, replacing *iiii li.viis.viid.* crossed out.

The account of Brother John Haldenby, keeper of the offices of sacrist and the fabric of the Monastery of St German of Selby from the festival of St Michael the Archangel (29 September) A.D. 1446 to the same festival of St Michael A.D. 1447.

Arrears (*Arreragia*)	None because Thomas Haldenby,[1] lately collector of the revenues of the aforesaid offices, answered for them at the end of his account of the year next preceding.

Total nothing.

Fixed rents (*Redditus assisus*)	But he answers for 67s.5½d. from fixed rents of the freeholders belonging to the aforesaid offices according to the rental this year.

And for £13 8s.2d. from rents and farms of the holdings leased at will, with the tithes of West Tanfield, Fairburn, and the farm of the mills of Thorpe Willoughby and Sitlington, according to the aforesaid rental this year.

And for 20s. from the profits of the office of the deanery of Selby this year.

Total £17 15s.7½d.

Altarage with offerings (*Altaragium cum oblationibus*)	And for 16s.8d. from offerings coming to the high altar at the festival of the Burial of St German (1 October) this year.

And for 6s.8d. offered on the same day at the same altar by the cardinal and archbishop of York[2] this year.

And for 27s. from offerings of this kind at the festival of Christmas this year.

And for 30s.1½d. from offerings of this kind at the festival of the Purification of the blessed Mary (2 February) this year.

And for 38s.1½d. from offerings of this kind at the festival of Easter this year.

And for 6s. from offerings of this kind at the festival of the Death of St German (31 July) this year.

And for £9 14s.10d. coming from the money-box (*Stipite*) of St German this year.

---

[1] No evidence survives that he was a relative of the accountant. A Thomas Haldenby received a fee of 20s. from the abbey in the account roll of the bursar in 1431–32 (HUL, DDLO 20/1, *Feoda*).

[2] John Kempe, archbishop of York 1425–1452.

And for £6 1s.9½d. coming from the money-box of the blessed Mary at Stainer this year.

And for 2d. coming from the money-box of St Zita (*Cithe*)³ this year.

And for 2s.2d. offered at the new cross (*ad novam crucem*) this year.

And for 7s.5d. coming from the money-box of the Holy Cross (*sancte Crucis*) this year.

And for 19d. offered at the obit of Brother John Farnell this year.⁴

And for 19d. offered at the obit of Brother William Skipwith this year.⁵

And for 1½d. offered at the image (*ymaginem*) of St Leonard⁶ this year.

And for 1d. offered to St Stephen (*ad sanctum Stephanum*) this year.

And for 8d. offered on the day of the anniversary mass (*die anniversar'*) of Robert Stodley this year.

And for 16d. offered on the day of John Stephenson's obit this year.⁷

And for 4d. offered on the day of the anniversary mass of Elizabeth Manston this year.⁸

And for 4d. received for wax burned around the body of the same Elizabeth this year.

And for 15d. offered on the day of the anniversary mass of John Burton this year.⁹

And for 5d. coming on the day of offerings of candles by the boys of the monastery¹⁰ this year.

And for 3d. offered at the high altar on the festival of the Ordination of St German this year.

---

³ Presumably St Zita of Lucca, born 1218 and died 1278, now the patroness of domestic workers (see *New Catholic Encyclopedia*, New York, 1967, s.v. 'Zita, St.').
⁴ Brother John Farnell had entered the monastery in 1424 and been subsequently ordained a priest in 1427 (Borthwick Institute of Historical Research, Archbishop's Register 5A, *Sede Vacante* Register 1423–26, f.52; and Archbishop's Register 19, John Kempe, f.321).
⁵ Brother William Skipwith had entered the house in 1442 and been ordained a priest in 1445. His death appears to have occurred in 1447 (Borthwick Institute of Historical Research, Archbishop's Register 19, John Kempe, fos 220b & 283a; WDA, Se/Ac/16, *Solutiones*).
⁶ A sixth century hermit and later founder of a monastery, who lived at Noblac near Limoges. He was the special patron of prisoners and also of peasants and the sick. See *The Oxford Dictionary of the Christian Church*, ed. F. L. Cross and E. A. Livingstone, OUP, 2nd edition 1974, s.v. 'Leonard, St.'.
⁷ He was buried within the monastery. See below, p. 219.
⁸ Alvered Manston esquire, who died in 1440, received a fee of 20s. p.a. from the bursar in 1431–32 (HUL, DDLO 20/1, *Feoda*); but whether this Elizabeth was a relative is not known.
⁹ One John Burton was paid £66 13s.4d. by the Bursar in 1431–32, a sum that formed only a part of the money then owed to him (HUL, DDLO 20/1).
¹⁰ *die oblationum cereorum garcionum Monasterii.*

And for 3d. offered on the day of the anniversary mass of Abbot John Cave this year.[11]

And for 2d. offered on the day of the anniversary mass of Abbot William Pygott this year.[12]

And for 3d. offered on the day of maidens' offerings (*die oblationum puellarum*) this year.

And for 4d. offered on the day of the obit of Brother Richard Cave this year, and not more because he died at Snaith.[13]

Total £22 19s.11½d.[14]

Foreign receipts (*Forinsecum Receptum*)
And for 10s. from Brother Thomas Estoft[15] for 300[16] tiles sold in this way to the same for the chapel of the infirmary this year.

And for 3s.4d. from John Chaast for repair-work at the high altar this year.

And for 20d. from the same John for renewing one rail (*perticam*) before the image of St German this year.

And for 6s.8d. from the executors of John Stevenson on account of the burial of the same John within the monastery this year.

And for 20d. from various persons for wax sold to them at the festival of St Michael (29 September) this year.

And for 10s.4d. from John Chaast for the revenue and profit of selling one pipe of wine left by Brother John Fernell (*de remanentia Fratris Johannis Fernell*) this year.

And for 60s.3d. from the profit of two pipes of wine sold by the same John Chaast this year, in addition to the original purchase-price (*ultra primam emptionem*) as below.

Total £4 13s.11d.

Sum total of receipts £45 9s.6d.

---

11 Abbot of Selby 1429–1436.

12 Abbot of Selby 1408–1429.

13 The church of Snaith was appropriated to the abbey, which maintained the cure of souls by means of two resident monks, one of whom was known as the prior (see W. Dugdale, *Monasticon Anglicanum*, 1846, p. 493). Brother Richard Cave had entered the abbey in 1428 and was ordained a priest in 1432 (see Borthwick Institute of Historical Research, Archbishop's Register 19, John Kempe, fos 216a & 241b).

14 The total should be £22 19s.11d.

15 He had entered the monastery in 1428 and was ordained a priest in 1430. He is known to have served as precentor in 1431–32 and 1436; and he was still a member of the community in 1459. (See Borthwick Institute of Historical Research, Archbishop's Register 19, John Kempe, fos 216a & 236b; HUL, DDLO 20/1; B. Dobson, 'The Election of John Ousthorp as Abbot of Selby in 1436', p. 38; WDA, Se/Ac/18, *Solutio Denariorum*).

16 For lack of clear evidence to the contrary it is assumed that C = 100 in this account.

Pay and wages
(*Vadia et Stipendia*)

From which he accounts for the fee of this same accountant for his diligence in the said office this year 10s.

And for the fee of the sub-sacrist, with 2s. given to the same person as a present (*ad oblationem*) at the festivals of Christmas and Easter (9 April, 1447) in equal amounts (*equaliter*) this year, 5s.[17]

And for the reward given to Thomas Selby for work in the said office by order of the lord abbot this year 2s.

And for the wages of two clerks of the monastery within the office, each receiving 10s. this year, 20s.

And for presents (*oblationibus*) given to the same persons at the festival of Pentecost (28 May) 16d.

And for the service of the laundress of the office this year by agreement 5s.

And for the wage of John Ussher for sewing and repairing the purple copes and other trappings of the vestments within the office this year by agreement 6s.8d.

And for the wage of the clerk looking after the clock (*Horelogium*) this year 5s.

And for the wage of the clerk looking after and cleaning the passages (*aluras*) around the monastery this year 5s.

And for the reward given to John Ussher for his praiseworthy service in the said office this year 2s.

And for the wage of Thomas Goldale making the monastery's wax into candles this year by agreement 6s.8d.

And to the aforesaid sub-sacrist as a gratuity for his praise-worthy service in the said office this year 2s.

Total 70s.8d.

Running-costs of the office of sacrist
(*Resumptio officii Sacriste*)

And for 4000 hosts purchased at York for celebration of masses and the parishioners' holy communion this year, at 10d. for a thousand, 3s.4d.

And for 200 pounds of wax purchased there for making the candles of the monastery this year, at 46s.8d. for a 100 (pounds), £4 13s.4d.

And for the expenses incurred at York in purchasing the same wax

---

[17] The sub-sacrist was also a monk of the house (see B. Dobson, 'The Election of John Ousthorp as Abbot of Selby in 1436', p. 38).

this year, with 3d. given for transport thence by water to Selby this year (*sic*), 2s.3d.

And for one cask of lamp oil purchased from John Wassam containing 36 gallons 24s.

And for 1 quarter of charcoal (*Charcole*) purchased for the monastery's use this year 8d.

And for 4½ pounds of incense purchased for the monastery's use at 10d. a pound this year 4s.9d.[18]

And for 4 stones 10 pounds of paris candles purchased for the lighting of the monastery this year at 12d. a stone 4s.10d.

And for 12 pairs of gloves purchased and given to the bell-ringers (*pulsantibus campanas*) of the monastery this year 18d.

And for the customary breakfast of the priests at dawn on Easter Day 6½d.

And for the wage of the clerk collecting offerings on Candlemas (2 February) and Easter (9 April) days 12d.

And for the dinner given for the novices (*in cena novicorum data*) this year 3s.6d.

And for the wage of John Ussher making the mats in the choir of the monastery this year, by agreement 4s.1d.

And for 12 skeins (*zonis*) of thread purchased this year 5d.

And for the service of James Couper underpinning the water-spouts (*supponentis lez Spoutez*) on the north side of the monastery this year for 2 days, receiving 3d. a day with food provided by the lord (*ad cibum domini*), 6d.

And for nails purchased for repair of the monastery's aumbries[19] this year 2d.

And for silk purchased for repair of the albs[20] this year 3d.

And for the service of James Couper splitting fuel for melting wax for half a day this year 1½d.

And for 6 wainscot boards (*Waynscottez*) purchased for covering the walls of the high altar, by agreement 3s.4d.

And for thread purchased for repair of the albs and other vestments within the office this year 2d.

---

[18] The sum should be 3s.9d.
[19] A small recess in the wall of a church or sacristy, fitted with a wooden door, for the sacred vessels and books. (*The Oxford Dictionary of the Christian Church*, s.v. 'Aumbry').
[20] The alb was a priestly garment of white cloth, reaching to the feet, and enveloping the person. (*OED*)

And for the service of Henry Lucas cutting-down the boughs of trees growing in the cemetery this year 1d.

And for the wage of James Belfeld repairing one lock of the church 2d.

And for the repair of one lock of a certain cloister door this year 2d.

And for the wage of Nicholas Sawer sawing the wainscot boards this year 17d.

And for powder ( )[21] purchased from Anthony Swerdsliper for the Lenten veil[22] this year 1d.

And for 10 yards of linen cloth purchased for one alb at 5½d. a yard 4s.7d.

And for the service of William Payntour making 10 pounds of wax (for) before the image of St German this year 4d.

And for 100 pounds of rosin (*rosyn'*) purchased from John Methelay, by contract 4s.5d.

And for parures purchased from Brother John Farnworth[23] for one alb 13s.4d.

And for the service of John Ussher sewing together nine albs, at a cost per alb of (5d.)[24] plus 1d. in all for one principal alb, 3s.10d.

And for the service of the same person sewing together nine amices[25] this year 2d.

And for the service of the same person hemming (*fimbriantis*) four towels 2d.

And for one ounce of silk purchased for repair of the vestments of the office this year 1d.

And for silk purchased for repair of the crozier (*baculi pastoralis*) this year 16d.

---

[21] There is a blank space in the manuscript after the word *pulvere*, suggesting that a word defining the type of powder has never been added.

[22] The manuscript has *pro vero quadragesimali*, but I have concluded that *velo* is meant. The Lenten veil hung during Lent between the chancel and the nave (see Cardinal Gasquet, *Parish Life in Medieval England*, London, 5th edition 1922, p. 170).

[23] He entered the monastery in 1422 and was ordained a priest in 1427. He is known to have served as sacrist, as well as almoner and keeper of the refectory, in a long career as a monk that was still continuing in 1459. (See Borthwick Institute of Historical Research, Archbishop's Register 18, Henry Bowet, pt I, f.412r; and Register 19, John Kempe, f.231; HUL, DDLO 20/17; WDA, Se/Ac/15 and 18; Sheffield City Libraries, BFM 30). A parure is an 'ornament for an alb or amice' (*OED*).

[24] The amount appears to have been omitted by error in the manuscript.

[25] Part of the vestments of a priest, worn around the neck (see *The Dictionary of the Christian Church*, s.v. 'Amice').

And for three gallons of red wine purchased from Brother John Barlay[26] at 10d. a gallon 2s.6d.

And for rations purchased for the brethren chanting (*psallentibus*) at Stainer on the festival of the Assumption of the Blessed Virgin Mary (15 August) this year 2s.9d.

And for thread purchased on another occasion for repairing the monastery's albs this year 3d.

And for expenses incurred by the monastery's servants making the customary wax before Candelmas (2 February) 14d.

And for 6 footrests (*foteflekez*) purchased for the stall (*statione*) of the brethren of the monastery in the choir this year 12d.

And for one pound of incense purchased at York for the use of the monastery this year 10d.

And for wick purchased for 4 small candles this year 2s.8d.

And for the service of Thomas Goldale making the said candles this year, by agreement 21d.

And for the service of the same Thomas working up broken wax of the monastery (*facientis ceram fractam Monasterii*) in his own house this year 7d.

And for one yard of linen cloth purchased for celebration of mass (*ad celebrationem*) at the altar of St Katherine this year 4½d.

And for 2 pounds of incense purchased from William Barton of York at 10d. a pound 20d.

And for nails purchased for repair of the aumbry this year 1d.

And for 2 hair-cloths (*siliciis*) purchased for the altar of St Katherine and St Cuthbert this year 2s.7d.

And for props (*in ioc'*) purchased for the pageant (*pro ludo*) at Stainer on the festival of the Nativity of the Blessed Mary (8 September) this year 7½d.

And for the wage of John Ussher's wife washing the principal alb this year 2d.

And for one and a half yards of linen cloth for making one new alb this year 6d.

---

[26] His career at Selby Abbey was of impressive length, since he appears in the pittancer's roll as a novice in 1431–32 and was still receiving his pittance in 1498. During this period he is known to have served as pittancer and chamberlain 1446–50 and 1466–67, and as granger and kitchener at other times. (See HUL, DDLO 20/16, 22, 27, and 34; WDA, Se/Ac/16; Sheffield City Libraries, BFM 30).

And for the wage of Richard Wright making the money-box before the image of St Katherine this year 10d.

And for one dozen cinctures purchased for the albs at Selby this year 6d.

And for one sheep-skin purchased for repair of the organs this year 4d.

And for the service of Anthony Swerdsliper repairing the organs of the monastery this year 6d.

And for 1 sprent[27] purchased for the same person this year 2½d.

And for a hundredweight of rosin (C^a rosyn) purchased from John Methelay at another time for making large candles (torticis) from 4s.5d.

In respect of 22 gallons of wine from one pipe of wine left by John Fernyll (he claims) nothing here as an allowance because he is charged above under the heading of 'Foreign receipts'.[28]

And for 13 gallons 3 quarts of wine from the sacrist of the monastery purchased at 10d. a gallon this year 11s.5½d.

And for 6 gallons 1 pottle of red wine purchased for the use of the office from William Botiller at 6d. a gallon this year 3s.3d.

And for two pipes of wine purchased from Thomas Raghton this year £6.

Total £16 19s.11d.

Running-costs of the fabric office (Resumptio Officii Fabrice)

And for the wage of James Kerver of Hemingbrough making the shrine (tabernaculum) of the image of St Andrew this year, by agreement 13s.10d.

And for nails purchased for the same work ½d.

And for the service of John Chaumber repairing two windows of glass in the cloister of the monastery this year 8d.

And for one iron bar purchased from Robert Smyth for the door of the privy (necessariorum) this year 3d.

And for the service of Robert Hemper binding and locking two money-boxes before the images of St Andrew and St Katherine this year 2s.10d.

---

[27] i.e. young salmon.
[28] The meaning of this entry is not clear. The Latin entry reads: De xxii lagenis vini de reman' unius pipe vini de Johanne Fernyll nichil hic de alloc' quia oneratur superius in titulo de Forinsecum Receptum. See above, p.219.

And for the service of the same person repairing two carols (*carolas*) in the cloister of the monastery with iron work this year 13d.

And for the service of James Couper this year repairing the porch before the chapel of the Blessed Mary of Stainer for one day, providing his own food (*ad cibum proprium*), 6d.

And for the service of the same person doing various repairs within[29] the monastery on different occasions this year 4d.

And for the service of the same person repairing the monastery ladder this year 2d.

Total 19s.8½d.

Small Expenses (*Minute*)   And for glue (*glewe*) purchased for repair of the monastery organs this year 1d.

And for linen cloth purchased for the crozier this year 12d.

And for one lock with key purchased for safe keeping of the money-box of St Zita (*Cithe*) this year 2d.

And for three membranes of parchment purchased at York for repair of the legendary (*legende*)[30] of the monastery during Lent this year 20d.

And for the money paid to the suffragan bishop[31] for consecration of the altar of St Katherine this year 6s.8d.

And for the money given to the clerks of the same person this year 12d.

And paid to Oliver Writ for the scoring (*pro notatione*) of one gradual[32] this year, by agreement 13s.4d.

And for two thraves of wicks (*cirporum*) purchased for lighting of the lamps of the monastery this year 2½d.

And for the service of Robert Smyth repairing the water jar (*situlam*) at the Stainer font (*ad fontem de Stayner*) this year 4d.

And for the service of Anthony Swerdsliper making one leather baldric (*baudryk*) for one bell of the monastery this year 2d.

And for the service of this accountant's servant going to York in order to speak with Master Richard Wetwang concerning various matters of the office of the deanery this year 6d.

---

[29] *infra* is repeated in the manuscript.
[30] i.e. a collection of lives of the saints (see *OED*).
[31] i.e. an assistant bishop appointed to perform such episcopal duties as consecration and ordination, and essential to the functioning of a diocese at a time when the archbishop and bishop were often absent from it on business of the crown, etc.
[32] A gradual is the 'set of antiphons, usually from the Psalms, sung immediately after the first Scriptural lesson' (*The Oxford Dictionary of the Christian Church*, s.v. 'Gradual').

And for the reward given to William Fox for his[33] work with regard to Stainer this year 6d.

Total 25s.6½d.[34]

And for the service of William Byngham and John Barlay making one new house on the holding of James Couper for 17 days this year, each receiving 6d. a day whilst providing his own food, 7s.[35]

And for the service of Thomas Frothyngham working there on the same job for one day providing his own food 6d.

And for the service of one man carting timber from the abbey to the aforesaid holding this year 4d.

And for the service of John Scryvener carting one wagon-load of stones from the Monk Fryston quarry to the same holding this year 9d.

And for the service of Thomas Shawe carting three wagon-loads of stones from the monastery cemetery to the same holding for making the foundation of the walls there this year 3d.

And for the service of the same Thomas carting six wagon-loads of mud to the aforesaid house for daubing the same, receiving 1d. a wagon-load, 6d.

And for the service of Peter Cotes and his servant making the foundations of the walls there for one day 7d.

And for the service of Thomas Precuit and Thomas Walas daubing the walls of the same house this year, by agreement 15d.

And for one wagon-load of sand purchased for the same work this year 4d

And for the service of Thomas Wylde and his servant roofing there inside the house (*super domum interiorem*) for one day 6d.

And for the service of James Couper splitting 100 laths for the same work this year 7d.

And for 10 thraves of thatch (*damthak*) purchased for thatching and repair of the houses on the holding of John Webster this year 20d.

And for the service of William Butler mowing *damthak* purchased for repairs of the houses within the office this year, by agreement 20d.

And for the service of Thomas Thorp carting 5 wagon-loads of timber from Thorpe Willoughby to the houses on the holdings of the

---

[33] *suo* is repeated in the manuscript.
[34] The total should be 25s.7½d. The instruction 'turn over' (*vert'*) follows below this total; and the account continues on the dorse of the manuscript without a new heading.
[35] The amount should be 17s.

aforesaid James and John Webster this year, receiving 4d. a wagon-load, 20d.

And for the service of the said James carting timber from Hambleton wood to his holding this year 10d.

And for 200 medium spike-nails (*Midelspikyng*) purchased for making one fence on the holding of the aforesaid James this year 6d.

And for the service of Thomas Wylde roofing this year for two days on one house of the said James, receiving 5d. a day whilst providing his own food, 10d.

And for the service of his servant for the same time this year 5½d.

And for one wagon-load of quick-lime (*calcis vivi*) purchased from a certain man of Brotherton for doing various repairs within the office this year 2s.8d.

And for two quarters of lime purchased from the same person 7d.

And for 4 wagon-loads of sand purchased for mixing with the same (*pro mixtione eiusdem*) this year 16d.

And for 2500 brad-nails (*broddez*) purchased for the same work at 18d. a thousand 3s.9d.

And for transport of 1500 *thaktele* from the tile-kiln (*le telekilne*) at Cawood to the Ouse river this year 6d.

And for the service of Henry Sutton and Richard Rece transporting the said *thaktele* by water thence to Selby on the monastery's barge this year 16d.

And for the service of the carter carrying the said tiles in the monastery cart to the holding of the aforesaid James this year 2d.

And for the service of one woman carrying the said tiles from the boat to the cart this year 2d.

And for the service of Thomas Laxton daubing the walls there for 5 days this year, receiving 4d. a day whilst providing his own food, 20d.

And for 400 roofing-tiles purchased at Cawood this year 15s.

And for 18 ridge-tiles (*rigteles*) purchased at Selby for the same work this year 18d.

And for 40 corner-tiles (*cornertele*) purchased for the same work this year 20d.

And for the service of John Bysett roofing the aforesaid new house this year, by agreement 3s.4d.

And for the money spent on a certain lean-to (*tofall'*) and (its) erection on the holding of Thomas Forest this year 8d.

And for the service of the carter transporting stones from the monastery cemetery to the new tenement this year 2d.

And for the service of William Walker carting three wagon-loads of mud to the holding of William del Hill this year 11d.

And for the service of Thomas Frothyngham and his servant making the foundations of the walls there and daubing there for three days, each receiving 4½d. (a day), 2s.3d.

And for 300 tiles purchased from William del Hill for doing repairs in the new tenement this year, at a cost of 12d. per 100, 3s.

And for the service of John Bysett roofing there for 11 days, receiving 6d. a day whilst providing his own food, 5s.6d.

And for the service of his servant for as many days, receiving 4d. a day, 3s.8d.

And for one new door with bindings and iron-hinges purchased for the entrance there this year 16d.

And for the service of one man carting one wagon-load of mud to the holding of Robert Smyth for repair of the walls there this year 6d.

And for one pair of iron bindings purchased for the door of the malt-kiln on the holding of the aforesaid James this year 4d.

And for the repair of one wall on the holding of Ellis Smyth this year 4d.

And for the service of William Byngham and John Barlay repairing sundry defects in the houses on the holding of John Scales this year for 12½ days, each receiving 6d. a day whilst providing their own food, 12s.6d.

And for the service of Thomas Precius and John Warde daubing there for 6 days, each receiving 4d. a day, 4s.

And for the service of John Godsalff roofing there for 5 days this year, receiving 6d. a day, 2s.6d.

And for the service of his servant for as many days, receiving 4d. a day, 20d.

And for nails purchased from Robert Hesilwod for the aforesaid works this year, 3s.6d.

Total £4 16s.8½d.

Cost of ditches (*Custus fossatorum*)	And for the service of four men from Hambleton cleaning out the great ditch there from the western end of the same township to the point on the causeway called *le Fox* (*usque locum calcet' voc' le Fox*) for 4 days, each receiving 4d. a day, 5s.4d.

Total 5s.4d.

Transfer of rent
(*Resolutio redditus*)

And transferred to the keeper of the altar of the blessed Mary for the free rent yearly of one house in Gowthorp in the tenure of James Couper belonging to his office 3s.6d.

And to the kitchener of the monastery for the rent belonging to his office from the same house yearly 6d.

And to the same kitchener for the free rent yearly of the tenement formerly (in the possession) of John Escryke 2s.6d.

And to the same kitchener for the free rent of the new buildings in Gowthorp yearly 13s.4d.

And to the keeper of the infirmary for the free rent belonging to his office yearly 2d.

Total 20s.

Allowances
(*Allocationes*)

And this same accountant is allowed 2s.4d. for the decrease in rent of one cottage in Gowthorp in the tenure of James Couper, which used to return 13s.4d. and now returns only 11s. yearly.

And 3s. for decrease in rent of three tofts newly rented (*in novo redditu*) in the tenure of Richard Plommer, David Sawer, and John Levet which used to return 30s. and now returns only 27s. yearly.

And 2s.4d. for the decrease in the farm of Thomas Raghton for 2 acres of land in *Spryngriddyng*, 6 acres of land lying in *lez hagges*, and 2 acres of land lying in *Swartynglong*, formerly (in the possession) of John Escryke, which used to return 13s.4d. and now returns only 11s. yearly.

And 4s.8d. for the decrease in the farm of the tithes of sheaves and hay from Fairburn this year, which used to return 16s.8d. and now returns only 12s. yearly.

And 3s.4d. for the decrease in the farm of the tithes of sheaves and hay from West Tanfield this year, which used to return 13s.4d. and now returns only 10s. yearly.[36]

And 4d. for the decrease in rent of one assart lying near the marsh of *Todhill* formerly in the tenure of Robert Cloke, which used to return 12d. and now returns only 8d. yearly.

And 18d. for the decrease in the rent of 2 acres and 1 rood of land and meadow in the open fields (*campis*) of Barlby across the River

---

[36] West Tanfield is some 10.5 kilometres north-west of Ripon in the former North Riding, and its tithes were the only possession of the Selby monks in this area. Mr Haslop has noted that in the early 13th century the tithes were leased for 20s. a year (*YAJ*, 44, 1972, p. 161).

Ouse, and of 2 acres there lying in the place called *Thurstanynge* formerly in the tenure of Thomas Nelson, which used to return 6s. and now return only 4s.6d. yearly.

And 6d. for the decrease in rent of one assart called *Witlynland* formerly in the tenure of Richard Chaast, which used to return 2s.6d. and now returns only 2s. yearly.

And 16s. for the decrease in rent of the tofts and crofts formerly (in the possession) of John Scales in *Cowelane*, which used to return 26s.8d. and this year returned only 10s.8d., because for part of this year they remained in the lord's hand and are leased to John Webster for 15s. to be paid to the lord in the year next coming.

And 13s.4d. for loss of rent from Sitlington mill (*milne*)[37] because in a ruinous state and in the lord's hand for lack of tenant this year.

Total 47s.4d.

Total of all payments, liveries, and allowances £31 5s.3½d.[38]

And he owes £14 4s.2½d. From which he has paid to Brother Robert Whitwod,[39] bursar etc., as the price of wine, as shown by three tested tallies, 57s. And he owes £11 7s.2½d.[40] And afterwards he charges himself willingly (*grat'*) with 35s. received after the accounting from sundry creditors contained in certain lists of names and surnames delivered by the lord abbot to Brother William Snayth[41] to collect. And he owes £13 2s.2½d. Of which there is due from John Chaast, keeper of the inn, of the wine of this accountant as shown by 2 bills 18s.6d. And from Thomas Raghton for loss of ullage (*in defectu ulagii*) of wine purchased from him, namely 16 gallons at a price per gallon of 8d., 10s.8d.[42] And thus of the sum of 35s. above there is due from the accountant 5s.10d. And he owes £11 13s.0½d. net (*de claro*).

---

[37] Sitlington is in the parish of Thornhill near Wakefield. The mill was still untenanted in 1448 (*Ibid.*, p. 160 n. 4).

[38] The total should be £31 5s.2½d.

[39] He was bursar also in 1448 and granger in 1438–39. He entered the abbey about 1428 and was ordained a priest in 1432. He died in 1451. See Borthwick Institute of Historical Research, Archbishop's Register 19, John Kempe, fos 216a & 242b; HUL, DDLO 20/23 and 50; British Library, Additional Charter 45854.

[40] The following sentences to the end of the account have been added in a different hand.

[41] Brother William Snayth had an active career as an obedientiary, serving as pittancer and chamberlain 1435–36, 1440–42, and 1452–59, and as bursar 1459–60. He had entered the house about 1422; became a priest in 1427; and possibly died in 1470 or 1471, since he received his pittance for only part of that accounting year. (See Borthwick Institute of Historical Research, Archbishop's Register 18, Henry Bowet, f.412r, and 19, John Kempe, f.231; HUL, DDLO 20/20, 21, 25, and 30, 2/2; WDA, Se/Ac/18; B. Dobson, 'The Election of John Ousthorp as Abbot of Selby in 1436', p. 38.)

[42] For Chaast and Raghton see above, pp. 219 and 224. Ullage is the 'amount of wine or other liquor by which a cask or bottle falls short of being quite full'. (*OED*)

(b) The office of Keeper of the Choir of the Blessed Mary

The keeper of the choir (or alternatively altar) of the blessed Mary has left little record of his activities in the remaining Selby archives. A single account survives, and that one from the very last years of the abbey's history, 1536–37;[1] whilst just two other occupants of the office are known by name, Brother Thomas Howeden in 1475–76 and Brother James Marscheden in 1436.[2] The existence of the office can be traced back at least to the late fourteenth century, for the bursars of 1398–99 accounted for the transfer of 12d. rent to the keeper of the altar of the blessed Mary;[3] but there is no other concrete evidence of his responsibilities than the one account of more than a century later. Thus it has seemed better to include here a document considerably removed in time from the other accounts translated in this collection than none at all. The conservatism of medieval monks perhaps makes it feasible that the nature of the accounts would not have changed radically in the intervening period.

The keeper's function as it appears in this account was to maintain a single altar and provide for worship at it in much the same way that the sacrist cared for the abbey church and its services as a whole. The office links Selby Abbey with the widespread Marian devotion that produced Lady Chapels, dedicated to the Virgin Mary, in many monastic, cathedral, and parish churches. A popular situation in great churches was immediately behind the high altar, like the projecting eastern Lady Chapel at Winchester; whilst at Ely a spacious separate building was created by the monks at the north-east corner of the cathedral.[4] No evidence of such a chapel is known at Selby; and possibly the use of the word 'altar' as an alternative to 'choir' in the title of the official suggests a more modest provision for the cult.[5]

---

[1] Preserved in Hull University Library as DDLO 20/61. The income from rents recorded in the account is exactly as noted in the survey of Selby obedientiaries compiled shortly before the *Valor Ecclesiasticus*. Income in 1536–37 was 55s.11½d., whereas the survey assigns the office 44s.1½d.; but the difference is accounted for by 11s.10d. received by the keeper of 1536–37 from the sacrist and pittancer.

[2] The former of these references is in a lease recorded on the Selby court roll, and the latter in the list of Selby monks compiled for the 1436 abbatial election. See HUL, DDLO 20/30; and B. Dobson, 'The Election of John Ousthorp as Abbot of Selby in 1436', p. 38.

[3] See above, p. 54. A rental of the lands belonging to the altar of the blessed Mary also survives dated 1403 (HUL, DDLO 20/87).

[4] For a brief discussion of Lady Chapels, see L. Butler and C. Given-Wilson, *Medieval Monasteries of Great Britain*, p. 67. The Lady Chapel at Ely is 100 ft in length, 60 ft in height, and 46 ft wide (A. V. Franklin, *May I show you round? A Tour of Ely Cathedral*, St Ives, no date, p. 18).

[5] 'It is somewhat remarkable that we have no tradition of a Lady Chapel at Selby, beyond the entirely modern notion that the eastern bay of the choir was so used.' *The Coucher Book of Selby*, II, pp. liv–lv.

About the keeper of the choir in 1536–37, Brother Christopher Acastre, little is known. He had entered the house in 1511 and two years later became a full member of the community.[6] At the Dissolution in 1539 the name Acastre does not appear in the list of monks who received pensions, but it seems likely that he is there as Christopher Taylor, one of the most senior monks in the house and the recipient of £6 6s.8d. p.a.[7] His account is written on paper, utilizing one side of the sheet only, and is in legible condition throughout.

The Keeper of the Choir of the Blessed Mary's account for 1536–37

Table of Contents

[6] Borthwick Institute of Historical Research, Archbishop's Register 26, Christopher Bainbridge, fos 117v and 125v.
[7] W. W. Morrell, *The History and Antiquities of Selby*, pp. 113–114. In several cases it can be shown that the placenames by which the monks were known at Selby have been replaced by family name. The abbot, for example, is called Robert Rogers and not Robert Selby.

The account of Brother Christopher Acastre, keeper of the choir of the blessed Mary within the monastery from the festival of St Michael the Archangel (29 September) in the 28th year of the reign of King Henry the Eighth (1536) up to the same festival in the 29th year of the said king (1537), namely for one whole year just as appears below.

Arrears   None because this is the first account of the said
(*Arreragia*)   accountant in this office, as is clear (*ut apparet*).
    Total ( )

Fixed rent   But he renders account of the rent and farm of the
(*Redditus Assisus*) land and tenements in Selby, Burton, and Brayton,
                 with the land in Byram, yearly 40s.6½d.

And received from rent of the land and tenements in Pollington, Balne, and Whitley, yearly 2s.7d.

And received from rent of land in Barlby yearly 12d.

And received from the sacrist of the monastery in respect of rent passing from that office to his office (*exeunte de suo Officio ad suum Officium*) yearly 3s.6d.

And received[8] from the pittancer of the monastery for the same reason 8s.4d.[9]

Sum total of receipts 55s.11½d.

Transfer of rent and   The aforesaid accountant has transferred to the
wages (*Resolutio red-* kitchener of the monastery in respect of rent passing
ditus et stipendia)   from that office to his office yearly 4s.5d.

And paid to the aforesaid accountant for his diligence in that office this year as a gratuity (*ex curialitate*) 5s.

And paid to Thomas Nutbrowne for lighting the candles in the choir there yearly 2s.

And paid to the laundress of the said office yearly 8d.

And paid for 3 dozen gloves purchased for the monks (*Fratribus*) and the boys of the monastery this year as a present 3s.4d.

Total 15s.5½d.[10]

---

[8] *sol'* crossed out and *rec'* substituted.
[9] *id.* crossed out and *iiiid.* substituted.
[10] The total should be 15s.5d.

Purchases and pay-
ments (*Emptiones et
solutiones*)

And firstly he has paid for 24 pounds of wax purchased to make candles in that office against Christmas Day this year, at 6d. a pound. Total 12s.

And paid to John Goldall for making the said wax into candles at the same time and another time this year 20d.[11]

And paid for provisions at the time of working the said wax 14d.

And paid for 3 pounds of wax to make two candles called *lez Salvez*[12] against Easter Day (1 April) in that office this year 18d.

And given to the man going to ( ) for the same wax 4d.

And paid for one cord to hang the star there 3d.

And paid for 4 ells of linen-cloth purchased for one altar-cloth (*le Awter Cloth*) there this year, at 6d. an ell. Total 2s.

And paid for 3 ells of the same cloth[13] purchased for 2 towels there, at 5d. an ell. Total 15d.

And paid for 18 pounds of wax purchased from Richard Walker against the day of the Assumption of the Blessed Mary (15 August), at 6d. a pound. Total 9s.[14]

Total 29s.2d.[15]

Small expenses with
various things
(*Minute cum Variis*)

And firstly he has paid for the pricking (*le prik-kynge*)[16] of one mass of five parts, namely 'Mary has been taken up into heaven' (*assumpta est Maria*), 5d.

And paid for similar work in respect of one antiphon (*an*ᵃ) of five parts 2d.

And paid to John Bull for similar work in respect of one mass called 'Jesus Christ', and for ink and paper, 14d.

And paid for half an ell of linen-cloth for making and repair of the maniple (*manic'*) for 1 alb and for repair of the said alb belonging to that office 5d.

And paid for sewing (*philatione*) of various things purchased for that office this year as appears above 6d.

And given at the request of various monks of the monastery to the man from London chanting (*cant'*) there, because the lord abbot and bursar were away, 4d.

---

[11] *xd.* crossed out and *xxd.* substituted.
[12] i.e. salve-lights, candles 'lighted during the singing of the Salve' (*OED*).
[13] *panno* interlined.
[14] The last entry in this section has been written in a different ink.
[15] *xxviiis.iiiid.* crossed out and *xxixs. iid.* substituted.
[16] i.e. 'marking or writing by means of pricks, dots, etc.' (*OED*).

And paid for 2 pounds of rushes (*Rosell'*) for lighting the candles in that office this year 2d.

And paid for rushes (*cirpis*) for lighting the chandelier there ½d.

And paid for paris candles used there this year 2d.[17]

Total 3s.4½d.

Repair of houses (*Reperationes domorum*)	And firstly he claims allowance for the repair done this year of the house now in the tenure of John Rycall 12d.

And for the repair done this year of the house now in the tenure of Richard Sergeandson 8d.

And allowance for the wages of Thomas Skelton for repairing the candlestick and other defects in the aforesaid choir this year 2d.

Total 22d.

Sum total of allowances 49s.10d. And thus he owes at the view of this his account, as is clear, 6s.0½d.[18]

---

[17] *iid.* added in a different ink.
[18] The last sentence may have been added in a different hand. The amount owed should be 6s.1½d. on the accountant's figures.

IV

CHARITY AND HOSPITALITY

(a) The offices of Almoner and Keeper of the Skirlaw Chantry

A single perfectly preserved parchment roll from the abbacy of John de Cave (1429–36), the account of Brother John Acastre for the year Martinmas 1434 to Martinmas 1435, is all that remains of the records of the Selby almoner's office and its sub-department the Skirlaw chantry.[1] That it ranked as one of the major obediences is indicated by the fee received by its monk-official, 10s. p.a., on a level with the kitchener or the sacrist and fabric keeper; and at least one of the occupants of the office in the early fifteenth century went on to become abbot.[2] But nearly everything that is to be known about the functioning of the almonry and the scope of its activities is contained in, or must be deduced from, the document which follows this introduction; and there is only the evidence produced a century later by the build-up to the Dissolution for purposes of direct comparison.[3]

The foundation of the Skirlaw chantry was a relatively recent event in 1434–35. Bishop Walter Skirlaw of Durham had established it in 1398, when he granted the abbey property worth 10 marks p.a. (£6 13s.4d.) to provide revenues for various specified purposes.[4] Under the terms of the agreement between bishop and abbot the monks were to appoint one priest-monk to celebrate a daily mass at the altar of St Cuthbert[5]

---

[1] It is preserved in the Hull University Library as DDLO 20/55.
[2] John Ousthorp, almoner 1424–26 and abbot 1436–66.
[3] i.e. in the survey of obedientiaries and their revenues produced in 1535 for the *Valor Ecclesiasticus*. HUL, DDLO 20/60. For a general introduction to the almoner's functions in monastic houses, see the introduction by C. N. L. Brooke to *The Book of William Morton, Almoner of Peterborough Monastery 1448–1467*, ed. P. I. King, Northamptonshire Record Society Publications 16, 1954.
[4] Possible evidence of these transactions is to be found in the bursars' roll for 1398–99 translated above. See p. 51.
[5] The patron-saint of Durham.

Selby Abbey, the sacristy
(photograph by Dianne Tillotson)

established by Skirlaw in their church, and were to celebrate a yearly obit on the anniversary of his death. All monks present at that obit were to share in a distribution of 50s. for their efforts, whilst the priest serving at the altar of St Cuthbert was to be paid 14d. a week for celebrating the daily mass.[6] The organization of a regular succession of monks for the masses presumably formed part of the duties of the keeper of the chantry, for which he received an annual fee himself of 3s.4d.

Whether the Skirlaw chantry was attached to the almonry for administration from its inception cannot now be determined. Instances occur in the Selby records of particular monks described simply as keeper of the chantry, as in the cases of Brother Robert Pygot in 1421–22 and Brother John Ousthorp in 1423–24;[7] but the occasions are transfers of rent belonging to the chantry by another accountant, and the keepers may well also have been almoners without this information needing to be stated in that context. Certainly a hundred years later the chantry had become so much a part of the almoner's duties that the survey of the property of the office made in 1535 does not refer to its keeper at all, whilst it does record the continuing payment of 50s. as alms on the anniversary of Bishop Skirlaw's death.[8]

The Skirlaw chantry is an instance of a common practice in late medieval religion, the endowment of private masses for the spiritual benefit of specified souls, an essentially selfish use of wealth and position for religious objectives.[9] The almoner's office illustrates a more attractive, if often related, facet of the same religion: the duty of charity towards the unfortunate members of society by their superiors in property and status. For this was the monk-official principally concerned with providing charity from the community's resources for the poor and sick. His account gives an insight into monastic charity, its nature and its extent, at an abbey of substantial size and wealth in the north of England, where Durham Cathedral Priory set an impressive standard with its two small hospitals, two almshouses, and an almonry school maintaining some thirty poor scholars.[10]

---

[6] British Library, Cotton Vitellius E.XVI, fos 135v–136v. Skirlaw also established a perpetual chantry at Durham, where there were five in all in the first half of the 15th century (B. Dobson, *Durham Priory 1400–50*, p. 72), and York Minster (*Testamenta Eboracensia*, I, p. 306 n. 1).

[7] In the accounts of the serjeants of Stainer for these years; see WDA, Se/Ac/12 and HUL, DDLO 20/66.

[8] HUL, DDLO 20/60.

[9] For a full discussion of chantries, see K. L. Wood-Legh, *Perpetual Chantries in Britain*, Cambridge, 1965.

[10] Each hospital had a complement of only five brothers and sisters, but the two almshouses maintained 28 brothers and sisters and 15 persons respectively. The almonry school had a master who taught grammar for a yearly stipend of 40s. Even so Professor Dobson concludes: 'It would be impossible to maintain that the alms of the Durham monks ameliorated the lot of more than a handful of the poor unfortunates from the city and county.' (R. B. Dobson, *Durham Priory 1400–1450*, pp. 168–169.)

Before any judgements are made about the level of Selby Abbey's charitable endeavours, however, the full extent of its obligations in regard to alms needs to be understood, not all of which was the almoner's responsibility. Both the kitchener and certain abbey servants made customary doles of food commodities to the poor, as their surviving accounts show,[11] and if records survived from some other offices we would have further such evidence. As it is, the whole picture cannot be reconstructed now for the period around 1434, and we must go forward a century to the time of the compilation of the *Valor Ecclesiasticus* for a survey of abbey finances that gives particulars of regular annual alms expenditure in the context of total resources. In 1535 the almoner's income was assessed at £15 16s.7d., of which £7 10s. was earmarked for distribution to the poor and a further £2 10s. represented the sum distributed at the annual obit of Bishop Walter Skirlaw. In addition bursar, kitchener, and keeper of the spirituality of Snaith all had annual obligations to charitable payments recorded. For the bursar grain distributed by his officers, the proctors and serjeants, in parishes whose tithes had been appropriated to the abbey totalled 25 quarters; and this, with food and drink distributed at the monastery, was valued at a total of £13 11s.8d. The kitchener was recorded as giving out meat and fish on Maundy Thursday to the value of 16s.0d.; whilst the keeper of the spirituality of Snaith claimed to spend £1 on alms given to the poor on the anniversary of Henry Snaith's death, under the terms of his chantry foundation at Snaith.[12] When all these sums are added together, including the whole of the almoner's income, they produce a total of £31 4s.3d., less than four per cent of the gross income of the abbey as recorded in the same document.[13] One should stress, though, that these figures represent only those customary expenditures which could be claimed as deductions from taxable income, and not the full extent of the monks' charity in any year. Gifts of a casual and irregular kind did not qualify for inclusion in the 1535 returns, which thus need to be supplemented with the evidence of entries in the obedientiaries' accounts in order to arrive at a more realistic evaluation of charitable activities at late medieval Selby.

[11] For the kitchener see above, p. 189. In parishes where the abbey had appropriated parochial revenues, its officials made small distributions of grain to the poor: 1 quarter 2 bushels of wheat, and 1 quarter 2 bushels of beans and peas at Garthorpe, Luddington and Waterton in 1389–1390 (HUL, DDLO 20/62); 2 quarters 4 bushels of wheat in the account of the proctor of Whitgift and Reedness for 1397–1398 (HUL, DDLO 20/65); 1 quarter of wheat, 1 quarter 4 bushels of beans and peas, and 1 quarter of rye, at Hook and Carlton in 1426–1427 (HUL, DDLO 20/68).

[12] The foundation of this chantry in Abbot John de Shirburn's time is recorded in British Library, Cotton Vitellius E.XVI, fos 133v–135r.

[13] HUL, DDLO 20/60, where gross income is recorded as £819 2s.6½d. If only money actually expended on traditional alms to the poor is included in the calculation, the percentage is reduced to about 3 per cent, not far from the national average (see G. W. O. Woodward, *The Dissolution of the Monasteries*, London, 1966, pp. 21–23).

The almoner of 1434–35, Brother John Acastre, had a career remarkably free of the cares of office. He had entered the house in 1408, becoming a priest five years later;[14] and he died most probably in 1457, at which time he was the most senior monk in the community and its longest-serving member, the abbot alone excepted.[15] Yet during these 50 years he is known to have served only as almoner in this present account and in 1436, and as keeper of the spirituality of Snaith sometime before 1432.[16] He is otherwise notable only as one of the three scrutators of votes at the election of John Ousthorp as abbot in 1436.[17] The contrast between this freedom from administrative preoccupations and the careers as obedientiaries of other monks, like for instance his fellow scrutator of 1436 Brother John Haldenby,[18] argues perhaps a practical division in the Selby community between those whose emphasis lay with the duties of the choir-monk and those inclined towards administration.

---

[14] Borthwick Institute of Historical Research, Archbishop's Register 18, Henry Bowet pt I, f.39.

[15] WDA, Se/Ac/18. Abbot John Ousthorp had entered the house in 1404 (Borthwick Institute of Historical Research, Archbishop's Register 16, Richard le Scrope, f.310).

[16] HUL, DDLO 20/1 and R. B. Dobson, 'The Election of John Ousthorp as Abbot of Selby in 1436', p. 38.

[17] *Ibid.*, p. 34.

[18] For Brother John Haldenby, see above pp. 206–207.

The Almoner and Keeper of the Skirlaw Chantry's account for 1434–1435

Table of Contents

The account of Brother John Acastre for the offices of almoner and keeper of the chantry for the soul of Walter lord bishop of Durham in the monastery of Selby from the festival of St Martin in winter (11 November) A.D. 1434 to the same festival of St Martin A.D. 1435 for one whole year.

Arrears (*Arreragia*)	No arrears are held because (this is) the first year of this person as accountant and Brother Thomas Crull,[19] his predecessor, in his last account of the year next preceding exceeded income.
Total nothing.	

---

[19] For Brother Thomas Crull, see above p. 159 n.38.

Rents and farms
(*Redditus et Firme*)

Firstly the same person answers for £17 4s.10d. from rents and farms belonging to the office of almoner this year according to the rental.

And for 9s.6d. from increased rent of part of the toft in the New Lane (*le Newelane*) built by John Colyngham for the same John and Agnes his wife to hold for the term of their lives for 6d., and now in the tenure of Alice Birdar and Nicholas Benet for 10s. a year.

And for 9s. from tithes of corn sheaves and hay belonging to the aforesaid office sold for this to William Laweton this year.

And for £7 2s.6d. from rents and farms belonging to the office of keeper of the aforesaid chantry this year according to the rental.

Total £25 5s.10d.

Foreign receipts
(*Forinsecum Recep-tum*)

And for 16s.6d. received from Robert Stodelay for 1100 faggots made at *Milneriddyng*, sold for this to the same person at 18d. a hundred.

Total 16s.6d.

Total of receipts £26 2s.4d.

Transfers of rent
(*Resoluciones Red-ditus*)

From which he accounts for the transfer to Brother Thomas Normanton,[20] pittancer of the monastery, for rent belonging to his office from the office of the almonry this year 12s.2d.

And to Brother John Ousthorp,[21] keeper of the fabric, for the same reason yearly 2s.

And to the precentor for the same reason yearly 22d.

And to the kitchener for the same reason yearly 15d.

And to the third prior for the same reason yearly 12d.

And to the keeper of the altar of the blessed Mary for the same reason yearly 6d.

And to the chamberlain of the monastery yearly, namely for the clothing of this accountant, 20s.

---

[20] For Brother Thomas Normanton, see above p. 27.

[21] He became the next abbot of Selby in 1436 and ruled for 30 years, the second longest tenure of the office in the history of the abbey. He had entered the religious life at Selby in 1404; spent some years at Oxford University supported by a pension from the house, graduating as a bachelor in theology; and acted as his abbot's proctor at the provincial chapter of the Order in 1432, the year in which he seems to have become prior of the abbey. Earlier he had served as keeper of the chantry of the bishop of Durham 1423–24, and almoner 1424–26. See R. B. Dobson, 'The Election of John Ousthorp as Abbot of Selby in 1436', pp. 31–40; and HUL, DDLO 20/66 and 67.

And to the pittancer yearly, namely for the pittance of this accountant, 20s.

And to the lord prior for rent belonging to his office deriving from the office of the chantry yearly 6d.

And to the pittancer for the same reason yearly 5s.

And to the kitchener of the monastery for the same reason yearly 5s.11d.

And to the keeper of the refectory for the same reason yearly 2d.

And to the keeper of the infirmary for the same reason yearly 4d.

And to the sacrist for the same reason yearly 2s.

Total 72s.8d.

Wages with clothing (*Stipendia cum indumento*)	And for the wage of Thomas Wylson, servant in the office of the almonry this year 6s.8d.

And for 10 rods of russet cloth purchased from John Hovll for the clothing of three poor persons this year at 15d. a rod 12s.6d.

And for the making of three mantles from it 2s.

And for three pairs of shoes purchased for the same this year 21d.

And for the wage of John Muston, bearer of the mortuary roll (*Brevitour*) on account of Brother William Benefeld[22] this year, 9s.

Total 31s.11d.

Small expenses with various things (*Minute cum Variis*)	And for one stone of paris candles purchased for light in the office and for the boys[23] and the poor this year 14d.

And for wax tapers purchased for three poor persons at the feast of Candlemas (2 February) this year 1½d.

And for the service of the barber in shaving the said three poor persons this year 8d.

And for 3000 turves purchased for the fuel of the said poor persons this year at 7d. a thousand 21d.

---

[22] The object of the obituary roll was to secure for the soul of a dead monk the prayers of members of other religious communities; and it was carried from monastery to monastery by a professional breviator (see R.B.Dobson, *Durham Priory 1400–1450*, p.249). Brother William Benefeld had not long been a member of the community, since he was still a novice in 1433 (see Borthwick Institute of Historical Research, Archbishop's Register 19, John Kempe, f.ccxliiia).

[23] In 1413–14 one William Kay was paid a fee of 13s.4d. for instructing the monks and the boys in the almonry in grammar (HUL, DDLO 20/54b, *Pensiones et Feoda*).

And for 200 faggots purchased from the Bursar for the same persons' fuel this year 4s.10d.

And for paper and parchment purchased for writing the account and other things this year 4d.

And for the service of John Wyton making 1100 faggots at *Milneriddyng*, receiving 6d.[24] a 100, 5s.6d.[25]

Total 14s.4½d.

Purchase of grains and victuals (*Emptio bladorum et victualium*)	And for 6 quarters of rye purchased from Thomas Thomasson and others this year on account of the charitable distributions (*causa distributionum*) in Advent and at the festivals of the death (31 July) and the burial (1 October) of St Germanus,[26] at 4s.4d. a quarter, 26s.

And for one pig and 2 quarters of pig purchased on account of the charitable distributions on Monday *in Carniprivio*[27] this year 9s.

And for 1000 red herrings purchased from Thomas Bollyng on account of the charitable distributions at the festival of the death of St Germanus (31 July) this year 13s.4d.

And for one bullock purchased from William Eleson on account of the charitable distribution at the festival of the burial of St Germanus (1 October) this year 8s.6d.

Total 56s.10d.

Repairs of houses (*Emendationes Domorum*)	And for the transport of 4 cart-loads of mud from Bondgate to New Lane and elsewhere 6d.

And for the service of William Butler and his fellows plastering the walls of the house there in the tenure of Nicholas Benet for one day 8d.

And for 43 thraves of thatch (*thak*) purchased from the granger of the monastery at *BondKerr* this year, with 4s.8d. for mowing, binding, and transport of the same this year, 10s.8d.

---

[24] *ob.* crossed out.

[25] *xid.* crossed out and *vid.* substituted.

[26] Selby Abbey was dedicated to St Germanus of Auxerre, and its first abbot, Benedict, allegedly brought to England from the great French Benedictine monastery of St Germain d'Auxerre one of that abbey's most prized relics, the middle finger of St Germanus's right hand. See R. B. Dobson, 'The First Norman Abbey in Northern England', *The Ampleforth Journal*, 74 pt II, 1969, pp. 161–176.

[27] *Carniprivium* can mean the first days of Lent, or Septuagesima Sunday, or Sexagesima Sunday (C. R. Cheney (ed.), *Handbook of Dates for Students of English History*, London, 1970, p. 46). The Monday before Ash Wednesday, the first day of Lent, may be meant.

And for the service of William Broun of Wistow thatching (*tegentis dictum Thak*) for 6 days on the house in New Lane in the tenure of Roger Burwod and Thomas Marschall this year, receiving 6d. a day and providing his own food (*ad cibum suum proprium*), 3s.

And for the service of his mate on the said work for the same time 12d.

And for the service of Thomas Wylde for one day roofing and repairing defects at the house in Gowthorpe in the tenure of William Fox, with 2d. for the service of his mate, 7d.

And for 200 laths purchased for the beams (*lez bemes*) of the chapel of St Genevieve[28] this year 10d.

And for transport of 8 cart-loads of mud to the said chapel 12d.

And for the service of John Hilland and his three fellows for 2 days mixing the said mud and plastering the beams (*les bemes*) aforesaid this year, each receiving 4d. a day, 2s.8d.

And for the service of Richard Godsalve for one day and a half plastering the said beams (*bemes*) 6d.

And for planks (*plauncheours*) purchased for making benches from in the said chapel 10d.

And for the service of Robert Fynkhill for 3 days working up the said benches 15d.

And for nails purchased for the same work 4d.

And for boards purchased from Richard Goldale for the door of the garden of the said chapel, with the making of this door, 13d.

And for nails purchased for the same work 4d.

And for the service of Reginald Wright for 3 days working and repairing the defects of the house in the tenure of John Scales this year 15d.

And for nails purchased for the same work 6d.

And for the service of John Hill plastering the mud walls of the said house, by contract (*in conventione*) 16d.

And for 1000 tiles purchased at Cawood for paving various houses (*ad tecturam diversarum domorum super pavimentum*) this year 10s.

And for transport of the same thence to Selby 6d.

---

[28] It was in Gowthorpe. See *Coucher Book of Selby Abbey*, I, p.164, Doc. CCXIII. According to the Life of St Geneviève (c.422–c.500), she was specially blessed by St Germanus of Auxerre when she consecrated herself to God in childhood (*The Oxford Dictionary of the Christian Church*, p.555).

And for the service of William Grene roofing and pointing for 10 days on the houses in the tenure of Thomas Monkton, John Relyse, and others there this year, receiving 5d. a day and providing his own food, 4s.2d.

And for the service of his mate for the same time, receiving 3d. a day, 2s.6d.

And for posts (*stothes*) purchased from John Kirkeby for the house there in the tenure of Henry Waryn this year 14d.

And for 100 laths purchased for the same house 6d.

And for 30 stowers (*stoures*) purchased for the said house 9d.

And for the service of Peter Bynglay and Thomas Wayte, carpenters, working for 5 days this year on the said house and on the house attached to it formerly in the tenure of William Benyngholm, each receiving 5d. a day, 4s.2d.

And for 60 stowers (*stoures*) purchased (from) Brother John Selby[29] for the house formerly in the tenure of the aforesaid William this year 14d.

And for 1000 stowering-nails (*stouryngnaill*) purchased for the same work 16d.

And for 200 great spike-nails (*spyking*) purchased for the same work 8d.

And for medium-sized spike-nails (*middelspykyng*) purchased for the same work 8d.

And for the service of William Bower carrying 2 cart-loads of mud (from) Bondgate to the said houses 3d.

And for the service of William Butler and his fellows mixing the said mud and plastering the mud walls of the aforesaid houses, by contract 2s.

And for 1700 tiles purchased at Long Drax this year, with transport of the same, 9s.

And for porterage of the same 4d.

And for the service of William Grene renewing one chimney with the said tiles in the house in the tenure of Henry Waryn, by contract this year 6s.8d.

And for 2 cart-loads of lime purchased for the said chimney this year 5s.

---

[29] Brother John Selby was a novice at Selby in 1416, and held the offices of bursar, extern cellarer, granger and keeper of the guest house, before becoming prior of Selby's dependent cell at Snaith by 1436 (HUL, DDLO 20/1, 15 and 69; WDA, Se/Ac/8b and 14; B. Dobson, 'The Election of John Ousthorp as Abbot of Selby in 1436', p. 38).

And for 2 quarters of lime purchased from William Grene for the same work 2s.

And for 6 quarters of sand purchased at York this year 12d.

And for transport of the same thence to Selby 4d.

And for porterage of the same 4d.

And for 30 stowers purchased from William Mascald for the house in Ousegate in the tenure of Richard Wyndebore this year 12d.

And for the service of Reginald Wright for one day working on the said house 5d.

And for nails purchased for the same work 4d.

And for the service of John del Hill and John Selar for 2 days about the plastering of the same house 16d.

And for 8 stones of lead purchased from John Plummer for one drain (*gurgitem*) to be made from it this year 4s.8d.[30]

And for the service of William Plummer for 2 days on melting the said lead 12d.

And for the service of William Green placing the said lead in one drain between the chimney of Henry Waryn and the chamber attached to it, by contract 8d.

And for 6 thraves of thatch (*Damthak*) purchased for the roof of the house in the tenure of Peter Bynglay this year 18d.

And for the service of Thomas Wylde for 2 days roofing on the said house 10d.

And for the service of his mate for the same time 4d.

And for 7 posts (*stothes*) purchased from Richard Goldale for the almonry house this year 12d.

And for the service of William Heryng, carpenter, for one day working in the said house 5d.

And for the service of James Couper working there for 2 days 7d.

And for the service of Richard Godsalve making one stone foundation there, by contract 6d.

And for plaster (*plastre*) purchased from the wife of John Grewe this year 12d.

And for boards of 5 feet purchased from Richard Goldale for one louver (*lover*) at the poor-house this year 15d.

And for the service of Richard Goldale working on the said louver (*lover*) for one day 6d.

---

[30] *vs.iid.* crossed out and *iiiis.viiid.* substituted.

And for the service of John Webster making one fence on the western side of the garden within the guest house garden in the tenure of Robert Barbour from timber of the office for 5 days, receiving 5d. a day, 2s.1d.

And for nails purchased for the same work 12d.

And for one gudgeon (*gudyon*) and 2 iron *plates* purchased for the door of the said garden 4d.

And for one key called a *Cleket*[31] purchased for the smaller door of the guest house this year 2d.

Total 104s.3d.[32]

Charitable gifts from the almoner's office (*Dona caritativa ex officio Elemosinarii*) And for the charitable distribution to the poor on Maundy Thursday (14 April) this year 30s.

And for gifts to various poor strangers visiting this year on occasion 13s.4d.

Total 43s.4d.

Payments of money from the office of the chantry (*Solutiones denarii ex officio cantarie*) And for the payment made to various brethren of the convent celebrating Mass at the altar of St Cuthbert during 52 weeks for the soul of the said venerable father this year, at 14d. to each for every week, 60s.8d.

And to the same brethren on the anniversary day of the said venerable father this year 50s.

Total £5 10s.8d.

Allowances (*Allocationes*) And there are allowed to the same accountant 12d. from the decrease in rent (*de decremento redditus*) of three acres and a half of land in *Namanland* across the Ouse, formerly in the tenure of Robert Claybroke, belonging to the almoner's office, because it used to return 4s. and now it returns only 3s. a year.

And 12d. from the decrease in rent of one[33] assart called *longtodhill* in the tenure of William Mascald, because it used to return 10s. and now it returns only 9s. a year.

---

[31] A latch-key (*OED*).
[32] The items, including the revised one on p. 247, in fact add up to £5 3s.9d.
[33] *unius* repeated in the MS.

And 12d. from the decrease in rent of one house in Gowthorpe in the tenure of Thomas Goldsmyth, because it used to return 11s. and now it returns only 10s. a year.

And 16s.8d. from the decrease in rent of the house formerly in the tenure of William Benynghholm, because (it is) in the lord's hand this year[34] for want of a tenant.

And 16d. from the decrease in rent of the garden of the chapel of St Genevieve, because (it is) in the lord's hand this year for want of a tenant.

And 12d. from the decrease in rent of one house in Gowthorpe belonging to the office of the chantry, in the tenure of Robert Lyndesay, because it used to return 9s. and now it returns only 8s. a year.

And 12d.[35] from the decrease in rent of one house in Church Lane (*Kirkelane*) in the tenure of John Adcok, because it used to return 5s. and now it returns only 4s.[36] yearly.

And 14s. from the decrease in rent of one house at the minor church[37] in Selby, formerly in the tenure of John Crull, because (it is) in the lord's hand this year for want of a tenant.

And to this accountant himself for his diligence in the said offices this year by courtesy, with 3s.4d. for the office of keeper of the chantry, 10s.

Total 47s.

Total of all expenses, payments, and allowances £24 1s.0½d. And thus the accountant owes 41s.3½d.

---

[34] 'for Martin term' (*de termino Martini*) crossed out.

[35] *xxd.* crossed out and *xiid.* substituted.

[36] *iiis.iiid.* crossed out and *iiiis.* substituted.

[37] i.e. the chapel on or near the modern Church Hill, which served the townsmen of Selby as a parish church until the Reformation, when the abbey church took over the function. The chapel has not survived. See G.S.Haslop, 'The Abbot of Selby's Financial Statement for the Year ending Michaelmas 1338', p.161.

(b) The office of Keeper in the Guest House

Like other medieval monastic houses Selby Abbey provided hospitality for visitors as a matter of course. That such institutions should entertain guests in a manner befitting their status was an expectation of the age, which was given physical expression in the construction of special buildings within the monastic precincts to house visitors. At the Cistercian abbey of Fountains in Yorkshire, for example, the remains of the guest house can still be seen: two houses, each two storeyed, set together by the River Skell in the forecourt of the monastery outside the properly monastic area of the cloister.[1] Nothing remains of the guest house at Selby, but some details of its lay-out can be recovered from references in surviving records concerning its administration. It had a Hall, with a long table at which guests could dine; a superior apartment known as the High Chamber, consisting of an inner and an outer room and equipped in 1423–24 with a feather-bed; and at least two other rooms, *Le Baschaumbre* painted with red roses in 1425–26, and *Le Parlour* which contained a red bed in 1427–28. Outside the guests had their private garden.[2]

The task of the keeper was to supervise the running of this small household and maintain its facilities. His accounts record both the necessities of fifteenth century living, like the candles for lighting and rushes for the floor, and the luxury items that contributed to the rising standards of comfort of upper class life: curtains, coverlets woven with red roses and green *Pope Jayes*, a feather-bed, and silver spoons.[3] With an income of less than £3 a year, however,[4] his resources were not meant to meet the cost of food, drink, and other entertainment for the abbey's guests. The primary responsibility in these areas rested with the abbot himself, forming part of the general expenses of his household whenever he was present at Selby.[5] What was the full cost of hospitality to the house cannot be ascertained, because this item is not differentiated from other elements in the budget of the abbot's household. We can only suggest that it was likely to be considerable.[6]

---

[1] See the aerial view of Fountains Abbey in L. Butler and C. Given-Wilson, *Medieval Monasteries of Great Britain*, opposite p. 238.

[2] WDA, Se/Ac/8 and 14.

[3] WDA, Se/Ac/8 and 14.

[4] Income of the Guest House rose from £2 7s.3d. in 1413–14 to £2 11s.11d. in the years 1421–27, and again to £2 17s.9d. in 1427–32 after a new rental was made. In 1535 the rents and farms of the office brought in £3 6s.6d. See WDA, Se/Ac/8 and 14, and HUL, DDLO 20/60.

[5] When the abbot was absent from the abbey, the costs of food and drink might be met by the bursar, as they were in the account of 1398–99 (see above, p. 67).

[6] Three guests alone in 1398–99 cost 10s. for food and drink (see above, pp. 67–68); and considerable sums were outlayed in gifts to servants and other visitors in the same account (*ibid.* pp. 58–65). Visitors, including those coming on business, meant expenditure on wine of 45s. in 1416–17 (WDA, Se/Ac/9, s.v. *Expense supervenientium*).

Perhaps the most disappointing feature of the accounts of the keeper in the guest house is that they give no details whatever of the visitors who stayed at Selby, neither their names nor their number. The circle of friends, acquaintances, and contacts has to be pieced together from other sources, such as the lists in bursars' rolls of persons that came to the abbey and received small gifts from the abbot.[7] Even the visit of one of the king's sons makes no mark on the keeper's account for 1413–14; but we happen to know from another source that Thomas, duke of Clarence, was at Selby early in 1414. The account of the abbot's chaplain provides the information, with a record of money paid to a servant for announcing Clarence's arrival and of 20s. given to members of his household during his stay.[8]

Altogether twelve accounts of the keeper of the guest house have survived, in two bundles of five and seven documents respectively. Eleven of them form a continuous series of accounts covering the years 1421–1432; the twelfth is separated from the others by a few years and extends from Michaelmas 1413 to Michaelmas 1414.[9] Since all are in good condition and content varies little between individual accounts, the earliest has been chosen for inclusion here. Its accountant, Brother Thomas Bolton, has the particular interest that he is known to have been involved in hunting. His dogs and his hunting parties are mentioned in an account of 1416–17,[10] at which time Brother Thomas was acting as abbot's chaplain;[11] and it may be that this office included among its duties the entertainment of lay visitors for whom the abbot was providing hospitality.

Bolton had entered the abbey in 1404 and become a priest in 1406.[12] His career at Selby seems to have been active, but short. At the time that he was serving as keeper in the guest house in 1413–14, he was also one of the two kitcheners appointed that year; and, as mentioned above, he went on from here to be the abbot's chaplain in 1416–17.[13] During this latter year he travelled to London and stayed two weeks, at a total cost to the abbey of £6 0s.10½d. No reason for the trip is given in the bursar's account that records it, but it may have been connected with the important plea between the house and Sir Gerard Salvayn that was then proceeding in King's

---

[7] See, for example, the *Gifts* section of the bursars' account of 1398–99 (above, pp. 58–65).

[8] HUL, DDLO 20/54g. Thomas, duke of Clarence, was the second son of Henry IV, born in 1388. He died in March 1421. For a biography, see G. E. Cokayne, *The Complete Peerage*, III, pp. 258–60.

[9] These two bundles of accounts are preserved in the Westminster Diocesan Archives as Se/Ac/8 and 14. The account translated here is part of the former bundle.

[10] In the kitchener's account translated above. See p. 183.

[11] See WDA, Se/Ac/9, s.v. *Expense Domini Abbatis cum exhenniis datis.*

[12] Borthwick Institute of Historical Research, Archbishop's Register 16, Richard le Scrope, fos 310–311, and Register 5A, *Sede Vacante* 1405–07, f.100.

[13] HUL, DDLO 20/54a and 54c.

Bench.[14] In any case he used the opportunity to purchase seven pounds of pepper there for the kitchener.[15] He last appears in the Selby records in Lent 1418, when he was representing the abbot in the court of Selby.[16]

The Keeper in the Guest House's account of 1413–1414

Table of Contents

The account of Brother Thomas Bolton, keeper in the guest house of the monastery of Selby from the festival of St Michael the Archangel (29 September) A.D. 1413 to the same festival of Michael A.D. 1414, for one whole year.

---

[14] For the trip, see WDA, Se/Ac/9, s.v. *Forinsece Expense*. The plea, concerning the abbey's property in North Duffield, had begun as a plea of novel disseisin before Justices of Assize in Yorkshire, gone from there to Common Pleas, and been sent into King's Bench on a writ of error. It was in progress from 1413 to 1417, and still not terminated when the case disappears from the records. PRO, KB 27/622, M.CIX.
[15] See the kitchener's roll above, p. 163.
[16] HUL, DDLO 21/20.

Arrears   Firstly the same person answers for 4s.6½d. from
(*Arreragia*)   the arrears of the last account.[17]

  Total 4s.6½d.

Receipts   Firstly the same person answers for 44s.7d. from the
(*Receptum*)   rents and farms belonging to the aforesaid office
       yearly, as appears from the rental.

And for 2s.8d. received from tithe-sheaves belonging to the aforesaid
office this year, sold for this.

Total 47s.3d.

Total of receipts 51s.9½d.

Small expenses From which the same person accounts for 7 stones
(*Minute*)   of paris candles purchased from the candle-maker of
       Riccall for lighting in the office, at (*prout dat'*) 18d. a
       stone, 10s.6d.

And for 2 towels purchased from William Grene of Stapleton 12d.

And for 7 goblets (*ciphis*), of which (there was) 1 with a cover, 8d.

And for 12 ells of blanket cloth purchased for making blankets from,
at 13d. (an ell), 13s.

And for 12 plates, 12 dishes, 12 saucers, weighing 49 lbs., purchased
at London by John Haynson at 3¼d. a pound 13s.3¼d.[18]

And for 1 thrave of reeds (*Damthak*) purchased for strewing the
room of the old prior[19] and the rooms of the office with 3d.

And for rushes purchased for the same reason 8d.

Total 39s.4¼d.

---

[17] This entry substituted for the following deleted entry: 'None because the first year of this
accountant and Brother Peter Sutton, his predecessor, in his last account exceeded income'
(*Nulla quia primus annus ipsius computantis et Frater Petrus Sutton precessor suus in ultimo
compoto suo inde recessit in excessu*). Brother Peter Sutton entered the house about 1400 and
was ordained a priest in 1403. Keeper in the guest house is the only office that he is known to
have held before his death in late 1415 or early 1416. (HUL, DDLO 20/15; Borthwick
Institute of Historical Research, Archbishop's Register 16, Richard le Scrope, fos 285 and
304).

[18] The tableware was probably made of pewter. A similar account of 1422–23 records the
purchase of plates, dishes, and saucers of pewter weighing 48 lbs and costing 3¼d. a pound
(WDA, Se/Ac/8b, *Minute*).

[19] Possibly Brother Peter de Roucliff, mentioned as prior in a document of 1407, who died in
1432 or 1433 (British Library, Cotton Vit. E.XVI, f.132v; HUL, DDLO 20/17, pittancer's
roll 1432–33). The prior in 1413–14 was Brother John de Cave (see HUL, DDLO 18/1;
WDA, Se/Ac/9).

Wages
(*Stipendia*)
And for the wage of the laundress of the office during the time of the account 3s.

And for the wage of the page of the office during the time of the account 6s.8d.

And given to Robert Fullege, servant in the office, as a gift (*ad oblationem*) during the time of the account 12d.

And to the laundress for the same reason 4d.

And to the page of the office for the same reason 2d.

And to this accountant himself for his diligence in the office during the time of the account as a gratuity (*ex curialitate*) 3s.4d.

Total 14s.2d.[20]

Total of all expenses 53s.6¼d. And thus he exceeds (income by) 20¾d.

---

[20] The total should be 14s.6d.

APPENDIX

The attendance of Abbot John de Shirburn at parliament

For the long period of Abbot John de Shirburn's abbacy (1369–1408) the *Handbook of British Chronology*[1] lists thirty-eight parliaments. There is no evidence for eleven of these as to whether the abbot of Selby attended or not; but for the remaining twenty-seven the returns of parliamentary proxies preserved in the Public Record Office, London, supplemented by a register from the abbey and a surviving account roll of the bursary for 1398–99, supply the requisite information.[2] Abbot John de Shirburn can be shown to have attended only two parliaments, in 1382 and 1383, during the second of which he acted as one of the Triers of Petitions.[3] To the other twenty-five he appointed proctors to appear in his place; nor did he follow the practice of his predecessor, Abbot Geoffrey de Gaddesby, in appointing one of the Selby monks to act in this capacity and thus maintaining after a fashion the monastic presence in parliment.[4] A list of parliaments, with the names of proctors and the excuses for non-attendance proffered on the abbot's behalf, follows below:

1369, 3 June		No information
1371, 24 Feb.	Proctors:	William de Mirfeld, clerk; Elias de Sutton, clerk; James de Raygate.
	Excuse:	hindered by the concerns and difficulties of reforming the condition of the abbey.
	(PRO, SC 10/29/1447)	
1372, 3 Nov.	Proctors:	Henry de Barton and William de Mirfeld, clerks and canons of Lincoln.
	Excuse:	as in the last.
	(PRO, SC 10/30/1470)	
1373, 21 Nov.	Proctors:	Henry de Barton and William de Mirfeld, clerks and canons of Lincoln.

---

[1] F. M. Powicke and E. B. Fryde (ed.), *Handbook of British Chronology*, pp. 525–529.
[2] Parliamentary proxies for the period of Shirburn's abbacy are preserved in PRO, SC 10, files 29–43, and there is also a stray return for 1407 in C 49/48/no.10. The register is British Library, Cotton Vitellius E.XVI and Cotton Cleopatra D.III, and the account roll WDA, Se/AC/5. There are also occasional references in the printed rolls of parliament, *Rotuli Parliamentorum*, ed. J. Strachey and others.
[3] British Library, Cotton Cleopatra D.III, f.187v and *RP*, III, pp. 133 and 145.
[4] During the early 1360s, for example, Brother John de Goldale was one of Selby Abbey's proctors to parliament (PRO, SC 10/28/1372, 1391, and 1405.)

255

	Excuse: as in the last. (PRO, SC 10/30/1496)
1376, 28 Apr.	Proctors: Robert de Crull, clerk, and Adam de Chesterfeld, clerk. Excuse: as in the last. (PRO, SC 10/31/1524)
1377, 27 Jan.	Proctors: Robert de Crull, clerk, and Adam de Chestrefeld, clerk. Excuse: as in the last. (SC 10/31/1542)
1377, 13 Oct.	No information
1378, 20 Oct.	Proctors: John de Freton, clerk; Robert de Melton, clerk; and John de Waltham, clerk. Excuse: as previously. (PRO, SC 10/32/1590)
1379, 24 Apr.	Proctors: Richard de Ravenser, archdeacon of Lincoln, and John de Waltham, clerk. Excuse: poverty of the abbey and ill-health of the abbot. (British Library, Cotton Cleopatra D.III, f.186v; PRO, SC 10/33/1606)
1380, 16 Jan.	Proctors: Richard de Ravensere, archdeacon of Lincoln, and John de Waltham, clerk. Excuse: as in the last. (PRO, SC 10/33/1628)
1380, 5 Nov.	No information
1381, 3 Nov.	No information
1382, 7 May	No information
1382, 6 Oct.	The abbot attended this parliament (British Library, Cotton
1383, 23 Feb.	Cleopatra D.III, f.187v). The abbot attended this parliament and acted as one of the Triers of Petitions (British Library, Cotton Cleopatra D.III, f.187v and *RP*, III, pp. 133 and 145).
1383, 26 Oct.	No information
1384, 29 Apr.	No information
1384, 12 Nov.	Proctors: John de Waltham, canon of York; Thomas de Stanelay, clerk; and Robert de Melton, clerk. Excuse: as for 24 April 1379. (PRO, SC 10/35/1722)
1385, 20 Oct.	Proctors: John de Waltham, archdeacon of Richmond; John Scarle, clerk; Thomas de Stanelay, clerk. Excuse: as in the last. (PRO, SC 10/36/1755)
1386, 1 Oct.	Proctors: John de Waltham, archdeacon of Richmond; Thomas de Stanelay, canon of Lichfield; Thomas de Haxay, clerk. Excuse: as in the last. (PRO, SC 10/36/1772)
1388, 3 Feb.	Proctors: Thomas de Stanlay, clerk, and George de Louthorp, clerk. Excuse: as in the last. (PRO, SC 10/37/1816)

1388, 9 Sept.		No information
1390, 17 Jan.		No information
1390, 12 Nov.		No information
1391, 3 Nov.	Proctors:	Thomas de Haxay, clerk, and John de Rome, clerk.
	Excuse:	as for 24 April 1379.
		(PRO, SC 10/37/1847)
1393, 20 Jan.	Proctors:	Thomas Haxey, clerk; John Rome, clerk; and Robert de Brayton, clerk.
	Excuse:	as in the last.
		(PRO, SC 10/38/1872)
1394, 27 Jan.	Proctors:	Thomas de Haxay, clerk; John de Rome, clerk; and Robert de Brayton, clerk.
	Excuse:	as in the last.
		(PRO, SC 10/39/1916)
1395, 27 Jan.	Proctors:	Thomas de Haxey, clerk; John de Rome, clerk; and Robert de Brayton, clerk.
	Excuse:	as in the last.
		(PRO, SC 10/40/1952)
1397, 22 Jan.	Proctors:	Thomas Haxey, clerk, and John Rome, clerk.
	Excuse:	as in the last.
		(PRO, SC 10/40/1964)
1397, 17 Sept.		No information
1399, 30 Sept. and 6 Oct.[5]	Proctors:	Alexander de Stayndrop (WDA, Se/Ac/5, s.v. *Dona* and *Forinsece Expense*).
1401, 20 Jan.		The abbot excused from attendance at parliament because of infirmity (British Library, Cotton Vitellius E.XVI, f.129v).
1402, 30 Sept.	Proctors:	John de Rome, clerk; Peter de Crulle; John Pygot junior, clerk.
	Excuse:	poverty of abbey, and old age and sickness of abbot.
		(PRO, SC 10/41/2014)
1404, 14 Jan.	Proctors:	John de Rome, clerk; Peter de Crulle, king's esquire; John Pygot junior, clerk; John de Birne.
	Excuse:	poverty of abbey; abbot broken by old age and continual sufferer of ill-health.
		(PRO, SC 10/41/2049)
1404, 6 Oct.	Proctors:	John Rome, clerk, and Thomas Haxhey, clerk.
	Excuse:	abbey much burdened by adversity, and abbot broken by old age and bodily infirmity.
		(PRO, SC 10/42/2068)
1406, 1 Mar.	Proctors:	John de Rome, clerk; Thomas de Haxay, clerk; Robert de Selby, clerk; John Pygot, clerk; John de Birne.

[5] The writs of summons to the last parliament of Richard II were regarded as invalidated by his abdication on 29 September, and the assembly ended on the day of meeting. The same persons already present in London were then summoned to the first parliament of Henry IV on 6 October (see F. M. Powicke and E. B. Fryde (ed.), *Handbook of British Chronology*, p. 528, and E. F. Jacob, *The Fifteenth Century 1399–1485*, Oxford, 1961, p. 13).

Excuse: abbot broken by old age and continual sufferer of ill-health.

(PRO, SC 10/43/2121)

1407, 20 Oct. Proctors: John de Rome, clerk; Master Richard de Holme, canon of York; John de Birne.

Excuse: as in the last.

(PRO, C 49/48/no.10)

MONEY, WEIGHTS, AND MEASURES
USED IN THE ACCOUNTS

No attempt has been made here to list the many variations in medieval weights and measures. A full discussion of variations in time and place, and metric equivalents of English weights and measures, will be found in R. E. Zupko, *A Dictionary of English Weights and Measures from Anglo-Saxon times to the Nineteenth Century*, (University of Wisconsin Press, 1968).

Money

Farthing (¼d.)	one quarter of a Penny
Halfpenny (½d.)	one half of a Penny
Penny (1d.)	4 Farthings or 2 Halfpennies
Shilling (1s.)	12 Pennies
Pound (£1)	20 Shillings or 240 Pennies
Mark	13s.4d. or two thirds of a Pound

Weights

Ounce (oz.)	one sixteenth of a Pound, but also one twelfth of a Pound (e.g. for spices)
Pound (lb.)	16 Ounces, but also 12 Ounces
Stone	14 Pounds, but with many variations
Hundredweight (cwt)	112 Pounds, but with local variations
Ton	20 Hundredweights

Measures of Length

Inch (in.)	one twelfth of a Foot
Foot (ft)	12 Inches
Yard (yd)	3 Feet or 36 Inches
Ell	3 ft 9 ins or 45 Inches
Fathom	6 ft, but occasionally 7 ft
Rod	16½ ft or 5½ yds

Measures of Area

Rood	one quarter of an Acre
Acre	4840 sq. yds
Bovate	one half of a Virgate
Virgate	varied widely, but Virgates of 15, 16, 20, 24, 28, 30, 32, 40, and 60 Acres were the most common

MONEY, WEIGHTS AND MEASURES

Measures of Liquids

Pint	one eighth of a Gallon
Quart	one quarter of a Gallon
Pottle	half a Gallon or two Quarts
Gallon	8 Pints or 4 Quarts
Pipe	126 Gallons, but occasionally 120 and 125 Gallons
Tun	2 Pipes or 252 Gallons

Measures of Grain and other Dry Products

Peck	one quarter of a Bushel
Bushel	8 Gallons or 4 Pecks
Quarter	8 Bushels

Other Measures

Barrel	generally 31½ Gallons of oil; 30 Gallons of eels fully packed (but sometimes 42 Gallons); and 32 Gallons of sturgeon and most other fish
Chaldron	coal measure, first regulated in 1421, containing 32 bushels totalling 2000 lbs. But the chaldron of sea coal generally contained 48 bushels or 12 sacks of 4 heaped bushels each
Quire	24 or 25 sheets of paper
Thrave	generally 12 or 24 Sheaves

GLOSSARY

Allowances (*Allocationes*)	The section of the money account in which an accountant claimed as deductions from the income charged to him on the receipts side items of expected revenue that had not been received or had fallen short of the recorded sums.
Arrears (*Arreragia*)	The first section on the receipts side of a money account, which refers back to the final outcome of the account roll immediately preceding it of the same office. It records as part of the anticipated resources for the current year the sum, if any, owed by the accountant after all expenditures and allowances had been deducted from total receipts for the previous accounting period. See also 'Excess'.
Blanket	A white or undyed woollen cloth. See *OED*.
Brad	A thin flattish nail. See *OED*.
Brag	A large nail. See *OED*.
Brott	Refuse corn: short, broken straw. See J. Wright (ed.), *English Dialect Dictionary*.
Burnet	A quality wool-dyed cloth. See *OED*.
Canvas	A strong or coarse unbleached cloth made of hemp or flax. See *OED*.
Churching	The ceremony of thanksgiving following childbirth. See *OED*.
Clout	A plate of iron fitted to prevent wear. See *OED*.
Corrody	A yearly allowance of goods (food, drink, clothing) from the common store of a religious house, often with a provision for accommodation, granted sometimes in return for cash payment, sometimes as a reward for service, and sometimes at the request of a patron.
Damthak	Thatching material, presumably reeds taken from the Selby Dam or similar source.
Drawing (of thatch)	The process of sorting the long reeds, straws etc. from the short, pulling them out and laying them straight for the thatcher. See G. S. Haslop, *YAJ*, 48, 1976, n.50.
Dredge	A mixture of barley and oats.
Excess (*Excessus*)	The first section on the expenditure and allowances side of a money account, referring back to the final outcome of the account roll immediately preceding it of the same office. It records the sum owed to the accountant at the end of the previous account if expenditures and allowances had exceeded anticipated income, discharging him from this amount of his revenues for the present year. See also 'Arrears (*Arreragia*)'.

261

Foreign receipts (*Forinsecum Receptum*)	Items of income which were not a regular and anticipated part of the revenues of an office.
Gudgeon	A pivot, usually of metal, used with the specific meaning of the ring or 'eye' in the 'heel' of a gate which turns on the hook or pintle in the gate post. See *OED*.
Head-silver (*Hedesilver*)	A small annual tax on unfree tenants.
Lake	Fine linen. See *OED*.
Maslin	Mixed grain, especially rye mixed with wheat. See *OED*.
Mortuary	The due claimed by the incumbent of a parish from the estate of a deceased parishioner. Where the rectory had been appropriated, the abbey or other appropriator claimed the receipts as rector.
Nave	With reference to a wheel, it is the hub or central part into which the end of the axle tree is inserted, and from which the spokes radiate. See *OED*. With reference to a church, it is the main body of the building extending from the west end to the crossing and transepts, if any, or to the chancel and sanctuary.
Paris candle	A large wax candle. See *OED*.
Penny farm (*Penyferm*)	Money rent that replaced the rents in kind paid by tenants of holdings on some manors.
Pottage	A food dish of boiled vegetables, sometimes with meat, or a soup. See *OED*.
Ray	A striped cloth. See *OED*.
Reprise (*Reprisa*)	A deduction, charge, or payment (such as a rent-charge or annuity) made yearly out of a manor or estate.
Russet	A coarse woollen cloth. See *OED*.
Saucer	Dishes for holding sauces, salt, etc. on the table. See *OED*.
Selion	The area of land between two parallel furrows of the open field and variable in size.
Spike (*Spikyng*)	A large and strong nail. See *OED*.
Stamyn	A coarse cloth of worsted. See *OED*.
Stower	A stake, pole, or post. See *OED*.
Wort	The product in the process of brewing when the ground malt is mixed with hot water and mashed.

BIBLIOGRAPHY

Unprinted Sources

Durham, University of, Department of Palaeography and Diplomatic

Locellus XXV, no. 74   Letter of William Pygot, Abbot of Selby 1408–29, to Prior of Durham

Hull, University of, The Brynmor Jones Library

DDLO 4/2–3; 20/1–59, 61–75   Selby Abbey Account Rolls:

Abbot's Chaplain, 1413–14 (DDLO 20/54g)

Almoner, 1434–35 (DDLO 20/55)

Bursar, 1431–32, c.1450, ?1454, c.1452–55, 1479–80, c.1480, 1480–81, 1483–84, c.1490, 1496–97, 1526, 1527–28, 1531–32 (DDLO 20/1–2, 4–13)

Extern Cellarer, 1413–14, 1479–80, 1489–90 (DDLO 20/49, 54c, 56)

Granger, 1349–50, 1404–05, 1413–14, 1474–75, 1500–01 (DDLO 20/43–44, 46–47, 54e)

Infirmarer, 1400–1403 (DDLO 20/53)

Keeper of Choir of BVM, 1536–37 (DDLO 20/61)

Kitchener, 1412, 1413–14, 1438–39, 1475–76 (DDLO 20/50, 51, 54d)

Pittancer and Chamberlain, 1403–04, 1415–16, ?1416–17, 1431–32, 1432–33, 1433–34, 1437–38, 1438–39, 1441–42, 1447–50, 1450–51, 1452–53, 1460–61, 1467–68, 1468–69, 1469–70, 1470–71, 1472–73, 1474–75, 1497–98, c.1510, 1516–17 (DDLO 20/14–36)

Sacrist and Fabric Keeper, 1413–14, 1494–95, 1497–98, 1523–24, 1524–25, 1537–38 (DDLO 20/37–40, 42, 54a)

Abbey Servants, Acaster Selby 1535 (DDLO 20/75); *Doune* 1413–14 (DDLO 20/54f); Eastoft 1358–59, 1424–25 (DDLO 4/2–3); Garthorpe 1389, 1390–91, c.1390 (DDLO 20/62–64)

Hook and Carlton 1425–26, 1426–27, 1427–28, 1430–31 (DDLO 20/67–70); Queniborough 1413–14, 1528–29 (DDLO 20/54f and 73); Redbourne early 15th cent. (DDLO 20/48)

Stallingborough 1479–80 (DDLO 20/72); Stanford on Avon 1413–14 (DDLO 20/54f); Stainer 1423–24, 1523–24 (DDLO 20/66 and 74); *Stormesworth* 1413–14 (DDLO 20/54f)

Whitgift and Reedness 1397–98 (DDLO 20/65); Other c.1430 (DDLO 20/71)

Various Accounts: 1390 (DDLO 20/52), 1413–14 (DDLO 20/54b), c.1460 (DDLO 20/3), 1510–11 (DDLO 20/57), c.1520 (DDLO 20/58), c.1527–28 (DDLO 20/59), c.1530 (DDLO 20/41)

DDLO 20/60   Valuation of Selby Abbey Income 1535

BIBLIOGRAPHY

DDLO 20/87, 89–92; 21/173   Selby Abbey Rentals:
  Altar of BVM, 1403 (DDLO 20/87)
  Chapel of BVM Carlton, 1520–21 (DDLO 20/89)
  Hambleton, Over Selby, and Thorpe Willoughby, 7 Henry VIII (DDLO 21/173)
  Selby (fragment), early 16th cent. (DDLO 20/90)
  Thorpe Willoughby, Barlby, Brayton, Selby, early 16th cent. (DDLO 20/91)
  Tithes of various chapels, early 16th cent. (DDLO 20/92)

DDLO 1/1–9   Court Rolls, Brayton, 1485–c.1525

DDLO 2/1–24   Court Rolls, Brayton and Thorpe Willoughby, 1440–1519

DDLO 3/1   Court Roll, Crowle, 1426

DDLO 4/1   Court Roll, Eastoft, 1317/18

DDLO 14/1–2   Court Rolls, Monk Fryston and Hillam, 1411–12, 1432–33

DDLO 18/1–7   Court Rolls, Over Selby, 1399–1525

DDLO 21/1–105; DDX 145/1   Court Rolls, Selby, 1322–1537

DDLO 23/1   Court Roll, Selby Waterhouses, 1323–74

DDLO 24/1–2   Court Rolls, Snaith, 1458 and 1521

DDLO 25/1–14   Court Rolls, Thorpe Willoughby, 1449/50–1537

DDLO 20/76–86 and 88   Selby Abbey Miscellaneous Documents

Leeds, City Libraries, Archives Department

Towneley MS, Transcript (17th cent.) of lost Selby Abbey lease-book (including
  material for 1355–62)

Lincoln, The Castle, Lincolnshire Archives Committee

Crowle Manor 8/7   Selby Abbey Bursar's Account, 1480–81

CM 8/1–6, and 8   Rentals, Crowle, early 14th cent.–1500

CM 8/9   Rental, Brayton, c.1500

CM 1/1–201   Court Rolls, Crowle, 1310–1539

London, Public Record Office

C 49, file 46, no.40   Appointment of proxies by Abbot of Selby for Council, 1353
  file 48, no.10   Appointment of proxies by Abbot of Selby for Parliament, 1407

C 81, file 1786, nos 43–45   Requests by Abbot of Selby for secular aid against
  apostate monks, 1280, 1317, and 1359

C 84, file 29, nos 43, 47, 48   Petitions relating to Selby
  file 39, nos 43, 44, 46   Abbey elections 1368–69, and 1408

C 260, file 88, no. 18   Transcript of proceedings of Commission of Oyer and
  terminer, on complaint of Abbot of Selby 1375
  file 118, no. 3   Exemplification of plea in Common Pleas concerning advowson
  of church of Luddington, 1405

C 269, file 8, no. 43   Transcript of will of John Barbour of Selby 1398

BIBLIOGRAPHY

CP 40/651, m.258d   Plea in Common Pleas, 1423, Abbot of Selby V Richard Denyas, slater, concerning negligent workmanship

    m.531   Plea in Common Pleas, 1423, Earl of Westmorland V Abbot of Selby, concerning wardship of John FitzHenry

DL 42/8, Duchy of Lancaster Records, Misc. Books 8, Register of the time of Abbot Geoffrey de Gaddesby, 1342–68

E 28, file 28, no. 9   Petition of Abbot John de Cave concerning restitution of temporalities 1429

E 135/10/21, no. 3   Letter concerning grant by Abbot and Convent of Selby to king in defence of realm 1400

KB 27/622, m.cix   Plea in King's Bench, Abbot of Selby V Gerard Salvayn, knight, 1415–17

SC 10, 52 files   Letters from spiritual peers appointing proxies to represent them in Parliament

London, British Library, Department of Manuscripts

ADD CH 45854   Selby Abbey Account, Sacrist and Fabric Keeper 1447–1448

ADD MS 36579   Extent, Monk Fryston, Hillam, Hambleton, Stanford on Avon, and Queniborough, 1320–21

Cotton Vitellius E. xvi fos 97–162   Part of a Register of the time of Abbot John de Shirburn, 1369–1408

Cotton Cleopatra D. iii fos 184–202   Part of a Register of the time of Abbot John de Shirburn, 1369–1408

Oxford, Bodleian Library

Top. Yorks. d.2 (SC.35210)   Two leaves from a Selby Abbey Register, for 1341–42

Sheffield, City Libraries, Department of Local History and Archives

Bacon Frank MS 30   Selby Abbey Account Roll, Bursar, 1459

Bacon Frank MS 31   Representation of Selby Abbey concerning expenses incurred in upkeep of sewers etc., late 15th cent.

Westminster, Diocesan Archives of the Roman Catholic Archbishop

Se/Ac/1–23   Selby Abbey Account Rolls:
    Bursar, 1398–99, 1416–17, c.1531 (Se/Ac/5, 9, and 23)
    Extern Cellarer, 1492–93 (Se/Ac/20)
    Keeper of the Guest House, 1413–14, 1421–25, 1425–32 (Se/Ac/8 and 14)
    Keeper of the Refectory, 1421–22, 1423–24, 1436–37, 1459–60 (Se/Ac/11, 13, 15 and 19)
    Kitchener, c.1335–42, 1416–17 (Se/Ac/6 and 10)
    Pittancer and Chamberlain, 1362, 1412–13, 1446–47, 1453–59, 1496–97 (Se/Ac/2, 7, 16, 18, and 21)
    Sacrist and Fabric Keeper, 1446–47, 1522–23 (Se/Ac/17 and 22)

BIBLIOGRAPHY

Abbey Servants, Monk Fryston 1393–94 (Se/Ac/4); Stainer 1421–22 (Se/Ac/12); Whitgift and Reedness 1377–78 (Se/Ac/3)

Account of receipts from sale of timber, 6–19 Edward IV (Se/Ac/1)

Se/Ac/24 Rental, Monk Fryston, 15th cent.

Se/CR/1–14, and 16, Court Rolls, Selby 1377–1520
  15, and 17 Court Rolls, Thorpe Willoughby 1516 and 1524

Se/Misc/1–4 Selby Abbey Miscellaneous Documents

York, Minster Library, Dean and Chapter Archives

HH 21. 3 a–b Selby Abbey Account Rolls, Pittancer 1475–76 and 1479–80

York, Borthwick Institute of Historical Research

York Archiepiscopal Registers
  Reg. 5A *Sede Vacante* Registers
  Reg. 9A–B (William Melton, 1317–1340) to
  Reg. 28 (Edward Lee, 1531–1544)

Printed Sources

(Restricted to sources cited in notes to the text. For a useful bibliography of other printed account rolls and sources for late medieval monastic history, see D. J. Guth, *Late-medieval England 1377–1485*, Conference on British Studies, Bibliographical handbooks, Cambridge UP, 1976, XII Religious History)

Anon (ed.), 'Assessment Roll of the Poll-Tax for Howdenshire, 2 Richard II (1379), Houden' et Houdenshire', *Yorkshire Archaeological Journal*, 9, 1886, pp. 129–162.
  'Rolls of the Collectors in the West-Riding of the Lay Subsidy (Poll Tax) 2 Richard II', *Yorkshire Archaeological Journal*, 5, 1879, pp. 1–51, 241–266, 417–432; 6, 1881, pp. 1–44, 129–171, 287–342; 7, 1882, pp. 6–31, 145–193.

Atkinson Rev. Canon (ed.), 'Account Roll of Selby Abbey, 1397–8', *Yorkshire Archaeological Journal*, 15, 1900, pp. 408–419.

Baildon W. P. and Clay J. W. (eds), *Inquisitions post mortem relating to Yorkshire of the reigns of Henry IV and Henry V*, Yorkshire Archaeological Society, Record Series 59, 1918.

Birrell J. (ed.), *The 'Status Maneriorum' of John Catesby 1385 and 1386*, Dugdale Society, Miscellany I, 31, 1977, pp. 15–28.

Bishop T. A. M. (ed.), *Extent of Monk Friston, 1320*, Yorkshire Archaeological Society, Misc. IV, Record Series 94, 1937, pp. 39–72.

Bliss W. H. (ed.), *Calendar of Entries in the Papal Registers relating to Great Britain and Ireland: Petitions to the Pope*, I, 1342–1419, London, 1896.

—— Johnson C. and Twemlow J. A. (eds), *Calendar of Entries in the Papal Registers relating to Great Britain and Ireland: Papal Letters*, 1198–1492, London, 1893–1961.

BIBLIOGRAPHY

Caley J. and Hunter J. (eds), *Valor Ecclesiasticus temp. Henrici VIII, auctoritate regia institutus*, 6 vols, Record Commission, 1810–1834.

Clay C.T. (ed.), *York Minster Fasti*, II, Yorkshire Archaeological Society, Record Series 124, 1958.

—— *Yorkshire Deeds*, VII, Yorkshire Archaeological Society, Record Series 83, 1932.

Clay J.W. (ed.), *North Country Wills*, Surtees Society, 116, 1908.

Dugdale W., *Monasticon Anglicanum*, re-ed. J.Caley, H.Ellis, and B.Bandinell, 6 vols in 8, London, 1817–30.

Flower C.T. (ed.), *Public Works in Mediaeval Law*, 2 vols, Selden Society, 32 and 40, 1915 and 1923.

Fowler C.W. (ed.), *The Registrum Antiquissimum of the Cathedral Church of Lincoln*, II, Lincoln Record Society, 28, 1933.

Fowler J.T. (ed.), *The Coucher Book of Selby*, 2 vols, Yorkshire Archaeological Society, Record Series 10 and 13, 1891–93.

Haslop G.S. (ed.), 'A Selby Kitchener's Roll of the Early Fifteenth Century', *Yorkshire Archaeological Journal*, 48, 1976, pp.119–133.

—— 'The Abbot of Selby's Financial Statement for the Year Ending Michaelmas 1338', *Yorkshire Archaeological Journal*, 44, 1972, pp.159–169.

—— 'The Creation of Brother John Sherburn as Abbot of Selby', *Yorkshire Archaeological Journal*, 42, 1967, pp.25–30.

—— 'Two Entries from the Register of John de Shirburn, Abbot of Selby 1369–1408', *Yorkshire Archaeological Journal*, 41, 1964, pp.287–296.

Holt B. (ed.), *Two Obedientiary Rolls of Selby Abbey*, Yorkshire Archaeological Society, Misc. VI, Record Series 118, 1953, pp.31–52.

Kimball E.G. (ed.), *Some Sessions of the Peace in Lincolnshire 1381–1396*, The Lincoln Record Society, 49, 1955.

King P.I. (ed.), with an introduction by C.N.L.Brooke, *The Book of William Morton, Almoner of Peterborough Monastery, 1448–1467, transcribed and annotated by the late W.T.Mellows*, Northamptonshire Record Society Publications 16, 1954.

Lister J. (ed.), *The Early Yorkshire Woollen Trade, Extracts from the Hull Customs' Rolls, and Complete Transcripts of the Ulnagers' Rolls*, Yorkshire Archaeological Society, Record Series 64, 1924.

Lodge E.C. and Somerville R. (eds), *John of Gaunt's Register, 1379–1383*, Camden Society 3rd series 56 and 57, 1937.

McCann J. (trans.), *The Rule of St. Benedict*, Pb. edition, London, 1976.

Maxwell-Lyte H.C. (ed.), *Inquisitions and assessments relating to feudal aids*, London, 1920.

Myers A.R. (ed.), *English Historical Documents*, IV, 1327–1485, London, 1969.

Nichols J.G. (ed.), *Two Sermons preached by the Boy Bishop at St Paul's temp. Henry VIII, and at Gloucester temp. Mary, with an introduction giving an account of the Festival of the Boy Bishop in England, by E.F.Rimbault*, Camden Misc. VII, Camden Society, NS 14, 1875.

Nicolas N.H. (ed.), *Testamenta Vetusta*, London, 1826.

Oschinsky D. (ed.), *Walter of Henley and other treatises on estate management and accounting*, Oxford, 1971.

Pantin W.A. (ed.), *Documents illustrating the activities of the General and Provincial Chapters of the English Black Monks, 1215–1540*, 3 vols, Camden Society, 3rd series 45, 47, and 54, 1931–37.

Public Record Office, *Calendar of the Close Rolls preserved in the Public Record Office*, 1272–1509, London, 1892–1963.

—— *Calendar of the Fine Rolls preserved in the Public Record Office*, 1272–1509, London, 1911–1962.

—— *Calendar of Inquisitions post mortem and other analagous documents preserved in the Public Record Office*, XVI, 7–15 Richard II, London, 1974.

—— *Calendar of the Patent Rolls preserved in the Public Record Office*, 1216–1485, London, 1891–1916.

Raine J. and Raine J. (eds), *Testamenta Eboracensia*, I–II, Surtees Society, 4, 1836, and 30, 1855.

Riley H.T. (ed.), *Thomae Walsingham, Historia Anglicana*, II, Rolls Series, 1864.

Robinson F.N. (ed.), *The Works of Geoffrey Chaucer*, Oxford, 2nd edn, 1957.

Rothwell H. (ed.), *English Historical Documents*, III, 1189–1327, London, 1975.

Scaife R.H. (ed.), *The Register of the Guild of Corpus Christi in the City of York*, Surtees Society, 57, 1872.

Searle E. and Ross B. (eds), *Accounts of the Cellarers of Battle Abbey 1275–1513*, Sydney UP, 1967.

Sellers M. (ed.), *York Memorandum Book*, I–II, Surtees Society, 120, 1912, and 125, 1915.

Strachey J. and others (ed.), *Rotuli Parliamentorum; ut et Petitiones, et Placita in Parliamento*, 6 vols, 1783.

Thompson A. Hamilton (ed.), 'The Register of the Archdeacons of Richmond, 1442–1477, Pt I 1442–1465', *Yorkshire Archaeological Journal*, 30, 1932, pp. 1–134.

Works of Reference

Cheney C.R. (ed.), *Handbook of Dates for Students of English History*, London, 1970.

Cokayne G.E., *The Complete Peerage of England, Scotland, Great Britain, and the United Kingdom, Extant, Extinct, or Dormant*, revised edition, ed. V.Gibbs, H.A.Doubleday, G.H.White, and R.S.Lea, 12 vols, London, 1910–1959.

Constable G., *Medieval Monasticism: a Select Bibliography*, Toronto UP, 1976.

Cross F.L. and Livingstone E.A. (eds), *The Oxford Dictionary of the Christian Church*, Oxford, 2nd edn, 1974.

Emden A.B., *A Biographical Register of the University of Oxford to 1500*, Oxford, 1957–59.

—— *A Biographical Register of the University of Cambridge to 1500*, Cambridge, 1963.

Fisher J.L., *A Medieval Farming Glossary of Latin and English Words*, London, 1968.

Foss E., *The Judges of England*, 9 vols, 1848–64.

Gooder A. (ed.), *The Parliamentary Representation of the County of York, 1258–1832*, vol.I, Yorkshire Archaeological Society, Record Series 91, 1935.

Gorer J. E. B., Mawer A., and Stenton F. M., *The Place-Names of Northampton-shire*, English Place-Names Society Publications 10, Cambridge, 1933.

Guth D. J., *Late-Medieval England 1377–1485*, Conference on British Studies, Bibliographical Handbooks, Cambridge, 1976.

Horn J. M., Jones B. and King H. P. F. (compiled), *John Le Neve: Fasti Ecclesiae Anglicanae 1300–1541*, 12 vols, London, 1962–67.

Knowles D. and Hadcock R. N., *Medieval Religious Houses. England and Wales*, 2nd edn, London, 1971.

—— and St. Joseph J. K. S., *Monastic Sites from the Air*, Cambridge, 1952.

Latham R. E., *Revised Medieval Latin Word-List*, London, 1965.

Martin C. T., *The Record Interpreter*, 2nd edn, London, 1910.

Murray J. A. H., Bradley H., Craigie W. A., and Onions C. T. (eds), *Oxford English Dictionary*, Oxford, 1888–1933.

New Catholic Encyclopedia, New York, 1967.

The New Encyclopaedia Britannica, 15th edn, Chicago, 1974.

Ordnance Survey, *Map of Monastic Britain*, 2 sheets, Chessington, Surrey, 2nd edn 1954 (south sheet) and 1955 (north sheet).

Pevsner N., *The Buildings of England: Yorkshire, West Riding*, 2nd edn, Harmondsworth, 1967.

Powicke F. M. and Fryde E. B. (eds), *Handbook of British Chronology*, 2nd edn, London, 1961.

Public Record Office, *Lists and Indexes*, 9, List of Sheriffs for England and Wales from the earliest times to A.D. 1831, London, 1898.

Smith A. H., *The Place-Names of the East Riding of Yorkshire and York*, English Place-Names Society Publications 14, Cambridge, 1937.

—— *The Place-Names of the West Riding of Yorkshire*, English Place-Names Society Publications 30–37, Cambridge, 1961–63.

Wright J. (ed.), *The English Dialect Dictionary*, London, 1898.

Zupko R. E., *A Dictionary of English Weights and Measures from Anglo-Saxon times to the Nineteenth Century*, University of Wisconsin Press, 1968.

Secondary Authorities

Baildon W. P., *Notes on the Religious and Secular Houses of Yorkshire*, 2 vols, Yorkshire Archaeological Society, Record Series 17 and 81, 1895–1931.

Beresford M., *The Lost Villages of England, London*, 1954.

Brooke C. N. L., *The Monastic World, 1000–1300*, London, 1974.

Brown A., 'The Financial System of Rochester Cathedral Priory: a Reconsideration', *London University. Institute of Historical Research. Bulletin*, 50, 1977, pp. 115–120.

Burne R. V. H., *The Monks of Chester: the History of St Werburgh's Abbey*, London, 1962.

Burton T. (ed. and enlarged J. Raine), *The History and Antiquities of the Parish of Hemingbrough in the County of York*, Yorkshire Archaeological Society, Extra Series 1, 1888.

Butler L. and Given-Wilson C., *Medieval Monasteries of Great Britain*, London, 1979.

BIBLIOGRAPHY

Cheney C. R., 'Norwich Cathedral Priory in the Fourteenth Century', *Manchester University. Bulletin of the John Rylands' Library*, 20 (1), 1936, pp. 93–120.

Clay R. M., *The Hermits and Anchorites of England*, London, 1914.

Cobb G., *English Cathedrals: The Forgotten Centuries. Restoration and Change from 1530 to the Present Day*, London, 1980.

Cook G. H., *English Monasteries in the Middle Ages*, London, 1961.

Dickinson J. C., *Monastic Life in Medieval England*, New York, 1962.

Dobson R. B., *Durham Priory*, Cambridge, 1973.

—— 'The Election of John Ousthorp as Abbot of Selby in 1436', *Yorkshire Archaeological Journal*, 42, 1967, pp. 31–40.

—— 'The First Norman Abbey in Northern England. The Origin of Selby: a ninth centenary article', *The Ampleforth Journal*, 74, pt II, Summer 1969, pp. 161–176.

—— 'The Foundation of Perpetual Chantries by the Citizens of Medieval York', in *Studies in Church History*, ed. G. J. Cuming, IV, 1967, pp. 22–38.

—— *Selby Abbey and Town*, Selby, 1969.

Darwin F. D. S., *The English Mediaeval Recluse*, London, 1944.

Drew J. S., 'Manorial Accounts of St Swithun's Priory, Winchester', in *Essays in Economic History*, II, ed. E. M. Carus-Wilson, London, 1962, pp. 12–30.

East Riding County Record Office, *Brief guide to the Contents of the East Riding County Record Office*, Beverley, 3rd edn, 1966.

Evans S. J. A., 'The Purchase and Mortification of Mepal by the Prior and Convent of Ely, 1361', *English Historical Review*, 51, 1936, pp. 113–120.

Finberg H. P. R., *Tavistock Abbey: a Study in the Social and Economic History of Devon*, Cambridge, 1951.

Franklin A. V., *May I show you round? A Tour of Ely Cathedral*, St Ives, n.d.

Gasquet F. A., *Parish Life in Medieval England*, London, 5th edn, 1922.

Gilyard-Beer R., *Abbeys. An illustrated guide to the abbeys of England and Wales*, HMSO, 2nd edn, 1976.

Gorsuch E. N., 'Mismanagement and Ecclesiastical Visitation of English Monasteries in the early fourteenth century', *Traditio*, 28, 1972, pp. 473–482.

Haines C. R., *Dover Priory. A History of the Priory of St Mary the Virgin, and St Martin of the New Work*, Cambridge, 1930.

Harper-Bill C., 'Monastic Apostasy in late medieval England', *Journal of Ecclesiastical History*, 32, 1981, pp. 1–18.

Hartridge R. A. R., *A History of Vicarages in the Middle Ages*, Cambridge, 1930.

Harvey B. F., *Westminster Abbey and its Estates in the Middle Ages*, Oxford, 1977.

—— 'The Monks of Westminster and the University of Oxford', in *The Reign of Richard II: Essays in honour of May McKisack*, ed. F. R. H. Du Boulay and C. M. Barron, University of London, 1971, pp. 108–130.

Haslop G. S., 'The Fourteenth Century Fire at Selby Abbey', *Yorkshire Archaeological Journal*, 39, 1958, pp. 451–454.

Hatcher J., *Plague, Population and the English Economy 1348–1530*, London, 1977.

Hockey S. F., *Quarr Abbey and its Lands 1132–1631*, Leicester UP, 1970.

Jacob E. F., *The Fifteenth Century 1399–1485*, Oxford, 1961.

Jones E. D., 'The Church and "Bastard Feudalism": The Case of Crowland Abbey from the 1320s to the 1350s', *Journal of Religious History*, 10, 1978, pp. 142–150.

—— 'The Crown, Three Benedictine Houses, and the Statute of Mortmain 1279–1348', *Journal of British Studies*, 14, 1975, pp. 1–28.

Keil I., 'Corrodies of Glastonbury Abbey in the Later Middle Ages', *Somersetshire Archaeological and Natural History Society Proceedings*, 108, 1964, pp. 113–131.

Kemp E. W., *Counsel and Consent*, London, 1961.

Kershaw I., *Bolton Priory: the economy of a northern monastery, 1286–1325*, Oxford, 1973.

Knowles D., *Christian Monasticism*, London, 1969.

—— *The Monastic Order in England*, Cambridge, 1966.

—— *The Religious Orders in England*, 3 vols, Cambridge, 1948–59.

—— 'The Case of St Albans Abbey in 1490', *Journal of Ecclesiastical History*, 3, 1952, pp. 144–158.

Lambrick G., 'Abingdon Abbey Administration', *Journal of Ecclesiastical History*, 17, 1966, pp. 159–193.

—— 'The Impeachment of the Abbot of Abingdon in 1368', *English Historical Review*, 82, 1967, pp. 250–276.

Lincolnshire Archives Committee, *Archivists' Report* No. 4, 1952–53, 'MANOR OF CROWLE', pp. 13–21.

Lomas R. A., 'The Priory of Durham and its Demesnes in the Fourteenth and Fifteenth Centuries', *Economic History Review*, 2nd series 31, 1978, pp. 339–353.

Lunt W. E., *Financial Relations of the Papacy with England 1327–1534*, Cambridge, Mass., 1962.

—— 'The Collectors of Clerical Subsidies', in *The English Government at Work, 1327–1336*, II, ed. W. A. Morris and J. R. Strayer, Cambridge, Mass., 1947, ch. VI.

McDonnell K. G. T., 'The Archives of Selby Abbey', *Yorkshire Archaeological Journal*, 44, 1972, pp. 170–172.

McKisack M., *The Fourteenth Century*, Oxford, 1959.

McNiven P., 'The Betrayal of Archbishop Scrope', *Bulletin of the John Rylands Library Manchester*, 54, 1971–72, pp. 173–213.

Maddicott J. R., *Law and Lordship: Royal Justices as Retainers in thirteenth- and fourteenth-century England*, Past and Present, Supplement 4, 1978.

Mallet C. E., *A History of the University of Oxford*, vol. I *The Medieval University and the Colleges founded in the middle ages*, London, 1924.

Morgan M. M., 'The Suppression of the Alien Priories', *History*, 26, 1941–42, pp. 204–212.

Morrell W. W., *The History and Antiquities of Selby*, Selby, 1867.

Myers A. R., *England in the late middle ages*, Harmondsworth, 1952.

Myres J. N. L., 'Notes on the History of Butley Priory, Suffolk', in *Oxford Essays in medieval history presented to Herbert Edward Salter*, Oxford, 1934, pp. 190–206.

Owen D., 'The Muniments of Ely Cathedral Priory', in *Church and Government in the Middle Ages: essays presented to C. R. Cheney on his 70th birthday*, ed. C. N. L. Brooke and others, Cambridge, 1976, pp. 157–176.

Pantin W. A., *The English Church in the Fourteenth Century*, Cambridge, 1955.

—— 'English Monastic Letter-Books', in *Historical Essays in Honour of James Tait*, ed. J. G. Edwards, V. H. Galbraith, and E. F. Jacob, Manchester, 1933, pp. 201–222.

BIBLIOGRAPHY

—— 'General and Provincial Chapters of the English Black Monks, 1215–1540', *Royal Historical Society, London, Transactions*, 4th series 10, 1927, pp. 195–263.

—— 'Gloucester College', *Oxoniensia*, 11–12, 1945–47, pp. 65–74.

—— 'The Monk-Solitary of Farne. A Fourteenth Century English Mystic', *English Historical Review*, 59, 1944, pp. 162–186.

—— 'Two Treatises of Uthred of Boldon on the Monastic Life', in *Studies in Medieval History presented to Frederick Maurice Powicke*, ed. R. W. Hunt and others, Oxford, 1948, pp. 363–385.

Pearce E. H., *The Monks of Westminster: being a register of the brethren of the convent from the time of the Confessor to the Dissolution, with lists of the obedientiaries*, Cambridge, 1916.

Postan M. M., *The Medieval Economy and Society*, London, 1972.

Raftis J. A., *The Estates of Ramsey Abbey: a study in economic growth and organization*, Toronto, Pontifical Institute, 1957.

Ramsay N., 'Retained Legal Counsel, c.1275–c.1475', *Royal Historical Society, London, Transactions*, 5th series 35, 1985, pp. 95–112.

Renaud F., *Contributions towards a history of the ancient parish of Prestbury, in Cheshire*, Chetham Society Publications, Old Series 97, 1876.

Roskell J. S., 'The Problem of the Attendance of the Lords in Medieval Parliaments', *London University. Institute of Historical Research. Bulletin*, 29, 1956, pp. 153–204.

Ross C. D., *The Yorkshire Baronage 1399–1435*, Unpubl. D.Phil. thesis, Oxford, 1951.

Russell J. C., *British Medieval Population*, Albuquerque, New Mexico, 1948.

Salzman, L. F., *Building in England down to 1540. A Documentary History*, Oxford, 1967.

Saunders H. W., *An Introduction to the Obedientiary and Manor Rolls of Norwich Cathedral Priory*, Norwich, 1930.

Savin A. N., *English Monasteries on the Eve of the Dissolution*, in Oxford Studies in Social and Legal History I, London, 1909.

Searle E., *Lordship and Community: Battle Abbey and its Banlieu, 1066–1538*, Toronto, 1974.

Smith R. A. L., *Canterbury Cathedral Priory: a study in monastic administration*, Cambridge, 1943.

—— *Collected Papers*, London, 1947.

Snape R. H., *English Monastic Finances in the later middle ages*, Cambridge, 1926.

Somerville R., *History of the Duchy of Lancaster*, I 1265–1603, London, 1953.

Sweet A. H., 'Papal Privileges granted to Individual Religious', *Speculum*, 31, 1956, pp. 602–610.

Thomson R. M. (ed.), *The Archives of the Abbey of Bury St Edmunds 1020–1539*, Woodbridge, Suffolk: Boydell Pr. for Suffolk Records Society, 1980.

Tillotson J. H., 'Pensions, Corrodies, and Religious Houses: An Aspect of the Relations of Crown and Church in Early 14th–Century England', *Journal of Religious History*, 8, 1974, pp. 127–143.

Tout T. F., *Chapters in the Administrative History of Medieval England*, 6 vols, Manchester, 1928–37.

The Victoria History of the Counties of England, Lincoln 2, London, 1906; Yorkshire 3, London, 1913; Yorkshire, East Riding 3, Oxford, 1976.

Walker J. W., 'The Burghs of Cambridgeshire and Yorkshire and the Watertons of Lincolnshire and Yorkshire', *Yorkshire Archaeological Journal*, 30, 1930–31, pp. 349–419.

Weske D. B., *The Convocation of the Clergy*, London, 1937.

White R. B., 'Chaucer's Daun Piers and the Rule of St Benedict: the Failure of an Ideal', *Journal of English and Germanic Philology*, 70, 1971, pp. 13–30.

Wood S. M., *English Monasteries and their Patrons in the Thirteenth Century*, Oxford, 1955.

Wood-Legh K. L., *Perpetual Chantries in Britain*, Cambridge, 1965.

Woodruff C. E., 'Notes on the Inner Life and Domestic Economy of the Priory of Christ Church in the Fifteenth Century', *Archaeologia Cantiana*, 53, 1940, pp. 2–16.

Woodward G. W. O., *The Dissolution of the Monasteries*, London, 1966.

Youings, J., *The Dissolution of the Monasteries*, London, 1971.

INDEX OF PERSONS AND PLACES

[N.B. All references to the same combination of surname and Christian name (e.g. Smith, John) have been listed together, except in the case of Selby monks. They will not always refer to a single person.]

INDEX OF SUBJECTS